T0302041

The History of Ancient Chinese Economic Thought

This volume comprises twelve papers written by Chinese scholars on various aspects of the history of ancient Chinese economic thought. The contributions are preceded by an introduction which gives an overview of the development of the subject of history of economic thought in China, and which also provides an historical context to the individuals who constitute the major "schools" of ancient Chinese economic thought.

The authors of the papers are leading scholars who have dominated this research area since the founding of New China in 1949, while the broad range of topics covered by the contributions includes questions of methodology, detailed and sometimes controversial interpretations of texts and "schools", and the international influence and modern relevance of ancient Chinese thought. A recurrent theme is that ancient Chinese thought has at least as much to offer to the historian as ancient Western thought. As the first such volume of papers to be translated into English, this collection provides a unique opportunity for non-Chinese readers to sample the way in which Chinese historians of economics have attempted to understand their own intellectual heritage.

This book will be relevant to scholars interested in the history of economic thought, economic history and Chinese studies.

Cheng Lin is Chairman of the Department of Economic History and Associate Dean of the School of Economics at Shanghai University of Finance and Economics, China.

Terry Peach is Senior Lecturer in Economics at the University of Manchester, UK and Visiting Professor of Economics at Shanghai University of Finance and Economics, China.

Wang Fang is Associate Dean of the Institute of Advanced Research at Shanghai University of Finance and Economics, China.

Routledge studies in the history of economics

The History of Ancient Chinese Economic Thought

Edited by Cheng Lin, Terry Peach and Wang Fang

Routledge
Taylor & Francis Group

LONDON AND NEW YORK

First published 2014
by Routledge
2 Park Square, Milton Park, Abingdon, Oxon OX14 4RN

and by Routledge
605 Third Avenue, New York, NY 10017

First issued in paperback 2021

Routledge is an imprint of the Taylor & Francis Group, an informa business

British Library Cataloguing in Publication Data
A catalogue record for this book is available from the British Library

Library of Congress Cataloging in Publication Data
The history of ancient Chinese economic thought / edited by Cheng Lin,
Terry Peach and Wang Fang.
   pages cm
   Includes bibliographical references and index.
   1. Economics–China–History. I. Lin, Zheng.
   HB126.C4H57 2014
   330.0951–dc23   2013033955

ISBN 13: 978-1-03-209901-9 (pbk)
ISBN 13: 978-0-415-50014-2 (hbk)

Typeset in Times New Roman
by Wearset Ltd, Boldon, Tyne and Wear

Contents

Contents

Contributors

Hu Jichuang (1903–1993) studied at the LSE and held positions at Sichuan University, Northeastern University, Shanghai University of Finance and Economics, Beijing University and Beijing Normal University. He was also President of Zhejiang University of Finance and Economics, President of the Association of History of Chinese Economic Thought, and a member of the Shanghai Academy of Social Sciences. His major works include *History of Chinese Economic Thought* (vols 1–3, Shanghai: People's Publishing House, 1962, 1978, 1981), *A Concise History of Chinese Economic Thought* (Chinese version: Beijing: CASS Press, 1981; English-language version: Beijing: Foreign Languages Press, 1988) and *Brilliant Achievements of Ancient Chinese Economic Thought* (Beijing: CASS Press, 1981; published in English as *Chinese Economic Thought before the Seventeenth Century*, Beijing: Foreign Languages Press, 1984).

Li Chaomin (1963–) is a researcher at Shanghai University of Finance and Economics. His recent publications include *The Coming of China's War Finance Policies, 1931–1945* (Shanghai: The Oriental Press, 2011) and *A New China History of Defence Economics* (Shanghai: SDX Joint Publishing Company, 2010).

Ma Tao (1957–) is Professor of Economics at Fudan University, where he is also Deputy Director of the China Research Centre of Financial History and Deputy Director of the Institute of Economic Thought and Economic History. His major works include *Dawn in the Middle Ages – Enlightenment Trends in the Late Ming and Early Qing Period* (Shanghai: Shanghai University of Finance and Economics Press, 2003) and *History of Economic Thought* (Shanghai: Fudan University Press, 2002).

Tan Min (1949–) is the former President of Shanghai University of Finance and Economics and Vice Chairman of the Shanghai Social Sciences Association. He was previously President of the Association of History of Chinese Economic Thought. His major works include *History of Chinese Financial Thought* (co-authored with Hu Jichuang, Beijing: China Financial and Economic Publishing House, 1989) and *Chinese Origin of the Theory of the*

French Physiocrats (Shanghai: Shanghai People's Publishing House, 1992). Tan Min was the PhD student of Hu Jichuang.

Tang Renwu (1954–) holds positions including Vice Director of the Chinese Institute of Business Administration, Vice President of the Association of the History of Chinese Economic Thought, Vice President of the Beijing Institute of Politics and Public Management, Standing Director of China Research Institute of Enterprise Culture, and Standing Director of Chinese Academy of Business Education. He is the Associate Editor of *Reform* and editor of journals including the *Journal of Beijing Normal University*, *Pacific Journal* and *Journal of Capital University of Economics and Business*.

Wu Baosan (1905–1999) held positions including Director of the Institute of Economics of the Chinese Academy of Social Sciences and Vice President and Honorary President of the Association of the History of Chinese Economic Thought. His major works include his edition of *National Income of China* (1933), the first academic work on the national income of China (Shanghai: The Chinese Publishing House, 1947), *A Selection of China's Modern Economic Thought and Economic Policy Data* (1840–1864) co-authored with Feng Ze and Wu Chaolin (Beijing: Sciences Press, 1959) and *History of Economic Thought in the Pre-Qin Period* (Beijing: China Social Sciences Press, 1996).

Yan Qinghua (1951–) is Professor of Economics at Wuhan University and Vice President of the Association of the History of Chinese Economic Thought. His major works include *History of Chinese Economic Thought* (Hong Kong: Qianjin Press, 2004) and *Theoretical Innovation of China's Economic Development Model* (Haikou: South Press, 2001).

Ye Shichang (1929–) is Professor of Economics at Fudan University and Director of the Association of History of Chinese Economic Thought. His major works include *China's Monetary Theory around the Opium War* (Shanghai: Shanghai People's Publishing House, 1963), *A Concise History of Chinese Economic Thought* (vols 1–3, Shanghai: Shanghai People's Publishing House, 1978–1983) and *A General Financial History of China* (Beijing: China Finance Publishing House, 2002).

Ye Tan (1956–) is a Research Fellow at the Institute of Economics, Chinese Academy of Social Sciences, and Professor at the Graduate School of the Chinese Academy of Social Sciences. Her major works include *On Prosperity in the Song Dynasty* (Beijing: Beijing Publishing House, 1991), *A Major Political Reform – Emperor Shenzong of the Song Dynasty and the 11th Century Reform* (Beijing: Sanlian Press, 1996) and *Collection of Ye Tan: Confucianism and Economics* (Guangxi: Guangzi People's Publishing House, 2005).

Zhao Jing (1912–2007) was Professor of Economics at Beijing University and President of the Association of History of Chinese Economic Thought. His major works include *History of Chinese Economic Thought in Modern Times* (vols 1–3, co-authored with Yi Menghong, Beijing: The Chinese Publishing House, 1964, 1965, 1966), and *History of Modern Chinese Economic Thought* (ed., vols 1–4, Beijing: Beijing University Press, 1991–1998).

Zheng Xueyi (1953–2009) was Professor of Economics at Beijing University and President of the Association of the History of Chinese Economic Thought. His major works include *Historical Footprints to the World: Study of Modern Chinese Thought on Opening-up* (Beijing: Beijing University Press, 1990) and *History of Chinese Thought on Price* (Beijing: China Press, 1993).

Zhong Xiangcai (1954–) is a Research Fellow and Director of the Division of History of Economic Thought at Shanghai Academy of Social Sciences. His major works include *A History of Chinese Land Thought* (Shanghai: Shanghai Academy of Social Sciences Press, 1995) and *A History of Chinese Income Distribution Thought* (Shanghai: Shanghai Academy of Social Sciences Press, 2005).

Analytical table of contents

1 Considerations on the research methodology of the history of Chinese economic thought

Hu Jichuang

This chapter considers issues relating to the research methodology of the history of Chinese economic thought at what may be called the foundation stage of the discipline. It studies three major issues – the systemisation, comparative analysis and modernisation of ancient thought – and proposes a set of research methods for the subject. It also considers the challenges that are likely to be faced in future research and proposes criteria that should be satisfied by scholars in the area.

2 On the major fields and significance of the study of the history of ancient Chinese economic thought

Wu Baosan

This chapter argues for the importance of research in the history of Chinese economic thought through a comparative analysis of the evolution and significance of the research status of Chinese and Western histories of the subject. It is argued that the history of Chinese economic thought is an integral part of the history of international economic thought and that detailed study of feudal economic thought in China can play an important role in the promotion of Chinese culture and in enriching our understanding of ancient economic thought internationally. Examples are taken from Confucian, Daoist and other pre-Qin schools of economic thought. It is explained that research on the history of ancient Chinese economic thought mainly includes three aspects: philosophical thought as the basis or starting point for economic analysis; ideas and policies on various practical economic issues; and the analysis of relationships between economic phenomena and problems.

3 *Fu Guo Xue* and the "economics" of ancient China

Zhao Jing

It is argued in this chapter that there were concepts such as "the economy" and "economics" in ancient China, but that the "economics" of ancient China was quite different from "economics" in its modern sense. The study of economic issues in ancient China was mainly carried out under the banner of *Fu Guo*, which may be translated as "making the country rich", and *Fu Guo Xue*, the study of that subject. *Fu Guo Xue*, although not an independent discipline, presented many in-depth discussions of various issues and in doing so exhibited strong characteristics of an emerging theoretical discourse.

4 The Chinese origin of Physiocratic economics

Tan Min

The seventeenth and eighteenth centuries were a period of cultural exchange between China and Europe, especially France. In this chapter it is argued that the evolution of modern (Western) economics was greatly influenced by the ancient Chinese economic thought transmitted to Europe at that time. The paper analyses the relationship between ancient Chinese economic thought and Western thought, in particular the thought of the French Physiocrats. It is argued that Chinese thought was a major source for the economic theory of the Physiocrats, and that ancient Chinese thought not only was a brilliant achievement in its own right, but also provided the ideological origins of modern political economy.

5 On *Guanzi Qing Zhong*

Ye Shichang

Guanzi Qing Zhong ("Weighing and Balancing Economic Forces") is a work containing the greatest wealth of economic thought in ancient China, taking as its object the circulation process in the early feudal period. This chapter elaborates key aspects of the book's comprehensive analysis of circulation, including value theory, finance theory and monetary theory. The analysis in *Guanzi Qing Zhong* focuses on the role of national commercial capital and state usury capital, thereby recognising the coercive power of government as an integral part of the theory.

6 A comparison between Confucian and Daoist economic philosophies in the pre-Qin era

Tang Renwu

The two most influential schools of philosophy in ancient China were Confucianism and Daoism. The aim of this chapter is to compare Confucian and Daoist economic philosophies, thereby to shed light on the development of Chinese economic thought. Confucian and Daoist philosophies are mutually antagonistic: Daoism is concerned with *yin* and the nature of "Heaven's ways", while Confucianism is concerned with *yang* and the nature of "human ways". In terms of economic thought, Confucianism takes an overall perspective in which the restraint and channelling of desires is advocated, while Daoism adopts an individualistic approach and urges freedom from desires and indulgence. In terms of the design of utopia, Confucianism holds that an ideal society is one in which "the world is for all", while Daoism advocates "small country, small population". Additionally, Confucianism supports, while Daoism opposes, the institution of private property; Confucianism advocates "ethical" production, Daoism favours "natural" production; Confucianism supports cooperative work-sharing, Daoism endorses self-sufficiency; and, in the realm of distribution, Confucianism supports equality and the elimination of poverty among the masses, while Daoism advocates an even distribution of wealth among the population as a whole. Both philosophies have exerted a profound influence on later generations, but in different ways. Confucianism became an official, orthodox school of thought, while the Daoist influence was more subtle.

7 The start of family economics of Chinese feudal landowners: on Jia Sixie's *Important Arts for People's Welfare*

Zheng Xueyi

Important Arts for People's Welfare, written by Jia Sixie in AD 533–534, is one of the world's earliest extant works on agriculture; it is also a representative work of the "Knowledge of Livelihood" tradition of China's landed aristocracy in ancient times. As described by Jia Sixie, the family economics of feudal landowners is composed of three parts: first, the "Way of Livelihood" is the choice of the object or means of a family's business and of theories related to this choice; second, the "Theory of Livelihood' aims to provide guidance at the "micro" level, with the emphasis on concepts including thrift, management and efficiency; third, the "Strategy of Livelihood" gives practical advice on methods and measures of successful management. These three parts provided a foundation and direction for the formation and development of the household economics of China's feudal landowners.

8 Confucian thought on the free economy

Ma Tao

This chapter analyses and evaluates the strongly liberal strand of economic thought in Confucian philosophy, as represented by the writings of Confucius himself, and his followers including Mencius, Sima Qian, Ye Shi and Qiu Jun. Confucian liberal economic thought actively promoted the development of the commodity economy in ancient China, with its two peaks of the Spring and Autumn period through to the Western Han period, and the Song period through to the Ming. Those peaks were associated with dominance of Confucian economic thought and its influence on economic policies. The paper further suggests that Confucian liberal economic thought continues to exert great influence in East Asian countries, and it is argued that China should continue to take heed of Confucian thought in conducting its market reforms.

9 Etymological studies of "Chinese economics"

Ye Tan

This chapter begins with a study of the meaning and etymology of *Jingji* (the Chinese equivalent of "Economy"). By means of a contrast between the traditional Chinese understanding of "the study of economy" and the Western understanding of "economics", the chapter reviews the difficulties posed for China in accepting Western ideas and in preserving a distinctively "Chinese economics". The merits of treating the history of Chinese economic thought as an independent branch of Chinese economics are considered, and proposals are made for a more nuanced treatment of the complex relationships between economic theory, applications, and the different traditions of economic ideas.

10 The theory of division of labour in Chinese history

Yan Qinghua

Long before Adam Smith and other Western scholars elaborated their theories of the division of labour, the subject had been discussed by Chinese thinkers, of whom Mencius was a typical example, ever since the Spring and Autumn and Warring States periods (770–221 BC). Chinese thinkers had demonstrated the necessity for the division of labour in terms of multifaceted individual demand on the one hand, and one-sided individual capacity on the other. They described the positive role that division of labour, in various aspects, plays in enhancing professional skills, in producing economic benefit and in achieving a state of harmony between economic organisation and social life. It is argued that the theories of the division of labour articulated by writers including Mencius and Xunzi are among the richest literary treasures of ancient Chinese thought.

11 Harmony of Diversity and Great Uniformity: two trains of thought in the economics of ancient China

Zhong Xiangcai

In the history of China there were two economic trains of thought for building an ideal society: one was the theory of economic diversity based on the principle of harmony, and the other was the "Great Uniformity" (or "Great Harmony") social model stressing the abolition of private ownership. The two trains of thought reflected different philosophical methodologies, hence their policy suggestions are different and their social influences also vary greatly. According to the analysis in this chapter, the market economy of the present time shows the value of harmony increasingly clearly, although the danger of reverting to the Great Uniformity model has not disappeared completely.

12 The influence of ancient Chinese thought on the Ever-Normal Granary of Henry A. Wallace and the Agricultural Adjustment Act in the New Deal

Li Chaomin

This chapter argues that ancient Chinese thought of the Ever-Normal Granary and Green Sprout Money was the ideological basis for Henry Wallace's agricultural policies in the 1930s, which laid the foundation for the American agricultural legal structure and played an important role in combating the Great Depression. The chapter contends that the idea of the Ever-Normal Granary and the Green Sprout Money is an example of the significant influence exerted by ancient Chinese civilisation on the development of American economic thought.

Acknowledgements

Cheng Lin and Wang Fang would like to thank the following: Tian Linxia and Professors Zhou Jianbo and Zhang Yaguang (Beijing University) for their help with the translation of Zheng Xueyi's chapter; Professor Zheng Hongliang, Deputy Editor-in-Chief of *Economic Research Journal*, Feng Yuejian, Editor-in-Chief of *Journal of Chinese Economic History*, and Lu Rong, Editor-in-Chief of the *Journal of Finance and Economics* for their efforts in obtaining permission to republish papers; Lin Yue and Yan Huan, Research Secretaries at the School of Economics, Shanghai University of Finance and Economics, and Lu Nengbo, Master's student at the School of Economics, for help with translating and proofreading; and Zhang Shen and Yue Xingyu, also of the School of Economics, for their general editorial assistance. They also acknowledge the support from the Leading Academic Discipline Program, 211 Project for Shanghai University of Finance and Economics.

Terry Peach records his thanks to Tong Ping and Chen Zhixin for their help and support, and he seconds the thanks to Yue Xingyu for his outstanding assistance. He expresses his gratitude to Professor Cheng Lin and other colleagues at the School of Economics, Shanghai University of Finance and Economics, for their generous hospitality, friendship and guidance during his tenure of a Visiting Professorship at their institution. His greatest debt of gratitude is to Zhang Shen, whose efforts were more commensurate with those of an editor than an assistant.

Finally, the editors wish to commend Natalie Tomlinson of Routledge for her admirable patience in waiting for the delivery of the manuscript and for her general support and guidance.

Chronology

BC	Dynasty/Period				
2852–2357		Culture Heroes: Fu Xi, Shen Nong (Yandi), Huangdi (Yellow Emperor)			
2357–1950		Sage Kings: Yao, Shun and Yu			
1950–1550	Legendary Xia	Founded by Yu Terminated by Jie ("the robber")			
1550–1125	Shang (or Yin)	Founded by Tang Terminated by King Zhou			
1125–221	Zhou	Founded by King Wu. Succeeded by Cheng with the Duke of Zhou as regent during early years of reign			
1125–770	Western Zhou	*(Brace these four rows)*	680: Duke Huan of Qi (r. 685–643) becomes first Hegemon (*ba*) Guan Zhong (*c.*723–645) serves as Chief Minister		
770–480	Eastern Zhou/ Spring and Autumn period		571–480: traditional dates for Laozi (apocryphal)		
			551–479: traditional dates for Confucius		
		(Brace these five rows)	479–372: life of Mo Di tentatively ascribed to this interval	*(Brace these six rows)*	
			390–338: Wei Yang/Lord Shang		550–233: "Age of a hundred schools of philosophy"
480–221	Warring States period		370–290: Mencius; possibly also Zhuang Zhou around this time		
			312–?: Xun Qing (Qun Kuang)		
			280–233: Han Fei		
221–206	Qin	Li Si (d. 208) appointed as Chief Minister 213: Burning of books			
BC/AD					
206–9	Western Han	*c.*145–89: Sima Qian, *Records of the Grand Historian*			
25–220	Eastern Han				
265–317	Western Jin				
304–589	Southern				
317–420	Eastern Jin				
386–534	Northern Wei	*Important Arts for People's Welfare*, by Jia Sixie			
589–619	Sui				
619–907	Tang				
960–1127	Song	1021–1086: Wang Anshi			
1279–1368	Yuan				
1368–1644	Ming				
1644–1911/12	Qing	1839–1842	*(Brace)*	Opium Wars	
		1857–1860			
		1911: Chen Huanzhang's *Economic Principles of Confucius and his School*			
1911/12	Fall of Qing	Sun Yatsen declares *Jingji* as the translation of "Economics"			
1949–	People's Republic of China	1980: Inauguration of the Association of the History of Chinese Economic Thought (Hu Jichuang as first President)			

Editorial note

We have adopted the pinyin system of transliteration throughout this volume.

Our greatest challenge has been with the translation of papers. In the long iterative process that has taken place in compiling this volume we have attempted to retain the sense of the original Chinese versions while aspiring to produce readable English-language correspondents.

Translation of quotations from ancient sources has posed a particularly thorny problem. In cases where scholarly English-language translations exist, we have either substituted quotations from those texts (where we judge that no change of meaning is involved), or we have left the Chinese translations unchanged (where we judge that differences in meaning are minimal); also, in some cases we have given the received English-language translations in square-bracketed footnotes.

The production of bibliographical references in this volume has been subject to two constraints.

Ancient texts are frequently cited in the pages that follow. As there are so many editions and translations, generic references have been given, allowing the reader to locate the context of the quotation in whichever edition is to hand; and similarly for texts long established in more recent Chinese culture.

More conventional references are given for works published in the West and for modern Chinese works.

Where a specific translation is being quoted, bibliographical details are given.

Separately from this issue, we are bound by the references included when the papers that make up the twelve chapters of this book were originally published. In some cases, we have been able to interpolate additional footnotes (in square brackets) but in the majority of cases we have been obliged to follow the originals.

Note: Throughout this volume, when referring to Chinese personal names we have followed the Chinese convention of giving the family name first.

Introduction

This volume presents a collection of papers on the history of Chinese economic thought, mostly on or related to "ancient" thought (up to the Western Han dynasty, 206 BC–AD 9), written by Chinese scholars who have dominated the field since the founding of "New China" in 1949. The topics discussed in the papers range from fundamental questions of historiography (methodology) to detailed appraisals of the content, merit, influence and contemporary relevance of ancient Chinese thought.

As remarked by James L.Y. Chang (1987), works "on the history of Chinese economic thought are exceedingly scarce outside China",[1] and little has changed since those words were written. As China's global stature continues to grow, it seems fitting that a Western readership should have an opportunity to become acquainted with Chinese interpretations of the thought of their own ancient civilisation.

We are aware that non-Sinologists may find it daunting to engage with material that was mostly written for a Chinese readership. Within the main body of the text we have therefore interposed in square brackets a number of editorial footnotes with the aim of clarifying particular points. To the same end, we now offer sections that deal successively with overviews of the development of the history of economic thought in China, and the context and writings of the various individuals who make up the major "schools" of ancient Chinese thought.

The history of economic thought in China[2]

It was not until the late nineteenth and early twentieth century that studies were published on the history of Chinese economic thought, only after the Western subject of "economics" (or "political economy") had been introduced to China

---

1 "History of Chinese economic thought: overview and recent works", *History of Political Economy* 19.3, pp. 481–502.
2 In this section we draw freely on two unpublished papers: Cheng Lin and Wang Fang, "Evolution of the History of Chinese Economic Thought"; and Cheng Ling and Yue Xiangyu, "The Spread of Western Financial Theory and the Transition of Financial Thought and Institutional Arrangements in the Late Qing Dynasty".

in the turbulent aftermath of the Opium Wars (1839–1842, 1857–1860). Before that time, the very notion of a distinct subject-area of "economics" did not exist in China, let alone the history of that subject. The country remained cocooned in its "Celestial Empire", protected from what were viewed as the noxious influences and ideas of Western "barbarians" by a "Seclusion Policy" which, as it turned out, proved woefully inadequate to defend "all under Heaven" (the Chinese) from artillery deployed in the service of Western merchants and capitalists.

The defeat by Western powers compelled China to face what was referred to at the time, perhaps as an understatement, as "a tremendous change".[3] The opening of ports and granting of territorial concessions that had been forced on China in a succession of one-sided treaties had introduced foreign, capitalistic industrial and financial enterprises into the country, propelling China into the wave of capitalist expansion. Local enterprises, run by the Qing government and by private individuals, began to develop, resulting in the gradual embedding of new, capitalist relations of production, so prompting the gradual disintegration of the old "natural economy". Shocked and humiliated, it began to occur to the Chinese that there might be something to be gained from studying Western thought and practice (initially in the area of armaments, but later extending to areas even including fine art), a policy that became known as *ziqiang* or "self-strengthening", also referred to as "Chinese learning as the base, Western studies for use" and, more pointedly, as "learning from foreigners to defeat the foreigners".[4]

An early manifestation of the "Westernisation" movement was the establishment in Beijing of the *Tongwenguan* college, with similar institutions set up in Shanghai, Guangzhou and Fuzhou. Initially, the aim was to teach foreign languages, but the syllabus soon expanded to include other subjects, including Western economics/political economy. W.A.P. Martin, an American missionary who became Principal of the Beijing *Tongwenguan*, held that the dissemination of Western knowledge, including political economy, together with an introduction to the history of European and American history and civilisation, would help to dispel Chinese "myths" of their unique cultural superiority and guide them towards an appreciation of Western values (and religion). Martin would be the first to translate a book on Western political economy (Henry Fawcett's *A Manual of Political Economy*), published in China in 1880 but used as the basis for Martin's lectures from the 1860s.[5]

---

3 Li Hongzhang, *"Fuyi Zhizao Lunchuan Weike Caiche Zhe"* ("Proposal to Reconsider the Abolition of Ship Manufacturing") (1872) and *"Yin Taiwan Shibian Chouhua Haifang Zhe"* ("Proposal on Coastal Defence Planning after the Taiwan Incident") (1875). Quoted from Liang Qichao, *Li Hongzhang Zhuan* ("Biography of Li Hongzhang"), Tianjin: Tianjin Baihua Wenyi Press, 2008, Chapter 6.

4 Wei Yuan [1844], Hai Guo Tu Zhi (海国图志) ("Illustrated Treatise on the Maritime Kingdoms") (Changsha: Yue Lu Publishing House, 1998).

5 The publication of the Chinese translation of Fawcett's *Manual* was followed six years later by J. Edkins's translation of W.S. Jevons's *Primer of Political Economy*.

The defeat of China in the Sino-Japanese war of 1894–1895 lent more impetus to the "Westernisation movement", although the process was only to be accelerated after the Boxer rebellion and the occupation and vandalisation of Beijing by Western powers in 1900. One year later the Dowager Empress Cixi, earlier an opponent of radical change, issued an edict calling for, inter alia, the establishment of modern schools, the reform of the examination system (which had been based on the rote learning of the Confucian classics) and, notably, a "study-abroad" programme for Chinese students, with Japan, because of its proximity, as the favoured (but not exclusive) destination. Before 1900 it is estimated that there were approximately 200 Chinese students in Japan, a number that would swell to around 12,000 at its peak in 1905–1906.

Japan had embarked on its own "Westernisation" movement at the beginning of the Meiji period (1868–1912) and by the time the Chinese students were arriving the teaching of Western economics/political economy was firmly established on the curriculum. But it was not only the subject itself that the Chinese learned from the Japanese, it was also the name of that subject which, with an ironic twist, the Japanese had borrowed from the Chinese language: *Jingji* (经济).

Scholars concur that references to *Jingji* may be found in Chinese literature dating back to at least the fourth century BC. But its meaning at that time was not *Jingji* in the sense of eighteenth and early nineteenth century Western conceptions of economics/political economy. Rather, it referred much more broadly to national governance, "which included not only financial and economic aspects [in the "modern" understanding of those terms] but also politics, law, military studies, geography, construction and so-called 'foreign knowledge' as well".[6] Following the overthrow of the Qing dynasty in 1911, the nationalist leader, Sun Yatsen, pronounced that economics should indeed be referred to as *Jingji*, and so it has been ever since.

By the early twentieth century, then, the Chinese were making rapid strides in their study of "Western *Jingji*", and it was not long before they were exposed to Chinese versions of the history of the Western subject (Liang Qichao, a Chinese returnee from Japan, published his *Short History* in 1902, one year after Yan Fu's translation of Adam Smith's *Wealth of Nations*).[7] It was also around this time that the study of the history of Chinese economic thought began to attract attention.

It could be seen as inevitable that the absorption by the Chinese of Western conceptions of *Jingji*, and their acquaintance with histories of the Western subject, would lead them to construct their own "histories" following much the same pattern, and that is what happened. Nor is it particularly surprising, in view of the humiliation that Western powers had inflicted on their country, that they should seek and proclaim the splendour of their own contributions to the subject. In addition, a characteristic of many publications up until 1949 was to further the

---

6 Zhao Jing, this volume, p. 67.

7 It has been estimated that fifteen books were published in Chinese on the history of Western economic though in the period 1898–1911 (Ye Tan, this volume, p. 176).

nationalist cause of using "history" as preparation for the creation of a distinctively Chinese *Jingji*.

One of the first such publications was Liang Qichao's *A Modernised Interpretation of the Records of the Historian* in which it was argued that the "Biography of the Money-Makers", written by Sima Qian (*c*.145–89 BC) in the Western Han dynasty,[8] contained rich economic ideas that "have certain elements in common with Western economic thought and can help to boost the commerce of China once fully interpreted and utilised".[9] Indeed, Liang maintained not only that there were "common elements", but that China had already produced an "economics" similar to Western *Jingji* in the pre-Qin period (before 221 BC).

A second landmark study, the first to be published in (and at that time only in) English, was Chen Huanzhang's *Economic Principles of Confucius and his School* (1911), which had been written in part submission for the PhD he was awarded from Columbia University. As Henry R. Seager commented in the Preface to Chen's book:

> In presenting the economic teachings of Confucianism, Dr. Chen has adopted the same order of arrangement that has become usual in English treatises on political economy. The danger which this plan involves of creating the impression of a more systematic exposition of economic principles than is to be found in the sacred writings,[10] is much more outweighed by the large number of clear anticipations of the accepted economic teachings of today which it reveals.[11]

That Chen did indeed impose an "English" historiography, and highlight what were proclaimed, by Chen, as "clear anticipations of the accepted [Western] economic teachings of today", is amply born out as one peruses the 720 pages of his "learned and delightful book", as Keynes described it.[12] Thus, we are informed that "economic principles" are "quite abundant" in Confucius's own writings; that Confucian economic thought envisages three "factors of production", namely, men, land and capital; that Confucians fully appreciated the influences of scarcity, utility and cost-of-production on value (having presciently anticipated Alfred Marshall on this score, so it would seem); that they understood the principles of "supply and demand"; that they supported free international trade; and, remarkably, that they upheld a "productivity" theory of wages, by which they had meant "productive of utility". As to the contemporary relevance of "Confucian economics", imaginatively construed by Chen as a kind of

---

8 We return to Sima Qian and his famous essay below.
9 Liang Qichao [1907] (1989) 史记货殖列传今义 ("A Modernised Interpretation of 'The Biographies of the Money-Makers' in 'Records of the Grand Historian'") (Beijing: Zhonghua Book Company, [1907] 1989).
10 Seager is following Chen in portraying Confucianism as a "religion".
11 Seager in Chen Huanzhang, *The Economic Principles of Confucius and his School*. New York: Columbia University Press, 1911 p. ix.
12 Review of Chen (1911) in *The Economic Journal*, December 1912, pp. 584–588.

non-Marxist "religious socialism", it transpires that "Confucianism did not make China weak. She is weak not because she followed the teachings of Confucius, but precisely because she did not truly follow his teachings".[13] China's way forward was therefore a return to texts that had been written up to several millennia earlier.

More studies followed. The rate of publication increased rapidly during the late 1920s and 1930s, and courses were offered in the subject in at least ten educational institutions. Of the works published before 1949, Tang Qingzeng's *History of Economic Thought* (1936) is regarded by many within China as the most important. Based on a study of pre-Qin texts, Tang contended that there had been a "Western spread" of ancient Chinese ideas on *Jingji*: "ancient Chinese economic thought exerted a greater influence in Western countries than that of the Roman doctrine, Christian thought, and the Bible, especially on the French School of Physiocrats". The implication was that it was not only the name of the subject (*Jingji*) that had come from China; it was the very origin of the subject itself.[14]

To summarise, we can identify the following general characteristics of studies on the history of Chinese economic thought up to 1949: it was approached with a contemporary Western conception of *Jingji* and adopted the Western teleological practice of conceiving the subject's "history" as a search for anticipations of "correct" ideas, as embraced by contemporary economists; it was written by scholars who had been recently exposed to Western *Jingji*, in many cases from abroad; it focused overwhelmingly on ancient (pre-Qin) thought; it was often undertaken not merely as "historical study" but also to aid national reconstruction; and, through its "results", it played the role of promoting national pride in the wake of Western degradation.

The period 1956–1965 was marked by a renewal of interest in the subject, one difference with the earlier period being the introduction of Marxist terminology and historiography. Key works were published, including those by Hu Jichuang, Zhao Jing and Wu Baosan, whose contributions are represented in this collection. With the onset of the Cultural Revolution in 1965, however, research and publication activity came to an abrupt standstill, only to be resumed in earnest after 1978 (the inauguration of the Association of the History of Chinese Economic Thought, with Hu Jichuang as its first President, took place two years later). Since then research output has proliferated, with greater attention paid than previously to post-Qin and modern economic thought, comparative studies of Chinese and Western thought, and the relevance of historical studies to modern economic development and to contemporary political and social conditions.

Yet, for all the developments in the subject, the pre-1949 period continued to exercise a dominant influence on the research agenda. This is true not only in the sense that ancient thought has remained the most populated research area, but

13 Chen (1911) p. 720.
14 A variation on the same theme is argued by Tan Min in this volume.

also that scholars are still grappling with the issues raised in those earlier studies. For some, the point of the subject continues to one of celebrating the ancient Chinese contributions to "Western *Jingji*" (or, depending on taste, to "neo-Chinese *Jingji*"), while for others the aim has been to reject or qualify what is seen as the "modernisation" of ancient thought and to reconstruct it in its own terms and within its own distinctive historical context.

In the following section we provide an introduction to the historical milieu in which ancient thought emerged and, in mainly chronological sequence,[15] to the most important individuals and "schools" of that time.

Ancient Chinese thought: an introduction

Ancient Chinese political, philosophical and economic thought is conventionally represented as originating in the "Spring and Autumn" and "Warring States" periods, preceding the establishment of the Qin dynasty in 221 BC. With regard to economic thought, more narrowly, the period is extended to include the early Western Han (206 BC–AD 9) in order to accommodate two works (the *Guanzi* and *Shi Ji*, both discussed below) which are generally held to contain outstanding examples of early Chinese contributions to the subject.

Knowledge of pre-Qin China is limited and dates for particular periods and events can be taken only as rough estimates. Nevertheless, it is generally accepted that the Zhou dynasty was founded by King Wu around 1125 BC and that it endured as a powerful entity until *c.*770 BC. This period, known as the Western Zhou, was to be celebrated by many as a golden age of Chinese civilisation, with the Duke of Zhou (King Wu's brother) lionised as the very embodiment of the just and virtuous prince. The story told is that when King Wu died, his son and heir (King Cheng) was a child, so the Duke of Zhou ruled as regent. But as soon as Cheng reached the age of maturity the duke selflessly handed back the reins of power, allowing the continuity of the dynasty and enshrining his own place in history.

The Western Zhou was brought to an end by tribal invasions which forced the eastern relocation of the capital from Hao to Chengzhou (in the vicinity of modern-day Xi'an and Luoyang, respectively). Thereafter, the power of the dynasty began to decline, the seeds for its demise having been sown by its founder, King Wu, who had enfeoffed allies and family as feudal lords in the many states of the empire with a view to consolidating his power. The strategy appears to have worked well enough until the northern incursion, but after the central state had been weakened the vassals embarked on the path of strengthening their own positions both relatively to the central Zhou state and to each other, the final result being the conquest of "all under Heaven" by the Qin in 221 BC.

The division of the intervening centuries into the Spring and Autumn period (770–480 BC) and Warring States period (480–221) is possibly misleading to the

---

15 The principal exception being our discussion of Daoism, which we have found convenient to locate immediately following our review of Han Fei and Legalism.

extent of suggesting that states were not "warring" in the former period, which they most certainly were.[16] As reported by Sima Qian some 500 years later, from around 650 BC,

> the empire was torn by the strife of the warring kingdoms. Men honoured deceit and power and scoffed at benevolence and righteousness; they put wealth and possession first and courtesy and humility last.... The more powerful rulers annexed the smaller fiefs and made subjects of their lords, while in the weaker states the ruling families were wiped out and the sacrifices to their ancestors cut off forever.[17]

With the Zhou dynasty becoming increasingly enfeebled, although nominally still in existence, real power in the Spring and Autumn period devolved to a succession of feudal rulers who assumed the title of *ba* (hegemon), usually said to include Duke Huan of Qi (r. 685–643 BC), Duke Wen of Jin (r. 636–628 BC) and Duke Mu of Qin (r. 659 BC). But, by the end of the period even this pragmatic attempt to impose some measure of order had broken down.

It was the scale, ferocity and sophistication of inter-state warfare which increased during the Warring States period. At the beginning of the earlier period there had been in the region of fifteen major states. By 361 BC, the position as recounted by Sima Qian, was this:

> In the area east of the Yellow River and the mountains, six powerful states [remained] in existence, the ruler King Wei of Qi, King Xuan of Chu, King Hui of Wei, Duke Dao of Yan, Duke Ai of Hann, and Duke Cheng of Zhao being ranged side by side, while in the region of the Hui and Si rivers there were ten or more smaller states.... The Zhao royal house had sunk into insignificance and the feudal lords ruled by force, wrangling with one another and annexing each other's lands.[18]

By 249 BC the rump Zhao dynasty had ceased to exist altogether, with only three powerful states remaining (Qin, Chu and Qi) to continue the slaughter.

The cost in human lives and misery in the centuries after the demise of the Western Zhou is incalculable but, at the same time, this was a period of great technological, economic and intellectual advancement. Mining underwent rapid development, highly sophisticated copper and bronze (and later iron) artefacts, agricultural implements and weaponry were crafted, attention was paid to the

---

16 The naming of the earlier period has nothing to do with the presence of absence of war; it was an allusion to the *Spring and Autumn Annals*, which provided a chronicle of the state of Lu from 722 to 469 BC.

17 Sima Qian, *Shi Ji* ("Records of the Grand Historian") 30, "The Treatise on the Balanced Standard", in B. Watson (tr.), *Records of the Grand Historian: Han Dynasty II* (New York: Columbia University Press, 1993) pp. 84–85.

18 Sima Qian, *Shi Ji* 5, "The Basic Annals of Qin", in B. Watson (tr.) *Records of the Grand Historian: Qin Dynasty* (New York: Columbia University Press, 1993) p. 23.

better use of land, commerce flourished, and urbanisation increased. It was also a time when rulers of the various states would encourage itinerant scholars to proffer advice on the administration of their domains (in the fourth century BC, King Xuan of Qi established the Jixia Academy by offering honorary titles and generous financial inducements to attract scholars, who were expected to study and expound their various doctrines). This was the age of the "hundred schools of philosophy" (*c.*550–233 BC), inaugurated by possibly the most influential philosopher of them all, Kongfuzi (Master Kong Fu), better known in the West by his Latinised name, Confucius (*c.*551–479 BC).

Confucius was born in the state of Lu. From the little that is known of his life, it would seem that he was a man of political ambition and firm conviction in the righteousness of his teachings, travelling between states in the hope of achieving high office but without much success (as he reportedly lamented, "If only there were someone to employ me, in not more than a year's time things would become acceptable, and after three years there would be results"[19]). Such information as we have of his teachings comes mainly from the *Lun Yu*, the literal meaning of which is "selected statements", hereafter referred to by its Western title, *Analects*. This work was not composed by Confucius but was compiled by his "disciples" and their followers over an uncertain period, possibly extending to centuries. As to the provenance of the sayings, Arthur Waley wrote in his 1938 translation, "I think we are justified in supposing that the book does not contain many authentic sayings [of Confucius], and may possibly contain none at all"[20]: a view that has been echoed more recently.[21] We shall follow the convention of referring to the saying as if they emanated from an historical person, although we do so throughout with a silent caveat over their authenticity.

The Confucius of the Analects is portrayed as looking back nostalgically to the time of the Western Zhou and as seeking to reintroduce the values that had allegedly prevailed in that earlier, golden time ("we take Zhou as our model"[22]). In the ideal state, one in which "those who are close by are pleased and those who are far off are attracted",[23] the ruler would be advised by junzi ("gentle-men") who pursued the dao ("way") of good governance rather than personal profit.[24] Through the example of the ruler's own personal "humaneness", encompassing "courtesy, tolerance, good faith, diligence, and kindness",[25] by instilling

---

19 *Analects* XIII.10. Referees are to Raymond Dawson's translation of *The Analects* (Oxford: Oxford University Press, 1993) unless stated otherwise.
20 Waley [1938], Translator's Preface, *The Analects* (London: Everyman, 2000), p. 19.
21 Raymond Dawson, *Confucius: The Analects* (Oxford: Oxford University Press, 1993), p. ix.
22 *Analects*, III.14.
23 Ibid., XIII.16.
24 Other qualities of *junzi* include not competing with others; cultivating universal rather than partial sympathies; "reciprocity" ("Do not impose on others what you would not like yourself" *Analects* XII.2); helping the poor; not having a concern only with salary and not being carried away by sexual attraction; being conciliatory to the ruler, but also prepared to disagree; not being self-indulgent.
25 *Analects* XVII.5.

in "the people" a respect for "rites",[26] by promoting a taste for "elegant music"[27] and, in the last resort, by inflicting punishments to correct errant behaviour, the result of this governance would be a well-ordered, hierarchical state in which people were "good", "obedient" and "submissive", with a regard for their ruler akin to that of a respectful, well-mannered and grateful child to its father.

As to the "economic" content of the *Analects*, there is a smattering of passages that relate broadly to economic policy, although detailed discussions are lacking. To take some examples, the state should be "economical in expenditure" and employ people (for corvée labour in the service of the state) "only in due season" (when they are not required to work on the land);[28] it should ensure that there is "sufficient food";[29] help should be given to "those who are in straightened circumstances";[30] and officials should "get people to work hard by choosing tasks which may properly be worked hard at".[31] In addition, there is a small number of passages that have come to acquire an almost canonical status for Chinese historians. The first of them reads:

> Duke Ai enquired of Master You: "The year has seen famine and the revenues are inadequate, so what should be done in such circumstances?" Master You replied: "Why not take one-tenth of their produce in tax?" He said: "With two-tenths I would still not have enough, so in that case what would a one-tenth tax achieve?" The reply was: "If the hundred surnames [i.e. the people] have plenty, then with whom will your lordship share insufficiency; but if the hundred surnames do not have plenty, with whom will you share plenty?"[32]

---

26 A useful summary of the nature and function of "rites" is given in the *Li Ji* ("Book of Rites") (although the ascription to Confucius is even more doubtful than the attributions in the *Analects*):

> Yan Yan asked again, "Are the rules of Propriety [i.e. the rites] indeed of such urgent importance?" Confucius said, "It was by those rules that the ancient kings sought to represent the ways of Heaven, and to regulate the feelings of men ... [Those] rules are rooted on heaven, have their correspondence in earth, and are applicable to spiritual beings. They extend to funeral rites, sacrifices, archery, chariot-driving, capping [the ceremony of a boy's coming-to-age], marriage, audiences, and friendly missions.... [It is] by the universal application of the rules of propriety that the lot and duty (of different classes) are fixed."
>
> *Li Yun* ("Ceremonial Usages"), sections I.iv, II.xv, pp. 215, 220 in James Legge (tr.)
> [1885] (2008) *The Li Ji or Book of Rites*, Part I (republished by Forgotten Books at www.forgottenbooks.org)

27 *Analects*, XVII.16. Confucius and his follows set great store by the performance of music which, if suitably "elegant", would purportedly induce in its listeners a refinement of manners and harmony of mind.

28 Ibid., I.5.

29 Ibid., XII.7.

30 Ibid., VI.4.

31 Ibid., XX.2.

32 Ibid., XII.9.

The standard interpretation of this passage is that through the mouthpiece of his "disciple", Confucius had himself promulgated the 10 per cent taxation rule that was later to become a stock "Confucian" policy (although it might be noted that the advice given by Master You pertained specifically to a year of famine).

A second passage relates to distribution:

> I have that the possessors of states or noble families do not worry about under-population, but worry about the people being unevenly distributed; do not worry about poverty, but worry about discontent. For when there is an even distribution there is no poverty ... and when there is contentment there will be no upheavals.[33]

The object of the "uneven distribution" in the final sentence of the above passage is left frustratingly unclear. Within China, however, "it [has] been generally understood by Confucians that what was being talked about here was the relationship between the distribution of wealth and the problem of equality",[34] thus casting Confucius in the role of an egalitarian, if only in respect of "the people".[35]

A third passage or, more precisely, a sentence, comes from *Analects* XX.2. Confucius is asked, "What sort of person must one be so that one may take part in government?", to which he answers, a person who "honours the five excellences", the first being that "the gentleman is not wasteful although he is bounteous". Pressed to clarify what is meant by being bounteous but not wasteful, Confucius responds, "If he benefits the people on the basis of what the people will really find beneficial", which has been interpreted by some Chinese scholars as to "put no restraint whatever upon people's daily affairs, a Chinese version of the modern 'laissez-faire'."[36] However, were one to take issue with this interpretation it could be pointed out, first, that Confucius's (hopelessly ambiguous) "clarification" could be and has been read quite differently;[37] second, that he immediately goes on to say that "If *he* [i.e. the gentleman] gets people to work hard *by choosing tasks* which may properly be worked hard at, then who will feel resentful?", which is not prima facie suggestive of a "laissez-faire" approach; and third, that the second of the "five excellences" is that the gentleman "is not resented although *he* gets people to work hard": a position expressed

---

33 Ibid., XVI.1.
34 Hu Jichuang, *A Concise History of Chinese Economic Thought* (Beijing: Foreign Languages Press, 1988), p. 49 n. 19.
35 A more concrete proposal for "equality" – specifically, of equality in the distribution of *land* among the agricultural population – was to be made by Confucius's follower, Mencius, with his "well-field" scheme. See below, p. 14.
36 Hu Jichuang, *A Concise History of Chinese Economic Thought* (Beijing: Foreign Languages Press, 1988), p. 45.
37 Arthur Waley suggested as a possible reading something along the lines of "if he [the gentleman] promotes agriculture instead of distributing doles and largesses" (Waley [1938], *The Analects*, p. 221 n. 1). Agriculture *could* be promoted by encouraging a "laissez-faire" approach, but that is only one possibility.

elsewhere in the *Analects*.[38] At the least, non-"laissez-faire" readings would seem perfectly defensible.

For all but the most ardent believers in "Confucian economics", it would be challenging to argue that the "economic" pickings in the *Analects* are anything other than meagre. But with Meng Ke (*c.*370–290 BC), or Mencius to give him his Latinised name, the self-proclaimed advocate, defender and developer of Confucianism, the position is different. However, by the time that Mencius was expounding his doctrines it was not only the gathering pace of inter-state warfare to which he was responding; it was also to the circulation of new and antagonistic doctrines, among which Mohism was perceived as a singularly dangerous threat.

Mohism takes its name from Mo Di or Mozi (Master Mo) who lived between the time of Confucius's death and Mencius's birth (*c.*479–372 BC). Nothing is known about his life, other than his mission to persuade feudal rulers of his cause. Mo was appalled by the actions of those he depicts as "taking delight in the injury and extermination of the people of the world":[39]

> murdering men is a paltry way to benefit [mankind] and when we calculate the expenditures for such warfare we find that they have crippled the basis of the nation's livelihood and exhausted the resources of the people to an incalculable degree.[40]

He was also exercised by the "evil, violence, thievery and rebellion" within states.[41] It was to remedy these ills that he set out his programme, his ambitious objectives being to "rescue the world from chaos and restore it to order"[42] and ensure that the people have adequate food, clothing and rest.[43]

How were those objectives to be achieved? At the philosophical level, Mo's answer was that people (rulers, especially) should embrace the principle of "universal love"; they should regard other states, families and fathers as they would their own, and other individuals as they would regard their own person.[44] In such

---

38 "Zilu asked about government. The Master said: 'By giving them a lead, cause them to work hard.'" *Analects* XIII.1.

39 "Against Offensive Warfare", in *Mozi: Basic Writings* (hereafter *Mozi*) (B. Watson tr., New York: Columbia University Press, 2003), p. 58.

40 "Against Offensive Warfare", *Mozi*, p. 57.

41 "Explaining Ghosts", *Mozi*, p. 96.

42 "Against Music", *Mozi*, p. 114–115.

43 Ibid.

44 This principle has prima facie resemblance to Confucius's notion of "reciprocity" ("Do not inflict on others what you yourself would not wish to be done to you", *Analects* XV.24). But as one commentator has observed:

> for modern readers an immediate qualification is necessary: in practice … [the Confucian saying] has to be interpreted as doing unto others as you would have others do unto you *if you had the same social role as they*. Otherwise [it] would require fathers to treat their sons in the same manner that their sons treat them – a practice that no Confucian has ever considered appropriate
>
> (Paul R. Goldin, *Confucianism*, Durham: Acumen, 2011, pp. 15–16, emphasis in original)

a world, no ruler "would raise up his state to attack another"[45] and, similarly to Confucian thought in this regard, the people would be fed when hungry, clothed when cold, nourished when sick and buried when they died.[46]

At the more practical level, the first requirement was to ensure the recruitment of competent "gentleman" who would be charged with running the state. They should be attracted by "the promise of material benefits" and appointed regardless of their social position and familial contacts. Providing that they were suitably enriched, honoured, respected and praised, Mo was confident that there would be "no difficulty in obtaining a multitude of them".[47]

It would be the "gentlemen" who issued orders, began enterprises and directed the employment of the people.[48] But they would do so only with a view to *useful* production. To take an example:

> What is the purpose of making clothing? To keep out the cold in winter and the heat in summer. Therefore the way to make clothing is to design something that will provide warmth in winter and coolness in summer. Whatever is merely decorative and does not contribute to these ends should be avoided.[49]

The same principle of "usefulness" (or of functional utilitarianism, as it might be termed) would apply to *all* spheres of production.

The state must also ensure that people are not diverted from their "useful production" and that produced wealth is not squandered on useless activities. Rulers should be persuaded to "give up their passions for collecting jewels, birds, beasts, dogs, and horses",[50] lengthy mourning rites should be curtailed (they take people away from "useful" productive activity), and music and dancing for the edification of rulers and "gentlemen" should be dispensed with altogether (those who make, play or listen to musical instruments are removed from "useful" work, and dancers "lived entirely off the efforts of others"[51]).

The embrace of "universal love", the attraction of competent "gentlemen" by the lure of financial gain, the focus and direction of economic activity on "useful" production and, to the extent possible, the minimisation of expenditure on warfare, would go some way to achieving Mo's ideal state. But there remained the problem of ensuring "order" among the general populace. To this, Mo's answer was the fear of punishment, to be inflicted by corporeal and incorporeal agencies alike on all who "failed to identify with their superiors" or

---

45 An exception being to defend a small state against an "unrighteous" attack by a larger state: "Against Offensive Warfare", *Mozi*, pp. 62–63.
46 "Universal Love", *Mozi*, pp. 42–45.
47 "Honouring the Worthy", *Mozi*, pp. 20–21.
48 "Moderation in Expenditure", *Mozi*, p. 65.
49 Ibid.
50 Ibid., p. 66.
51 "Against Music", *Mozi*, pp. 112–116.

neglected the principles of "universal love".[52] At the corporeal level, Mo advocated the rigorous application of the "five punishments",[53] supplemented at the
incorporeal level by encouraging a belief in supernatural forces (ghosts) which
"have the power to reward the worthy and punish the wicked". Indeed, inculcating a belief in ghosts was to be made "a cornerstone of policy in the state" which
would "provide a means to bring order to the state and benefit to the people".[54]

The emphasis on punishments rather than "rites" as a corrective to wayward
behaviour, the promotion of "universal love", the acceptance of "gentlemen"
who were motivated by personal profit, the condemnation of lengthy mourning
rituals and "music", and (arguably) the somewhat more *dirigiste* approach to
economic activity (exemplified by the promotion of "useful" production), were
all departures from standard Confucian teaching. Little wonder, then, that Mo
should have dismissed Confucian learning as "of no use in deciding what is right
for the age", to which he added a vitriolic ad hominem attack on Confucius and
his followers.[55] Little wonder also that his views should have been condemned
by Mencius as heresy and a block on the road to morality.[56]

Born and raised in the small state of Zou, Mencius had studied Confucian
philosophy as a young man. Later, he followed the (by then) well-trodden path
of toting his philosophy and policy prescriptions from one state to another in the
hope of gaining influence. No less so than Mo, he was trenchantly opposed to
sending "people to war, making pulp of them, for sake of gaining further
territory".[57] What people needed, he believed, was a "true king": one who prac-
ticed "benevolence and rightness", was a good "father and mother to the people",
and would employ his (not-for-profit) "gentlemen"[58] in the mission to ensure that
the people's material needs were met and that they were educated in rites and
morality.

Although Mencius believed that rites and the "transforming influence of
morality",[59] rather than severe punishments,[60] would conduce to a benevolent
and tranquil state, he also recognised that providing for material needs must take
precedence:

> [A] clear-sighted ruler ensures that ["constant means of support"] are suffi-
> cient, on the one hand, for the care of parents, and, on the other, for the
> support of wife and children, so that the people always have sufficient food

---

52 "Identifying with One's Superior", *Mozi*, p. 39; "Universal Love", p. 51.
53 These were: tattooing, amputation of the nose, amputation of limbs, castration and execution.
54 "Explaining Ghosts", *Mozi*, p. 107.
55 "Against Confucians", ibid.
56 *Mencius* III.B.9.
57 Ibid., VII.B.1.
58 "Surely a gentleman should never allow himself to be bought" ibid., II.B.3. Mencius did
   concede that it might be necessary to appoint "gentlemen" solely on the basis of merit, regardless of family relationship and social rank, but only when "there is no choice" (ibid., I.B.7).
59 Ibid., II.A.3.
60 He advised that punishments should be reduced: ibid., I.A.5.

in good years and escape starvation in bad; only then does he drive them towards goodness.[61]

In effect, he had made economic policy the state's first priority.

Mencius's key suggestion was that land should be divided and distributed according to the *jing* or "well-field" system:

> A *jing* is a piece of land measuring one *li* square, and each *jing* consists of 900 *mu*. Of these, the central plot of 100 *mu* belongs to the state, while the other eight plots of 100 *mu* each are held by eight families who share the duty of caring for the plot owned by the state. Only when they have done this duty dare they turn to their own affairs.[62]

The character for *jing*, meaning "well", is "井", which gives a rough pictographic representation of the system that Mencius was envisaging.[63]

In addition, the ruler (and his "gentlemen") should instruct the people in the basic principles of cultivation and animal husbandry, make tours of inspection and dispense aid when necessary, and arrange for the planting of the mulberry "in every homestead of five *mu* of land, [so that] those who are fifty can wear silk".[64] Families would therefore have equal *means* of supporting themselves in the form of a 100-*mu* plot of land, although whether they would have the same material standard of living would presumably depend on their own efforts.

The "constant means" policy, hailed by Hu Jichuang as "one of Meng Ke's outstanding economic ideas",[65] applied to agriculture. Although this was the activity in which the overwhelming majority of the population of the time would

---

61 Ibid., I.A.7. More epigrammatically, Confucius is reported to have espoused a similar viewpoint:

> When the Master went to Wei, Ran You drove his carriage. "How dense is the population!" exclaimed the Master. "When the people have multiplied, what more should be done for them?" said Ran You. "Enrich them," he replied. "And when they have been enriched, what more should be done for them?" "Instruct them," he replied.
>
> *Analects* XIII.9

62 *Mencius* III.A.3. The *li* was approximately 416 metres (m), and one *mu* equalled approximately 139 m², giving each family (and the state) a landholding of approximately 4 hectares or 2 acres.

63 Mencius's description of the well-field system has some similarities with the Daoist "utopia" in *Laozi* (the *Daodejing*). Mencius wrote:

> Neither in burying the dead, nor in changing his abode, does a man go beyond the confines of his village. If those who hold land within each *jing* befriend one another both at home and abroad, help each other to keep watch, and succour each other in illness, they will live in love and harmony.
>
> Ibid., III.A.3

On the Daoist position see below, p. 25.

64 Ibid., I.A.3 cf. I.A.7, VII.A.22.

65 Hu Jichuang, *A Concise History of Chinese Economic Thought* (Beijing: Foreign Languages Press, 1988) p. 64.

have been engaged, Mencius also acknowledged the existence of "a hundred different crafts" including specialist weavers, potters and blacksmiths.[66] To encourage their activities he advocated that taxation should be reduced to "one in ten, to be levied in kind"[67] (a slightly less onerous rate than the one in nine taxation effectively levied on the *jing* households). At the same time, he was emphatic that taxation could not be reduced below these levels without reducing the state to "barbarity". In the "Central Kingdoms" it was necessary to fund expenditure on city walls, ancestral temples, sacrificial rites, gifts and banquets, not to mention the salaries of "numerous officials".[68] The "low" taxation policy of (around) one in ten was therefore dictated as much by the requirements of the state for its own expenditure as it was by the "benevolent" wish to promote the livelihood of the people.

In the kind of society described by Mencius in which social division of labour and specialisation had occurred, there would evidently have to be some provision for commodity exchange. The necessity for people to trade "the surplus fruits of their labours to satisfy one another's needs" was fully recognised and accepted by him, and it was also acknowledged, if only in passing, that exchangeable value must reflect the skill of the labourer ("If a roughly finished shoe sells at the same price as a finely finished one, who would make the latter?).[69] However, Mencius was perfectly aware that society had moved beyond a pure state of "simple commodity production and exchange" (as Marx would call it) and that profit-seeking merchants had become a fact of life. His attitude towards merchants, and to profit-seeking behaviour generally, poses some interesting questions.

Mencius recounted the following story:

> In antiquity, the market was for the exchange of what one had for what one lacked. The authorities merely supervised it. There was, however, a despicable fellow who always looked for a vantage point and, going up on it, gazed into the distance to the left and to the right in order to secure for himself all the profit there was in the market. The people all thought him

---

66 *Mencius* III.A.4. *Per force*, Mencius had recognised the social division of labour, for which he has earned plaudits, but he has also been pilloried for his "reactionary" position on the social division between "gentlemen" (*junzi*) and "small men" (*xiaoren*):

> There are affairs of great men, and there are affairs of small men. ... There are those who use their minds and there are those who use their muscles. The former rule, the latter are ruled. Those who rule are supported by those who are ruled

(ibid., III.A.4)

For his influential evaluation of Mencius's position see Hu Jichuang, *A Concise History of Chinese Economic Thought* (Beijing: Foreign Languages Press, 1988) p. 67.

67 *Mencius*, III.A.3.
68 Ibid., VI.B.10.
69 Ibid., III.A.4.

despicable, and, as a result, they taxed him. The taxing of traders began with this despicable fellow.[70]

The moral of the story appears to be that trade undertaken for profit, and only trade undertaken for profit, should be taxed for its wickedness. This would fit with the attitude displayed elsewhere by Mencius towards profit-seeking behaviour, depicted by him as antithetical to morality and a threat to the state's very existence. Nor were his strictures directed only against princes, "gentlemen" and traders (merchants): they applied equally to "commoners", or "those below".[71]

In light of the above it might seem odd to find Mencius advocating policies including tax-free passage for merchants at border posts and low taxation in markets, never mind commending an outcome in which "all merchants enjoy the refuge of [the state's] market place", but that is what he did.[72] Perhaps he was genuinely conflicted on the subject, or believed that profit-seeking merchants were a necessary evil to facilitate exchange. What does seem to emerge is that he had no desire to promote the wider spread of such "despicable" or "greedy" behaviour, i.e. behaviour that went beyond the exchange of "what one had for what one lacked".

Let us suppose that Mencius's economic policies were in place: the people have their means of support and are neither cold nor hungry, merchants are tolerated, and the state has sufficient resources to aid the needy and meet the expenses of the king and his "gentlemen". What then? Mencius counselled as follows: "This is the way of the common people: once they have a full belly and warm clothes on their back they degenerate to the level of animals if they are allowed to live idle lives, without education and disciple."[73] Although, according to Mencius, all human beings have "capacities" for humaneness, rightness, propriety and wisdom, they are capacities that can be overwhelmed by external circumstances unless they are carefully nurtured. It is only "exemplary persons" who do not lose at least some part of their innate "goodness" (or "original mind").[74] As for lesser persons – "the common people" – education in the rites and morality ("rightness") becomes essential to teach them the basics of "human relationships": "love between father and son, duty between ruler and subject, distinction between husband and wife, precedence of the old over the young, and faith between friends".[75] Only when these wholesome values have been instilled would "the Empire be at peace".[76]

Of course, the Empire was not at peace, although there was no shortage of itinerant philosophers to advise on how it could be made so. Among them was

---

70 Ibid., II.B.10. We have given here D.C. Lau's translation (*Mencius*, London: Penguin Classics, 2004). "Greedy" is substituted for "despicable" in the more recent translation by Irene Bloom (New York: Columbia University Press, 2009).
71 *Mencius*, VI.B.4, I.A.1; see also IV.B.33, VII.A.25.
72 Ibid., I.B.5, II.A.5, I.A.7.
73 Ibid., III.A.4.
74 Ibid., VII.A.6–10, 14.
75 Ibid.
76 Ibid., IV.A.11.

Xun Kuang (also known as Xun Qing, *c.*312–?BC), who offered his own variation on the Confucian theme.

All we know of Xun Kuang, apart from his writings, is that he was born in Zhao, studied and taught in Qi when he was about fifty years old, and then moved on to Chu. At one level he could be read as endorsing what had become, and remained, standard Confucian refrains:

> Lead the people by magnifying the sound of virtue, guide them by making clear ritual principles, love them with the utmost loyalty and good faith, give them a place in government by honouring the worthy and employing the able, and elevate them in rank by bestowing titles and rewards. Demand [corvée] labour of them only at the proper season, lighten their burdens, unify them in harmony, nourish and care for them as you would little children.[77]

However, there were also differences with received (particularly Mencian) Confucianism, some of them profound.

One stark difference was Xunzi's (Master Xun's) basic thesis, in direct opposition to Mencius, that "man's nature is evil":

> he is born with a fondness for profit … with feelings of envy and hate … with the desires of the eyes and ears, [and] with a fondness for beautiful sights and sounds [which can] lead him into license and wantonness.[78]

It was precisely these "evil tendencies" which required correction by rites and the imposition of harsh punishments in order to make the "little children" obedient and submissive.[79] Indeed, it was *because of* man's evil nature that rites had been invented in the first place.

Xunzi would appear to be the first Chinese philosopher to explain the origin of rites, and the necessity for social stratification, in blunt materialistic terms:

> What is the origin of ritual? I reply: man is born with desires. If his desires are not satisfied for him, he cannot but seek some means to satisfy them himself. If there are no limits and degrees to his seeking, then he will inevitably fall to wrangling with other men. From wrangling comes disorder and from disorder comes exhaustion. The ancient kings hated such disorder, and therefore they established ritual principles in order to curb it, to train men's

---

77 "Debating Military Affairs", in *Xunzi: Basic Writings* (hereafter *Xunzi*) (B. Watson tr., New York: Colombia University Press, 2003) p. 77.

78 "Man's Nature is Evil", *Xunzi*, p. 161.

79 "The Regulations of a King", ibid., p. 52. Xunzi's emphasis on punishment is reminiscent of Mo Di's position: "If anyone is found acting or using his talents to work against the good of the time, condemn him to death without mercy" (ibid., p. 36); "punishments shall be meted out without error [and 'in public']" (ibid., p. 44); "employ the five punishments as a warning" (ibid., p. 51).

desires and to provide for their satisfaction. They saw to it that desires did not overextend the means for their satisfaction, and material goods did not fall short of what was desired. Thus both desires and goods were looked after and satisfied. This is the origin of rites.[80]

On this account, rites were devised and imposed as a solution to a form of "scarcity" problem. Consumption is limited to the available supply of material goods, not by price signals but by training desire through the imposition of ritual: suitably brainwashed (in effect) individuals only *want* to achieve a level of material consumption that actually *can* be achieved given the available supply of material produce. In this way, people are relieved of the "anxiety" that comes from paying "undue attention to external objects" and, as they cease to be "the slave of [external] things", the society becomes more orderly.

But why should society require stratification and different levels of "ritualised consumption"? At one point Xunzi merely asserts that where "ranks are all equal there will not be enough goods to go around",[81] but a possibly more compelling reason (for him) is that a "hierarchical order" is required in order to create the authoritarian class who must "join together" and, rather euphemistically, "watch over those below" (inculcating rites and forcing their observance), thus bringing about the social order that would be impossible in an anarchic world populated by "evil" self-seeking individuals.[82]

In addition, "those above" were charged with imposing an *economic* order on the state by determining not only the "ritualised" levels and content of material consumption, but also by their detailed supervision and direction of production, subject to the requirement that "no man of ability [is] left unemployed".[83]

Output would be closely monitored:

Clothing should be of a fixed type, dwellings of a fixed size … Likewise, the vessels and trappings used in mourning should all be fixed in accordance with social rank.… All decorations that do not follow old patterns should be given up; all vessels and trappings that are not like those of earlier times should be discarded.[84]

As to the supervision of "suitable" productive activity, it would be the duty of "the administrator of the fields" to "decide what type of grain should be planted, examine the harvest and see that it is properly stored away" and to ensure more generally "that the farmers remain honest and hardworking and do not turn to other occupations".[85] Likewise, the "director of artisans" would be required to

80 "A Discussion of Rites", ibid., p. 93.
81 "The Regulations of a King", ibid., p. 38.
82 Ibid., p. 38.
83 Ibid., p. 44.
84 Ibid.
85 Ibid., p. 50.

judge the merits of the various artisans, determine the most appropriate time for their work, judge the quality of their manufactures, encourage efficiency and high quality, and see that all necessary goods are made available, making sure that no one dares to manufacture sculptured or ornamented decorations privately at home.[86]

This vision of a state-controlled economy is closer to Mo Di's than anything to be found in the *Analects* or the *Mencius*, the principle difference with Mo Di being that Xunzi effectively redefines "useful production" to include a greater proportion of ritual material objects.[87]

There was one area of economic activity – mercantile trade – which Xunzi appeared content to see operated by private, profit-seeking individuals. "Goods and grain shall be allowed to circulate freely," he declared, "so that there is no hindrance or stagnation in distribution; they shall be transported from one place to another as the need may arise, so that the entire region among the four seas will become like one family".[88] To facilitate circulation, a "director of markets" should "keep the roads in repair, eliminate thieves and highway bandits, ensure a fair assignment of public buildings and market stalls … so that travelling merchants can conduct their business in safety".[89] The peculiarity of this position is that Xunzi was endorsing the activities of the very people who were, on his own terms, "evil" in their pursuit of profit. Perhaps, as we suggested for Mencius, he believed them to be both evil *and* necessary.

Xunzi appeared confident that his policies would achieve a "well-ordered state", the very antithesis of which he expressed as follows:

These are the signs of a disordered age: men wear bright-coloured clothing, their manner is feminine, their customs are lascivious; their minds are set on profit, their conduct is erratic, their music is depraved, and their decorative arts are vile and garish. In satisfying the desires of the living they observe no limits, but in burying the dead they are mean and niggardly. They despise ritual principles and value daring and shows of strength. If they are poor, they steal, and if they are rich, they commit outrages.[90]

We are left in no doubt as to the kind of state that Xunzi would prefer.

---

86 Ibid., p. 51.
87 In spite of the affinity, however, Xunzi does not have a single positive word to say about Mo, who is harshly criticised, in particular, for not understanding the social value of classical music ("When music is moderate and tranquil, the people become harmonious and shun excess. When music is stern and majestic, the people become well behaved and shun disorder" "A Discussion of Music", *Xunzi*. p. 117). In his typically centralising fashion, Xunzi counselled that a "director" should abolish all "licentious" or "strange and barbaric" tunes ("The Regulations of a King", *Xunzi* p. 50).
88 Ibid., p. 45.
89 Ibid., p. 51.
90 "A Discussion of Music", *Xunzi*, p. 123.

It has been said that

> it is unfortunate for [Xunzi's] reputation as a Confucian that the two most famous of [his disciples] should have been Han Feizi, who became the leading exponent of the Legalist school, and Li Si, the statesman who assisted the First Emperor of the Qin in the unification of the empire, both men whose names are inseparably linked with the ridicule and persecution of Confucianism.[91]

But, while it may be unfortunate in that regard, the development of Xunzi's doctrine in a Legalist direction is scarcely surprising in view of his emphasis on law, punishment and state control, all of which were music to the ears of the Legalists.

Legalism did not originate with Han Feizi or Li Si. It has been traced back to Guan Zhong (*c.*723–645 BC), the Chief Minister of the state of Qi under Duke Huan (r. 685–643), to whom we return, and to Wei Yang (or Gongsun Yang), who became Lord Shang under the reign of Duke Xiao of Qin (r. 361–358 BC).

Sima Qian reports that Wei Yang (as he then was) "spoke to the duke, urging him to change the laws, impose penalties,[92] encourage agricultural pursuits within the state,[93] and on the foreign front to reward those who would fight and die in battle".[94] In addition, the duke was advised to abandon the rites and ignore the advice of (other) philosophers. Inconveniently for Lord Shang (as he had become), after he had been accused of treason following Duke Xiao's death, his attempt to flee was (allegedly) thwarted by his own legislation:

> [He] tried to put up at [a] guest house, but the keeper of the lodge, unaware of who he was, said, "Lord Shang's laws stipulate that anyone giving lodging to a person who lacks proper credentials will be prosecuted." Lord Shang sighed and said, "I made the law – and this is what I get!"[95]

What he ultimately received was to have his body torn in two by carriages, and to have his entire family "wiped out".[96]

Some four centuries later, Han Feizi (*c.*280–233 BC), born into the ruling family of the state of Han, was to advocate similar policies, and to meet a

---

91 Watson, *Xunzi*, pp. 2–3.
92 "The people were to be grouped in units of five and ten households, exercising mutual surveillance and mutually responsible before the law. Anyone failing to report an offence was to be cut in two at the waist." Sima Qian, *Shi Ji* 68, "The Biography of Lord Shang". In Watson (tr.) *Records of the Grand Historian: Qin Dynasty* (New York: Columbia University Press, 1993) p. 92.
93 Those "who engaged in secondary activities for profit [e.g. merchants and artisans] … were to be rounded up and made government slaves". Ibid., p. 93.
94 Sima Qian, *Shi Ji* 5, "The Basic Annals of Qin". Ibid., p. 24.
95 Sima Qian, *Shi Ji* 68, "The Biography of Lord Shang". Ibid., p. 99.
96 Ibid.

similarly premature death.[97] As with Lord Shang, laws and penalties were seen as the perfect way to maintain order in the state:

> for correcting the faults of superiors, chastising the misdeeds of subordinates, restoring order, exposing error, checking excess, remedying evil, and unifying the standards of the people, nothing can compare to law. For putting fear into the officials, awing the people, wiping out wantonness and sloth, and preventing lies and deception, nothing can compare to penalties.[98]

In the "enlightened" state envisaged by Han Feizi, "law supplies the only instruction":[99] there are "no books written on bamboo slips" (a reference to the writings of other philosophical schools);[100] there is no "talk about deeds of benevolence and righteousness" (a clear reference to Mencius);[101] and there are no wandering philosophers.[102]

As to the "economic" content of Han Feizi's teaching, we have, first, his own interpretation of the "scarcity" issue:

> In ancient times ... [the] people were few, there was an abundance of goods, and so no one quarrelled. Therefore, no rich rewards were doled out, no harsh punishments were administered, and yet the people of themselves were orderly. But nowadays ... the number of people increases, goods grow scarce, and men have to struggle and slave for a meagre living. Therefore they fall to quarrelling, and though rewards are doubled

---

97 He was poisoned on the instruction of Li Si, a fellow student of Xunzi. Li Si was minister to the King of Qin. For an account of the episode see B. Watson, Introduction to *Han Feizi: Basic Writings* (hereafter *Han Feizi*) (New York: Columbian University Press, 2003), pp. 3–4.

98 "On Having Standards" in ibid., p. 28.

99 "Eminence in Learning", ibid., p. 112.

100 Ibid. Notoriously, this policy was implemented under the Qin at the suggestion of Li Si, whose words are reported by Sima Qian as follows:

> I request that all records of the historians other than those of the state of Qin be burned. With the exception of the academicians whose duty it is to possess them, if there are any persons anywhere in the empire who have in their possession copies of the *Odes*, the *Documents*, or the writings of the hundred schools of philosophy, they shall in all cases deliver them to the governor or his commandant for burning. Anyone who ventures to discuss the *Odes* or *Documents* shall be executed in the marketplace. Anyone who uses antiquity to criticise the present shall be executed along with his family.
>
> (Sima Qian, *Shi Ji* 6, "The Basic Annals of the First Emperor of the Qin", in Watson (tr.) *Records of the Grand Historian: Qin Dynasty* (New York: Columbia University Press, 1993) p. 55.)

> A slightly less harsh account is given in *Shi Ji* 87, "The Biography of Li Si", ibid., p. 185, where miscreants would escape execution in favour of "tattooing and ... 'wall drawn' labour" (penal servitude).

101 "Eminence in Learning", *Han Feizi*, pp. 128–129.

102 Ibid., p. 126; "The Five Vermin" pp. 108, 111.

and punishments are piled on, they cannot be prevented from growing disorderly.[103]

Contrary to his teacher, Han Feizi gives the impression that humankind is not intrinsically evil and that scarcity arises not because of uncontrolled greed but rather because of population growth. Nevertheless, once it had become a fact of life, how was it to be dealt with?

As one might expect, Han Feizi's answer was that it should be dealt with by the ruler: he alone should exercise control over the wealth and resources of the state, and he alone "deliberates on scarcity and plenty".[104] Having deliberated for him, Han Feizi's principal suggestion, reminiscent of Xunzi's (and Mozi's) to an extent, was to cut back on "useless" activities, and "useless" people, and focus on "essential" production:

> An enlightened ruler will administer his state in such a way as to decrease the number of merchants, artisans, and other men who make their living from wandering from place to place [i.e. philosophers], and will see to it that such men are looked down upon. In this way he lessens the number of people who abandon primary pursuits [i.e. agriculture] to take up secondary occupations.[105]

As things were, Han Feizi complained, "merchants and artisans spend their time making articles of no practical use and gathering stores of luxury goods, accumulating riches, waiting for the best time to sell, and exploiting the farmers", while the wandering philosophers "get clothing and food without working for them". These classes of people, he declared, are "the vermin of the state" and should be "wiped out",[106] leaving "essential production", and the military, as the only pursuits that would hold out the prospect of securing a tolerable income.

Assuming that the "vermin" had been successfully eviscerated from society, or "encouraged" to work in functionally useful activities (as with Mo Di's proposal), and passing over the question of how goods are distributed in the absence of merchants,[107] Han Feizi seemed confident that the state would have sufficient resources to dispense charity and reduce its direct demands on the people. But these measures had nothing to do with the Confucian imperatives of humaneness, benevolence and rightness:

> If too much compulsory labour service is demanded of the people, they feel afflicted, and this will rise to local power groups. When local power groups have arisen, they will begin exercising the right to exempt the people from

103 "The Five Vermin", ibid., p. 98.
104 "The Way of the Ruler", ibid., pp. 17–18 and "The Five Vermin", ibid., p. 100. This position is not prima facie suggestive of the "non-intervention" interpretation advanced by Young Back Choi, "Political economy of Han Feizi", *History of Political Economy*, 1989, 21.2, pp. 367–390.
105 "The Five Vermin", *Han Feizi*, p. 117.
106 Ibid., pp. 118, 105.
107 One might suppose that this would be the state's responsibility.

labour service, and once they are able to do this, their leaders will grow rich on bribes.... Hence it is said, if labour services are few, the people will be content; if the people are content, there will be no opportunity for men to exercise undue authority on the lower levels and power groups will disappear. Once power groups have been wiped out, then all rights to dispense favours will reside with the sovereign.[108]

Moreover, those who became destitute as a result of "laziness or extravagant living" would find themselves ineligible for state aid under any circumstances,[109] thus providing a salutary lesson to the "diligent and frugal" to remain that way. No wonder that Han Feizi's "enlightened ruler" did not talk about "benevolence and righteousness".

In that last respect, at least, there is a correspondence between the behaviour of the Legalists' ruler and the Daoists' sage. But, in nearly all other respects, except for the Legalists' appropriation of the Daoist language of *wu-wei* (or "inaction"), itself a derivative notion to be discussed further below, the positions of these two "schools" could not be further apart.

There are two foundational texts for Daoism, the *Daodejing* or *Laozi* and the *Zhuangzi*. Parts of both texts have been traced to the mid-fourth or early third centuries BC, but it has been found impossible to date them precisely or to say which had precedence. The *Daodejing* is divided into two sections, the first entitled *Dao* (usually rendered "The Way"), the second *De* ("The Life Force" or "Virtue"), the complete title being along the lines of "The Book of the Way and The Life Force". Traditionally, authorship of the book was credited to an individual denominated as Laozi, or "Old Master", but most scholars now agree that it is doubtful if such a person ever existed. In the case of the *Zhuangzi* ("Master Zhuang"), it may be that there was an historical author, Zhuang Zhou, possibly a contemporary of Mencius, but there is nothing that can be reported of his life with any confidence.

Attempting to construct a single doctrine of "Daoism" from the two texts is made difficult by their different orientations: the *Daodejing* inclines more to describing the qualities that a sagacious Daoist ruler must have, whereas the *Zhuangzi* exhibits a greater concern with giving a Daoist modus vivendi for a "disordered" world. Nevertheless, there are some points in common, particularly with the description of the *wrong* "way".

The idea that rulers and individuals should follow some particular *dao* ("way") can be found in the *Analects* and had an even older provenance as the "Way of Heaven" based on the *Zhouyi* or *I Ching* (*The Book of Changes*), a work that may date back to the second millennium BC. In the opinion of the Daoists, however, many of the earlier "ways" were, one might say, wrong turns. As Zhuangzi writes with clear reference to Mencian Confucianism, "the rules of benevolence and righteousness and the paths of right and wrong are all hope-

---

108 "Precautions within the Palace", *Han Feizi*, p. 88.
109 "Eminence in Learning", ibid., p. 122.

lessly snarled and jumbled. How could I know anything about such discriminations?"[110] Confucianism, to the Daoists, was no better or worse than Mohism: both involved impenetrably complex and often mutually contradictory sets of rules and rites to regulate behaviour, and both arose only because the "the [true] Way was lost".[111]

As to the "right" way, and particularly the right way to govern, the *Daodejing* is more forthcoming than the *Zhuangzi*. The basic idea is straightforward: mostly by setting an example to the people through his own behaviour, and also through his policies, the ruler creates an environment in which people regain the simplicity of their "original" natures and lead a contented and harmonious existence, free of excessive material desires. In more detail, the ruler does not promote the worthy, so the people do not compete with each other for "position";[112] he gets rid of profiteering, so that "thieves and robbers are no more";[113] he does not esteem scarce or valuable objects;[114] he does not pursue a sumptuous lifestyle;[115] he never proclaims his own excellence;[116] he provides for those who do not have enough;[117] and he would use weapons defensively only as a last resort.[118] Such is the transformative power of his example, he has no need to rule people by "prohibitions or ordinances" (unlike the Legalists),[119] or directly control their consumption (unlike Mozi or Xunzi),[120] or control their behaviour with rites and rules (unlike the Confucians). Rather, the people have embraced a simple, non-competitive lifestyle, behaving well of their own accord.[121]

The style of governance described in the *Daodejing*, known as *wu-wei* or "inaction", did not originate with the Daoists. As we find in the *Analects*: "Among those who 'ruled by inaction' surely Shun must be counted. For what action did he take? He merely placed himself gravely and reverently with his face due south, that was all."[122] Shun was a divine sage who, like the Daoist sage, could rule solely on the basis of his own personal example. The Confucian sage was only an approximation to the "classical" sage, because he had to rely also on rites, rules and punishments, whereas the Legalist ruler, who was similarly claimed to practice *wu-wei*, relied solely on the rigour of his subordinates

110 "Discussion on Making All Things Equal", in *Zhuangzi: Basic Writings* (hereafter *Zhuangzi*) (B. Watson, tr., New York: Columbia University Press, 2003) p. 41.
111 *Daodejing*, 38, cf. 16, 19 (from *Laozi: Daodejing*, E. Ryden, tr., Oxford: Oxford University Press, 2008).
112 *Daodejing*, 3.
113 Ibid., 19; cf. 8.
114 Ibid., 3, 9, 12, 64.
115 Ibid., 75, 70, 53.
116 Ibid., 24, 34.
117 Ibid., 77.
118 Ibid., 31.
119 Ibid., 57.
120 Ibid., 72.
121 Ibid., 57.
122 *Analects* XV.5. "Facing due south" was the position traditionally adopted by Chinese rulers.

directing activities through the threat of penalties and punishments.[123] In effect, then, the *Daodejing* and the *Zhuangzi* in places,[124] were advocating a policy of returning to the practices of fabled antiquity to an extent unparalleled in the writings of any other school of philosophy in pre-Qin China.

But what of the "economic" characteristics of the Daoist state? As we can discern already, it would be one on which people's material ambitions were modest and competition and profit-seeking absent, suggesting that any trade would take the form of exchanging the surplus products of labour. The *Daodejing* expatiates as follows:

> Let the state be small and the people few;
> Let weapons of platoons and brigades be unused;
> Let the people respect death and renounce travel.
> Though there be boats and carriages, yet none do ride therein;
> Though there be armour and weapons, yet none do take them out.
> Let it be that people go back to the days of knots in ropes and use them.
> They relish their food,
> Embellish their dress.
> They cherish their ways,
> Embellish their home.
> Neighbouring states view each other.
> They hear the cries of chicken and dog,
> Yet people reach old age without meeting each other.[125]

Here, according to an admiring Joseph Needham, we find "the poetical expression of a cooperative collectivist society".[126] Economic activity would be minimal – no merchants, no production for profit and, it seems, no desire for economic growth – but that would be the way people wanted it to be. They would be content with their lot.

The Daoist "utopia" of "small state, few people", as it has come to be known, is often contrasted with the depiction of the "Grand Harmony" in the *Li Ji* ("Book of Rites"):

123 As described in the *Huainanzi*, a work compiled during the early Han dynasty (206–220 BC), the Legalist conception of *wu-wei* was not that the ruler "froze and was inert but that nothing any longer emanated from the ruler personally". "The Ruler's Techniques" in *The Essential Huainanzi* (Major, J.S., Queen, S.A., Meyer A.S., Roth, H.D., eds, tr., New York: Columbia University Press, 2012) 9.23, p. 100.

124 "The government of an enlightened king? His achievements blanket the world but appear not to be his own doing. His transforming influence touches the ten thousand things but the people do not depend on him." *Zhuangzi*, "Fit for Emperors and Kings", p. 92.

125 *Daodejing*, 80. There are obvious parallels here with Mencius's ideal *jing*-field system. See above, p. 10.

126 *Science and Civilisation in China* Volume II (Cambridge: Cambridge University Press, 1956) p. 59. Needham went on to describe the "cooperative collectivist society" in quasi-Marxian terms as the society "towards which mankind is inevitably moving as the scope and potentialities of the highest social organisations continue to increase." Ibid., p. 60.

When the Grand Harmony was pursued, a public and common spirit ruled all under the sky; they chose men of talents, virtue, and ability; their words were sincere, and what they cultivated was harmony. Thus men did not love their parents only, nor treat as children only their own sons. A complete provision was secured for the aged till their death, employment for the able-bodied, and the means of growing up to the young. They showed kindness and compassion to widows, orphans, childless men, and those who were disabled by disease, so that they were all sufficiently maintained. Males had their proper work, and females had their homes. (They accumulated) articles (of value), disliking that they should be thrown away upon the ground, but not wishing to keep them for their own gratification. They laboured with their strength, disliking that it should not be exerted, but not exerting it (only) with a view to their own advantage. In this way (selfish) scheming was repressed and found no development. Robbers, filchers, and rebellious traitors did not show themselves, and hence the outer doors remained opened, and were not shut. This was (the period of) what we call the Grand Harmony.[127]

As to the authorship of the passage, Hu Jichuang has pronounced thus: "That the ideal was formulated by early Confucians is certain, for the article was recognised as a canon by all Confucians from the second century BC onward".[128] However, the glaring strangeness of this attribution, as pointed out by James Legge and Joseph Needham, among others, is that the "Grand Harmony" is more suggestive of a Daoist position (perhaps with Mohist influences) than anything to be found in the extant writings of any pre-Qin Confucian thinker:[129] the values of the "cooperative collectivist society" (as Needham described the Daoist "utopia") could hardly be expressed more clearly, while the affirmed principle of "universal love" is in direct conflict with Confucian teaching. Yet, these and other oddities notwithstanding, the Confucian pedigree of the "Great Harmony" is widely taken for granted.[130]

We turn to the essays collectively known as the *Guanzi*. In general, their authors share one thing in common with the Daoists, namely, a disregard for

---

127 *Li Yun* ("Ceremonial Usages") I.2.
128 Hu Jichuang, *A Concise History of Chinese Economic Thought* (Beijing: Foreign Languages Press, 1988), p. 58.
129 James Legge [1885] (tr.) *The Li Ji or Book of Rites* (Forgotten Books, 2008), Part I of II, p. 215 n. 651; Joseph Needham, *Science and Civilisation in China Volume II* (Cambridge: Cambridge University Press, 1956), pp. 167–168.
130 It may suffice here to mention one further peculiarity. The passage immediately following I.2 describes what happened after the "Great Harmony fell into disuse and obscurity", one baleful result being the invention and application of the "rules and propriety and of what is right" in a world that pursued private advantage and warfare. Then, in the succeeding paragraph, "Confucius" is asked, "Are the rules of Propriety indeed of such urgent importance", to which he answers, "It was by those rules that the ancient kings sought to represent the ways of Heaven": a position that is difficult to reconcile with the views expressed in I.3 or I.2. Overall, there must be a suspicion that the "Great Harmony" passages may have been foreign interpolations to an existing text.

sermons on "benevolence and righteousness". However, in other respects their position was closer to Han Feizi's, although they were more forthcoming than him about the policy measures by which objectives including the development of "essential" production and, above all, the strengthening of state finances, might be achieved.

Guanzi takes its name from the eponymous minister of Qi during the reign of Duke Huan (r. 685–643 BC), whose policy was described by Sima Qian in these terms:

> Duke Huan of Qi, following the advice of his minister Guan Zhong, initiated a system of buying up goods when the price was low and selling them when it was high, and of exploiting the resources of the mountains and sea, until he had the other feudal lords paying court to him and, with what had up until then been the little and out-of-the-way state of Qi, had won for himself the title of dictator.[131]

But it was not only Qi and Duke Huan who benefitted, for as Sima Qian reports: "Guan Zhong himself, though only a court minister, owned the mansion called the Three Returnings, and his wealth exceeded that of the lord of a great feudal kingdom".[132]

The historical accuracy of Sima Qian's account of Guan Zhong's policies cannot be known, but it accords well with the general drift of the policy prescriptions in the *Guanzi*, particularly with those offered in the *Qing Zhong* section of the collection.

The authorship of the *Qing Zhong* essays is unknown, as is their date(s) of composition, with estimates for the latter ranging from the mid-Warring States period to the first century BC. The *qing zhong zhi fa* (*qing zhong* method) of governing that emerges from these chapters has been usefully summarised by *Guanzi*'s modern translator as follows:

> This method involved using money to acquire grain and other critical commodities when they were plentiful and cheap [*qing*, also meaning "light"], and to sell them when they were in short supply and expensive [*zhong*, also meaning "heavy"] in order to control the profits of merchants and gain income for the state. Thus … *qing zhong* may refer merely to taking advantage of market conditions to manipulate prices, or it may refer to a broad range of economic policies involving such things as government monopolies, loans to producers, foreign trade and territorial expansion, currency control, and work incentives.[133]

---

131 *Shi Ji* 30 "The Treatise on the Balanced Standard", in Watson (tr.) *Records of the Grand Historian: Han Dynasty II* (New York: Columbia University Press, 1993) p. 84.
132 *Shi Ji* 129, "The Biographies of the Money-Makers", ibid., p. 435.
133 W. Allyn Rickett, *Guanzi* vol. 2, p. 339 (Princeton: Princeton University Press, 1998).

Through the state's purchase and sale of commodities, the adept prince ensures that "all the people will be bound to him":[134] people are prevented from retaining their own surpluses, opportunities for private profit are restricted, and the people are directed to "essential" productive activities. As for merchants, through the state's purchase of commodities and consequent manipulation of prices, they find themselves in a position where their profitable trading opportunities are either limited or completely non-existent. Thus, premised on the idea that people are profit-seekers,[135] the state uses its purchases and sales to direct productive activity through price signals, at the same time arrogating to itself "the surpluses of the people"[136] by acting as the sole (or dominant) merchant. It therefore achieves objectives of a clear Legalist bent through an economic mechanism, although manifestly not of a "free market" variety. The aim of "*qing zhong* economic policies" – of what amounts to the policies of a centrally directed economy – is "to establish an encompassing framework to control [the] people"[137] and, of course, to enrich the state.

Recognition of man's profit-seeking propensity did not begin with the *Guanzi*: it was something that had been acknowledged from Confucius's time onwards, one aim of the various philosophical systems being to constrain or channel it through different combinations and interpretations of rites and rules, laws and penalties, and exemplary behaviour on the part of the ruler and his "gentlemen". What was strikingly new about the policies advocated in the *Guanzi* is that profit-seeking would be directed through state-manipulated price signals. The further step taken by Sima Qian (*c.*145–89 BC) was to depict a system directed by prices in the absence of government intervention.

Sima Qian is known to us through his *Shi Ji* ("Records of the Grand Historian"), described by Burton Watson as "one of the most widely read and influential of all works of early Chinese literature".[138] In Sima Qian's own words, he had "wished to examine into all that concerns Heaven and humankind, to penetrate the changes of the past and present, putting forth my views as one school of interpretation".[139] But before the manuscript had been completed, catastrophe

---

134 *Guo Xu* ("The State's Store of Grain"), ibid., p. 377.

135 This idea is expressed vividly in a chapter outside the *Qing Zhong* section:

> Indeed, it is the nature of men that whenever they see profit, they cannot help chasing after it, and whenever they see harm, they cannot help running away.... Thus, wherever profit lies, even though it be atop a thousand-*ren* peak, there is no place people will not climb. Even though it is at the bottom of the deepest depths, there is no place people will not enter.
>
> *Jin Cang* ("On Maintaining Restraint") ibid., pp. 219–220

136 *Guo Zhun* ("Maintaining Stability in State Finance"), ibid., p. 445. Cf. *Chen Cheng Ma* ("Planned Fiscal Management") ibid., p. 362; *Shi Yu* ("Discourse on Economic Matters") ibid., p. 369; and *Guo Xu* ("The State's Store of Grain") ibid., p. 377.

137 Ibid., p. 379.

138 Introduction to Watson (tr.) *Records of the Grand Historian: Qin Dynasty* (New York: Columbia University Press, 1993) p. ix.

139 Sima Qian, letter to Ren An (?91 BC), ibid., p. 236.

struck. Having spoken out in defence of a Han general who had surrendered to the enemy rather than committing suicide, as would have been expected at the time, Sima Qian was sentenced to undergo the penalty of castration. Being unable to find the money to commute the sentence, the normal course for a "gentleman" would be to take his own life, but Sima Qian chose the penalty, his reason being "that I grieve that I have things in my heart that I have not been able to express fully, and I am ashamed to think that after I am gone my writings will not be known to posterity".[140] Fortunately, his writings are known to us, consisting of 130 chapters in which he recounts his history of China from the earliest times known to him to his own present.

The chapter that has received the most attention for its "economic" content is *Shi Ji* 129, "The Biographies of the Money-Makers". Based on the "assumption" of pervasive profit-seeking behaviour ("Jostling and joyous, the whole world comes after profit; racing and rioting, after profit the whole world goes!"[141]), he wrote:

> Society obviously must have farmers before it can eat; foresters, fishermen, miners, etc., before it can make use of natural resources; craftsmen before it can have manufactured goods; and merchants before they can be distributed. But once these exist, what need is therefore government directives, mobilisations of labour, or periodic assemblies? Each man has only to be left to utilise his own abilities and exert his strength to obtain what he wishes. Thus, when a commodity is very cheap, it invites a rise on price; when it is very expensive, it invites a reduction. When each person works away at his own occupation and delights in his own business then, like water flowing downward,[142] goods will naturally flow forth ceaselessly day and night without being summoned, and the people will produce commodities without having been asked. Does this not tally with reason? Is it not a natural result?[143]

This oft-quoted passage provides a clear indication of Sima Qian's grasp of an economic system in which production is guided by price signals without government intervention.[144]

---

140 Ibid.
141 Watson (tr.) *Records of the Grand Historian: Han Dynasty II* (New York: Columbia University Press, 1993) p. 436.
142 Cf. the *Guanzi*: "Grain moves to wherever the price is highest like water flowing downhill." *Shan Zhi Shu* ("The Best Methods for Ensuring Fiscal Control"), Rickett, *Guanzi* vol. 2, p. 411 (Princeton: Princeton University Press, 1998) p. 411. Interestingly, the flowing water simile was also used by Mencius, but in his case the destination was rather different: "The people turn to the benevolent as water flows downwards" *Mencius* IV.A.9.
143 Watson (tr.) *Records of the Grand Historian: Han Dynasty II* (New York: Columbia University Press, 1993) p. 434.
144 This facet of Sima Qian's thought is emphasised in Joseph J. Spengler (1964), "Suma Qian, Unsuccessful Exponent of Laissez Faire", *Southern Economic Journal*, 30.3, pp. 224–243.

Shi Ji 129 gives a highly positive account of market-oriented behaviour for almost any category of economic agent one can imagine, including farmers, independent craftsmen, large producers, merchants, (usurious) money-lenders, slave-owners and monopolists, even extending to those who acquired their initial "capital" by gambling and grave-robbing. A list of "outstanding and unusually wealthy men", including monopolists and slave-owners, is presented as particularly worthy examples of those who "simply guessed what course things were going to take and acted accordingly, kept a sharp eye out for the opportunities of the times, and so were able to capture a fat profit"; they "gained their wealth in the secondary occupations and held on to it by investing in agriculture;[145] they seized hold of it in times of crisis and maintained in in times of stability."[146]

Sima Qian's attitude to monopolists deserves further attention. He wrote:

> In addition, there are many other men who exerted themselves at farming, animal-raising, crafts, lumbering, merchandising, and trade and seized the opportunities of the moment to make a fortune, the greatest of them dominating a whole province, the next greatest dominating a district, and the smallest dominating a village.[147]

What becomes clear is that Sima Qian's perspective is very much that of the "producer". *Shi Ji* 129 is, in effect, a manual for those would aspire to become rich in a market system, the great monopolist ("dominating a whole province") being the shining example. Thus, whatever else one might select as Sima Qian's outstanding achievements, it would surely not be his outline and commendation of a *perfectly* competitive economic system.

There is a further question raised by Sima Qian's acknowledgement that the "outstanding and unusually wealthy men" had acquired their wealth "in times of crisis". Turning to *Shi Ji* 30, "The Treatise on the Balanced Standard", there is an account of precisely such a time (around 120 BC):

> The rich merchants and big traders, however, were busy accumulating wealth and forcing the poor into their hire, transporting goods back and forth in hundreds of carts, buying up surplus commodities and hoarding them in the villages; even the feudal lords were forced to go to them with bowed heads and beg for what they needed. Others who were engaged in smelting iron and extracting salt from sea water accumulated [vast] fortunes … and yet they did nothing to help the distress of the nation, and the common people were plunged deeper and deeper into misery.[148]

---

145 Ibid., p. 453. They would do so because agriculture involved less "personal danger" than the secondary occupations: ibid., p. 449.
146 Ibid., p. 453.
147 Ibid.
148 Ibid., p. 68.

The peculiarity is that these "rich merchants and big traders" are none other than the "outstanding and unusually wealthy men" who are seemingly applauded in *Shi Ji* 129. The complex message appears to be that the benefits of the "market system" as envisaged by Sima Qian depend critically on one's place and time within it (a penetrating insight in its own right).[149]

The *Shi Ji* and *Guanzi* are often celebrated as containing the most developed examples of "economic" reasoning in ancient China, rightly so. But, as our cursory review has shown, "economic" phenomena of an identifiably "classical" Western sense had been recognised in earlier writings, including (without exhausting the possible list) those of the social division of labour and specialisation, production, trade (of both an individual and mercantile nature), desire, scarcity, exchangeable value, welfare, monopoly, distribution, and distinctions that prefigure "classical" dichotomies between "productive" and "unproductive" labour. Just how far these and other insights deserve to be elevated to the status of "theories" is likely to remain a contentious issue, notwithstanding the fact that the writers of the following essays in this volume tend to favour affirmative answers. However, there is at least one aspect of these ancient writings that surely cannot be gainsaid, namely, that they contain remarkable examples of widely differing programmes for state *economic policy* based on behavioural "assumptions" and objectives, which have all the characteristics of "theoretical" discourse. In that respect alone, they are deserving of our attention, as are the efforts of Chinese scholars to engage with them.

---

149 A similar change in focus, or orientation, is evinced by Sima Qian's account in *Shi Ji* 30 of the time of the "warring kingdoms":

> Men honoured deceit and power and scoffed at benevolence and righteousness; they put wealth and possession first and courtesy and humility last. Thus it happened that commerce grew so rich that their wealth was counted in the hundreds of millions, while among the poor there were those who could not even get enough dregs and chaff to fill their bellies.
>
> (Ibid., pp. 84–85)

1 Considerations on the research methodology of the history of Chinese economic thought[1]

Hu Jichuang

Any discipline, especially a discipline in the social sciences, is bound to face questions about methodology at its inception, such as the controversy over deduction and induction, "from the abstract to the concrete" and "from the concrete to the abstract". Thus, it is not surprising for History of Chinese Economic Thought, as a new subject, to encounter some disagreements on methodology. Although the disagreements on research methodology applicable to the history of Chinese economic thought that emerged in the 1960s did not lead to heated debates, they still linger on in the minds of some scholars even in the 1980s. Those disagreements are different from the general disciplinary methodological debates, such as what system to adopt to describe the discipline, whether to make comparative analyses of ancient and modern or Chinese and Western, and the so-called problem of "modernisation of ancient thought". In a strict sense, they are not entirely methodological in nature, but are different views based on disciplinary features and caused by the lack of appropriate analytical tools of Marxist theory under certain historical conditions. Such disagreements first appeared in the research on Chinese philosophy and history, and the problems that have arisen in the research on history of Chinese economic thought are mainly subject to their influences. It seems that the disagreements in philosophy have now been eliminated, and historians also have gradually lost interest in them. However, in the study of the history of Chinese economic thought, although the disagreements have been largely resolved, they are still not eliminated completely. Further clarification thus remains necessary.

Systemisation

Different systems can be employed for writing the academic works of any discipline. Each system has its advantages and disadvantages, and only in certain situations can we judge which system is relatively appropriate. This is not a problem related to methodology in nature. However, the problem of system was

1 Originally published as "中国经济思想史研究的方法论歧见" ("Considerations on the research methodology of the history of Chinese economic thought"), *Academic Monthly*, 1986 Issue 3, pp. 20–27.

first proposed based on the grounds that the analysis of the economic thought of a particular thinker or a particular era should not be expressed by economic categories such as wealth, production, circulation, distribution, money and finance. The reason given is that Chinese economic thought has its own characteristics of development and we should use a proper system of its own in narrating its development rather than borrow some framework from the history of Western economic theory. If a system of the above-mentioned economic categories is utilised for description, it will still "have the shortcoming of applying mechanically the framework of history of Western economic theory to Chinese economic thought to some extent".[2] As this viewpoint relates to whether to borrow some "framework" of history of Western economic theory, it is thus somehow associated with methodology. Such a view was quite understandable in the 1950s and 1960s, because in that period, with its emphasis on class conflict, anything related to the West was completely denied with no exception for academic works. Yet, in the 1980s it seems to be no longer necessary to adhere to that point of view. As for what system to adopt for compiling the history of Chinese economic thought, I submit the following opinions for consideration.

First, we should take the economic thought of a certain major historical figure, school or historical period as a clue in compiling any history of thought and, in particular, a history of Chinese economic thought. Marx's *Theories of Surplus Value* is written in terms of such a system. This is not the "framework" unique to the history of bourgeois economic theory, so there should not be any disagreement. Some scholars advocate the system of thematic studies by breaking the format of compiling by era or figure. This compiling style has the advantage of giving readers a systematic understanding of each topic, but meanwhile it has a serious drawback, that is, tearing apart the economic thought of a certain historical stage from the whole picture of the entire development process, which does not meet the basic requirement of historical academic work. Therefore, historical works written in this system can only be named "historical study" rather than "history" directly. Furthermore, this system is generally the resort adopted by an author who does not fully grasp the overall knowledge of his research field and it is by no means a typical compiling style from the viewpoint of the science of history.

Second, when narrating the economic thought of a certain historical figure, school or period, should we base it on a variety of economic categories such as wealth, production, distribution, money, and so on? This is the core of the so-called "system" differences. Some scholars in opposition to this compiling style think that this is the framework of history of bourgeois economic theory. But that is a complete misunderstanding. Any history of thought has its own specific theoretical category and only by describing the development of that category can we display its own characteristics. If all histories of thought invariably depict class struggle and social relations of production without the specific category of

2 [The author is here responding to views expressed in "Several issues on the research of Chinese Economic Thought", *Quarterly Journal of Shanghai Academy of Social Sciences* 1983(12).]

its own discipline, who can distinguish between history of philosophy, history of political science, history of economic thought and other intellectual histories? This does not mean denying class analysis or social relations of production; on the contrary, it is actually through the analysis of a specific category that class essence or social relations of production can be reflected more accurately. Marxist viewpoints are the guiding principle of any scientific research, yet the guiding principle must not be in lieu of any specific content of a science. Is it acceptable to compile a history of chemistry mainly through class struggle and production relations instead of such "frameworks" of history of Western chemistry as alchemy, elements, molecular structure, and so on? Some may think that social science and natural science are different and thus cannot be compared. We will then take the history of social science as our example. In Marx's *Pre-Capitalist Economic Formations*, *Theories of Surplus Value* and some other works, economic categories of wealth, production, money, interest and profit have been frequently discussed in the narration of economists, so why should we stay away from these categories in compiling a history of Chinese economic thought?

Third, since there were no professional economic thinkers in ancient times and people's economic views were often mixed with philosophical and political discourse, it is hard to separate them strictly if we do not describe their economic views by respective categories in the study of history of ancient economic thought, whether Western or Chinese. This is not a set "framework", nor unique to the history of Western economic theory, but a style of compilation that must be adopted not only in the history of economic thought but also in the intellectual history of various disciplines, with the only difference that various disciplines have their own specific categories to be described. The same category, taking the economic category for example, can be either defined as a bourgeois economic category if viewed from a bourgeois economic perspective, or as a category of proletarian political economy if guided by the viewpoints of Marxist political economy, and can also be transformed into a socialist economic category. Is it not common to see the wide use of such categories as commodity, capital, interest and profit in all socialist countries? We will inevitably use these categories in the future compilation of history of economic thought in socialist China. Can such a practice be accused of using the framework of history of bourgeois economic theory? The key to the question is whether Marxism and Mao Zedong Thought are employed as the guide and whether the standpoint is socialism. Using economic categories as the system for the history of economic thought does not mean being subject to the limitations of a certain framework. If possible, scholars are free to propose the compiling system that is regarded by themselves as the best, but should not consider a system of economic categories as a set "framework".

Fourth, Chinese economic thought before the nineteenth century indeed has its own characteristics and is quite different from modern economic thought in logical thinking, terminology, and so on. This is also one of the major reasons for disagreement. Traditional Chinese economic thought is generally subject to ethical requirements in the whole process of its formation and development, while modern economics has long shaken off the chains of ancient European codes of ethics ever since the classical school of economics. As a result, the contents of ancient and modern Chinese economic categories towards the same object may have various degrees of difference. Take the category of wealth, for example. Modern economics mainly studies the nature and source of wealth, while the traditional Chinese concept of wealth, like that in ancient European studies, largely discusses under what conditions people can acquire wealth in line with "justice". Therefore, some scholars propose that we should not classify how to acquire wealth and similar views of this kind into the wealth category, which is inconsistent with historical analysis.[3]

As for the use of terminology, the differences between ancient and modern times are even more significant. Most ancient and modern terms towards the same economic object are quite different. For example, the so-called ancient *Min Shu* is referred to as *Ren Kou* (population) in modern times, the ancient term *Que* of the Western Han dynasty means monopoly, *Ping Zhun* is price regulation, and *Cheng Ti Zhi Shu* of the Southern Song dynasty refers to the principles of paper currency management in the modern sense, and so on. On the other hand, some ancient terms such as *Feng Jian* (feudalism) and *Jingji* (economy) are sharply different in connotation from so-called feudalism and economy in the modern sense. Ancient China also has some particular economic concepts such as *Qing Zhong* (Light-Heavy Theory), *Zi Mu Xiang Quan* (Balance Theory of Money) and *Nong Zhan* (Farming and War) for which it is difficult to find equivalents in modern economic categories; there are also some categories that did not yet form specific terms but were in fact discussed in ancient China, such as "division of labour", "distribution", "desire", "supply and demand"; and, of course, there are also many terms that share almost the same meaning with modern economic

---

3 Here we discuss a related issue. Some people have repeatedly asserted that the traditional Chinese "View of Righteousness and Benefit" is unique to China, which is mistaken. The economic views of all ancient countries that have been uncovered by now, be it India, Greece or Rome, all stress the ethical constraints on the acquisition and use of wealth, which is a common feature of ancient economic thought all over the world. The code of ethics mentioned is the so-called "righteousness" while the acquisition and use of wealth is "benefit" in the view of "righteousness and benefit" in ancient China. The Chinese and foreign expressions towards this issue are different, but the connotations are completely consistent. Therefore, China's "Righteousness and Benefit View" actually reflects the common economic thought of the whole ancient world, which is certainly not unique to China. Not only in ancient economic thought, even in modern Western economics, while the chains of ancient code of ethics on the acquisition and use of wealth have long been shaken off, the ethical influence is still not clearly eliminated. The major difference between the so-called "normative economics" and "positive economics" in modern economics is that the former emphasises the role of ethics in distribution, while the latter proposes to abandon the constraints of ethics. Therefore, as put in traditional Chinese terms, there is still the controversy between "righteousness" and "benefit" even in modern Western economics. Therefore, the "view of righteousness and benefit" is not a characteristic of Chinese economic thought whether in ancient or modern times.

categories such as money, price, monopoly and tax, with only minor differences in connotation.

However, such differences in logic, thinking and terminology cannot justify the use of old economic thought as the compiling system for the history of Chinese economic thought; on the contrary, the existence of those differences requires us to compile the history of Chinese economic thought by a system that is based on modern economic categories and also takes into account the characteristics of the old system. The reason is that in our age, people are familiar with modern ways of thinking and modern economic categories; if a familiar system is not used, how can we make it easy to understand, let alone use Marxist views to systemise, analyse and criticise the heritage of old economic thought? Let us take an example from the history of philosophy to illustrate this point. Huang Zongxi's *Song Yuan Xue'an* and *Mingru Xue'an* have always been regarded as famous masterpieces elaborating the schools of academic thought of the Song, Yuan and Ming dynasties.[4] In modern language, what they provide is a history of philosophy of the Song, Yuan and Ming dynasties written in terms of old intellectual categories with their unique adaptive system. If such a system is suited to current needs, it can be considered to have maintained the true colours of the thought of the ancients and it is thus unnecessary to rewrite the works of history of Chinese philosophy after the May Fourth Movement,[5] especially the Song, Yuan and Ming parts, by a system of modern philosophical logic, thinking and terminology. As to whether to follow the guidance of Marxism, that is another issue to be considered. Such is the case of history of Chinese philosophy, and the same is applicable to history of Chinese economic thought.

Therefore, it is not only irreproachable but also inevitable to take the economic categories in modern use as the basis for the compiling system for history of economic thought in ancient China. In fact, in all the existing works of history of Chinese economic thought, whether published before or after liberation [1949], the general compiling system is based on a sequence of historical figures and relevant economic categories, the principal difference being whether to follow the guidance of Marxism. There are diversities only in historical data and analytical focus, but this does not belong to a system-difference problem. Even in the works of some scholars who are opposed to the economic category system and place the emphasis on such ancient terms as *Yi Li Lun* (Theory of Righteousness and Benefit), *She Jian Lun* (Theory of Luxury and Thrift), *Mou Dao Bu Mou Shi Lun* (Theory of Searching for Truth rather than a mere Living), modern economic categories of production, distribution, desire, value and finance have been heavily used. This fully shows that it is impossible to compile a history of Chinese economic thought understandable to modern readers without such economic categories. On the other hand, in the current academic works of the

4 [Huang Zongxi (1610–1695), scholar and reformer in the early Qing dynasty.]
5 [The name given to the intellectual "revolution" of 1917–1921, which encompassed trenchant criticism of the influence of Confucianism and a desire to learn from the West in order to promote China's development.]

discipline, not a single one has exclusively used the system of modern economic categories, and some special ancient theories that cannot be expressed in modern economic categories, such as *Qing Zhong* (Light-Heavy Theory), *Zi Mu Xiang Quan* (Balance Theory of Money) and *Cheng Ti* (Principles of Paper Currency Management). Thus, the use of modern economic categories as against ancient terms is only a matter of degree and cannot be regarded as a difference in system. The issue of so-called "system difference" is therefore pointless and requires no further discussion.

Comparative analysis

As far as research in this discipline is concerned, so-called comparative analysis means to make ancient and modern comparison or Chinese and Western comparison of various economic perspectives in ancient China, to the extent possible. In the 1960s and 1970s, whether to engage in ancient and modern comparison has been discussed, while in recent years the discussion is mainly about whether to make Chinese and Western comparison. Some scholars oppose ancient and modern or Chinese and Western comparisons on the same theoretical basis that different social forms or production modes have their corresponding economic concepts that are essentially different and cannot be compared. They believe that the economic thought of ancient China reflects the particular characteristics of a slave mode of production, especially a feudal mode of production, which surely cannot be compared with economic views that reflect the capitalist mode of production. Besides, popular economic views of modern China are bourgeois economic views imported from the West, which cannot be compared with ancient economic thought; and Western society is a typical capitalist mode of production, which does not lend itself to a Chinese and Western comparison.

Scholars who hold such opinions ignore the following considerations. First, China's ancient history is also divided into periods of slavery and feudalism, yet the works of these scholars analyse the two systems side by side without distinction. Is that not also to compare different natured economic views of a slave mode of production and a feudal mode of production? Second, their works also borrow a large number of categories from modern bourgeois economics, which puts them into comparative analysis with economic viewpoints under the slave and feudal systems. Third, these scholars think they are using the economic views of scientific socialism for criticism and reference of ancient Chinese economic thought. Without comparative analysis, how can they make criticism and reference? This is actually a self-denial argument. However, these are all minor problems or even non-problems. Let us start by discussing the necessity of comparative analysis. If it is necessary, then we can make both ancient and modern and Chinese and Western comparisons.

Before discussing why it is necessary to make a comparative analysis of ancient Chinese economic thought we need first to understand from Marxism the economic categories under various social forms. Historical investigation tells us that various economic categories can be roughly divided into three types:

economic categories common to any social form; economic categories unique to certain social forms; and economic categories characteristic of several social forms.

Labour, as an economic category common to any social form, is "the simplest abstraction, which expresses an immeasurably ancient relation valid in all forms of society".[6] However, it was "a quite simple category"[7] in ancient times, "the practical truth"[8] in the capitalist society, and becomes "life's prime want"[9] in the communist society. Despite these qualitative differences, the category of labour is still common to all social forms, with the possibility of comparison. The same is true of other economic categories such as production and consumption.[10]

Surplus value under capitalism, distribution according to need under communism, and the like, fall into the type of economic categories unique to certain social forms. Except for the particular economic categories of socialism and communism that we will not discuss for now, the specific capitalist economic categories also appeared in China in its semi-feudal and semi-colonial period, thus they cannot be regarded as something entirely Western. As for many economic categories specific to various pre-capitalist social forms, they also existed in China and Western countries. Only by the comparative analysis of these specific economic categories can we find their concrete differences between different countries under the same social form and between different stages of historical development of the same country. For some particular categories that have emerged under certain historical conditions of China but never existed in the same social form in the West, such as *Qing Zhong* (轻重, Light-Heavy Theory), although we are not able to make a direct comparative analysis, yet only by overall comparison of the Chinese and Western specific economic categories under the same social form can we discover some characteristics of ancient Chinese economic thought.

Several social forms based on the private ownership of means of production, such as the slave, feudal and capitalist social forms, share a larger number of economic categories such as commodity, trade and currency. Some scholars insist that the economic thought of ancient China based on slave and feudal systems must not be compared with the economic thought under the capitalist social form because the various social forms are essentially different. This view is similar to that of Dühring, which was criticised by Marx and Engels. In "From *Kritische Geschichte*", Marx has clearly pointed out that certain phenomena such as commodity production, trade and interest-bearing capital, are "common to both ancient and modern societies", so the "principles" and "theorems" used in modern bourgeois economics have also been "utilised by the writers" of ancient times, which "form the theoretical starting points of the modern science".[11]

---

6 Marx: *A Contribution to the Critique of Political Economy*.
7 Ibid., p. 165.
8 Ibid., p. 167.
9 Marx: *Critique of the Gotha Programme*.
10 See the Preface and Appendix to Marx's *A Contribution to the Critique of Political Economy*.
11 Anti-Dühring.

When applying this guideline of Marx to the study of the history of Chinese economic thought, we can either compare the economic thought of ancient China with that of its semi-colonial period, or with the Western economic thought from the slave system to the capitalist mode of production. This is by no means equivalent to ignoring the essential differences between modes of production. The reason is simple. There is no doubt that a certain social form is bound to have its own specific economic categories, but this does not mean that the social form does not share some common economic categories with other social forms. On the contrary, although economic categories unique to a certain social form play a dominant role, they are very few in number, otherwise they would not be referred to as "unique", while the economic categories shared with other social forms are many. Therefore, some scholars insist that economic categories of different social forms cannot be compared, which lacks the theoretical basis of Marxism. We can compare not only the economic categories common to different social forms, but also those unique to certain social forms. Without comparative analysis, how can we identify that they *are* "unique"?

In fact, in the academic works of those who adhere to the viewpoint that economic categories of different social forms cannot be compared, we often find an analysis of the "righteousness and benefit", the "fundamental and incidental" and other categories with a continuity of ancient to modern times. These writers have not only made comparison of economic categories of slave, feudal and semi-colonial societies, but have even regarded them as common categories across different social forms. That being the case, on what ground can they oppose comparative analysis of ancient Chinese economic thought and non-unique economic categories of capitalist society, and call this comparison "rigidly applying the Western capitalist economic theory model since the seventeenth century to the economic thought of feudal China for several thousand years"[12]?

As far as the study of history of Chinese economic thought is concerned, comparative analysis is all the more essential. Economic thought of the long period of ancient China to the mid-nineteenth century has evolved and developed with its own specific way of thinking and terminology. Since the latter half of the nineteenth century, some forward-looking Chinese scholars have actively sought for "truth" from the West. Whether they found that "truth" or not, Western bourgeois economics thereby began to enter and expand, which finally replaced the dominance of traditional Chinese economic thought at the beginning of the twentieth century. The whole set of theoretical system, thinking mode and terminology were borrowed from Western bourgeois economics mainly through Japan; even the basic terms of "economy" and "economics" and their connotations were copied from Japan, not to mention other economic categories. Whether we like it or not, since then the whole set has become the pattern that people are accustomed to when discussing any economic theory or problem, and there is no exception even for those who are specialised in the

12 [The quotation is from Ma Bohuang, "Several issues on the research of Chinese Economic Thought: discussions about the ancient part", *Journal of Social Sciences*, 1983 (12).]

study of the history of Chinese economic thought. Although Marxist scientific economic theory is completely opposite to bourgeois economics in viewpoint and methodology, the economic categories used in the classics of Marxism still follow those of classical bourgeois economics, at least in terminology. Therefore, when translating the classics of Marxism into Chinese, their economic categories are consistent with those in general use at least in terms of terminology, which helps speed up the spread of Marxism. Under such objective conditions, for any scholar who studies history of Chinese economic thought, including those who are against comparative analysis, whether he follows the guidance of Marxism or starts from the bourgeois standpoint, he must employ the economic categories familiar to people's understanding. There is no other way. This is actually making comparative analysis already.

By comparative analysis of ancient and modern economic thought we can know the clues for the development of, and changes in, economic thought around the mid-nineteenth century: which of the old economic ideas have been discarded, which ones are preserved, which ones have changed to bourgeois viewpoints in the new economic conditions, and which ones are still meaningful for socialist construction. On the other hand, only by means of the comparative analysis of old Chinese economic thought and Western economic thought of ancient and modern times can we know what contributions our ancestors have made to economics under their historical conditions and what position these contributions hold in the history of economic thought of the world. Despite the glorious achievements of ancient Chinese economic thought, if we are opposed to comparative analysis by the economic categories that are in long and common use by Chinese people in modern times, it will be impossible to know where the glory lies; on the other side, if we compare the ancient and modern economic thought behind closed doors, we will have no idea of the extent of the glory. Only by making Chinese and Western comparative analysis can we truly understand the brilliant achievements of ancient Chinese economic thought. My work *Brilliant Achievements of Ancient Chinese Economic Thought before the Seventeenth Century* in both Chinese and English versions[13] has attracted more attention than my *History of Chinese Economic Thought* both at home and abroad, including the United States, Britain, France, Netherlands and Japan. This illustrates that the comparison of ancient and modern, especially Chinese and Western economic thought, is conducive to promoting patriotism. In present times, some Chinese economists have been committed to comparative economics, which will soon become a subject of economics. Thus, it is far from keeping up with the times for the still existing disagreements to persist as to whether there should be comparative analysis in the study of history of Chinese economic thought.

---

13 [The English version was published with the title, *Chinese Economic Thought before the Seventeenth Century*. See above, p. xvii.]

Modernisation of ancient thought

Literally, "modernisation of ancient thought" means to explain the thought of ancients and their relevant works with modern theoretical categories and terms. For instance, scholars of oracle bones inscriptions (the ancient Chinese characters carved on tortoise shells and animal scapulas) use modern Chinese to describe more than 1,000 unidentified characters; archaeologists identify unearthed cultural relics with modern technology; some documents on the ancient economy of the pre-Qin dynasty as well as the Qin and Han dynasties are annotated in modern Chinese, and so on. It is not the case only in China. Many modern economists in Western countries also employ advanced mathematics to analyse the theories of economists of early periods such as William Petty, Francois Quesnay, and David Hume, even Marx's Reproduction Theory, to indicate their accuracy. Those are typical examples of modernisation of ancient thought. There is nothing wrong with this. However, the approach proposed by some scholars since the 1950s and 1960s is endowed with a totally different connotation, which means to impose on ancient scholars some categories and thought that modern people might have but would never have been possible for ancient people to understand. I believe that any scholar with a pure academic attitude would never agree with such an approach. Any discussion of this matter thus has little theoretical significance. Yet, disagreements on this point continue to spring up now and then, so it may be helpful to conduct a simple analysis.

The disagreement about modernisation of ancient thought never occurred in Western economics. The reason is that the basic concepts and terminologies in contemporary theories of Western economics mainly develop from the primary recognition and idioms of ancient Greece and Rome. With the same origin, there are only differences in depth, precision or scope. No dissension or opposition to modernisation will arise, for modernisation is automatically realised in the development.

As pointed out above, the theoretical systems, thinking patterns and terminologies of ancient economic thought are greatly distinct from those that have been widely applied since the early twentieth century. Besides, differences between ancient and modern Chinese make modernisation of ancient thought and relevant works the first obstacle to overcome for scholars who study the history of any academic field of ancient China. There are at least three fundamental processes in order to remove this obstacle. The first is to translate ancient Chinese into modern Chinese. The second is to match ancient categories and terms with those that are widely used in modern times. The third is to refine ancient heritage in terms of modern thought. It is needless to go into detail about translating ancient Chinese into modern Chinese as there is no controversy over this point. The analysis below is on the second and third processes.

Matching is a very necessary process and an arduous and meticulous task. I will cite a couple of examples to illustrate the point. *Yin and Yang*, a part of the sentence "all the creatures under the sun are composed of *yin* and *yang*" in *Laozi*, is a universal category in ancient times. Some people define it as a kind of dialectic thought, which is a match between ancient and modern categories. For another example, some people define *Xiao Yao You* (carefree journey) in *Zhuangzi* as a kind of theory of absolute freedom, which is also tantamount to a match. In both examples, an ancient concept has been matched with a modern one, no matter whether the two matches are faithful. Should we omit this matching process and blindly believe in the annotations of the pundits of previous generations, we will become more and more confused as we delve further into ancient ideas. How could we make rational comment on them and use them as a source of reference without understanding the original meaning of ancient concepts? Let us take another example. Some people point out that the so-called *Tian* in ancient times is an equivalent of "natural object" of modern times, while *Dao* is an equivalent of "objective law". There are many other ancient categories, like *Zhi* (reference), *Ming* (name), and *Lei* (category) in the logical thought of pre-Qin days, which are unintelligible without being matched with modern categories or terms. The overwhelming majority of the concepts and terms of our ancient philosophy and social science require a matching process. Otherwise, we will preoccupy ourselves with the study of philosophy and logic, focusing all our attention on *Yin and Yang*, *Tian Da* (divine order), *Zhi Wu* (referent), *Ming Shi* (name and nature). In that case, we will be completely disconnected with each other. How could we relate to each other and how could we undertake relevant analysis? It is natural that there will be some discrepancies in the process of matching. Take *Dao*, for example. Some people define it as a kind of objective law, which must be naïve materialistic thought, while some others take it as the noumenon of absolute mind, which belongs to idealistic thought. As there are countless such examples it is unnecessary to cite more of them. In short, matching is an undeniably necessary process no matter whether some inaccuracies arise during the process.

Refining is also sometimes essential. A great many ancient ideas have not generated relatively definite categories or terms but can be expressed with definite categories and terms in modern times. For instance, philosophical terms such as materialism, idealism and *Weltanschauung* were not created in ancient times, but such mental characteristics indeed existed at that time which requires us to systemise or process the ancient treatises and distinguish materialism from idealism and other categories. Without this processing it would be impossible to recognise the thought of Xun Qing and Wang Chong [27–?100] as materialistic thought and the thought of Zhu Xi [1130–1200] and Wang Yangming [1472–1529] as objective idealism and subjective idealism, respectively, because there are no such modern philosophical terms in these people's works. Chinese scholars in the history of philosophy devote most of their time to refining work. For another example, the records of revolutionary peasants in Chinese history are nothing but the words of rumour-mongering and slandering, such as *Fei* (bandit), *Dao* (robber), *Fan Pan* (rebel) and *Jian Lu Shao Sha* (raping, burning and killing), which require the modern historian to undertake some refining and illustration in order to depict a kind of revolutionary struggle. Due to the refining of modern scholars, we finally realise that

"Discourses on Salt and Iron"[14] is actually a dialogue concerning political, economic, military, diplomatic and cultural policies for the feudal ruling class. As for the thought of Jin Rang, Shui Hui, Mu Ji and Huo Han, recorded in "The Biographies of the Money-Makers" in [Sima Qian's] *Records of the Grand Historian*, the refining of modern scholars enables us to know that they are actually thoughts of the circular agricultural economy in ancient China. In consequence, processing is also an arduous, meticulous and indispensable process in systemising our ancient heritage.

Modern translation, matching and refining are all indispensable and arduous tasks for all people engaged in research in any history of intellectual thought, scholars of Chinese history of economic thought included. It is mainly aimed to modernise ancient thought, which is beyond reproach. Although there are some mistakes in the process, like the misconception in the modern translation of ancient economic documents, they are no more than the oversight of scholars engaging in modern translation rather than the mistake of the requirement of the modernisation of ancient thought itself.

Impending challenges

In the 1960s, due to imperfect understanding of Marxist Philosophy and Political Economy, lack of access to bourgeois economics and doctrine, and the rare study of the historical origins of commonly used economic categories and terminology, it is understandable that some unnecessary disagreements arose over systems, comparative analysis and modernisation of ancient thought in the research on history of Chinese economic thought. I fully believe that the disagreements will be eliminated in the near future. Especially, under the brilliant leadership of the Central Committee of the Party, who continue with the opening-up policy, call on us to take some reasonable Western elements for reference in establishing new socialist economic theory, and propose the policy of "one country, two systems" that has impressed the whole world – in short, under these new historical conditions – nobody could continue to keep alive the residual disagreements that appeared since the 1960s. Although the disagreements will soon melt away, their clarification will be helpful in order to avoid an unnecessary detour in the development of this discipline.

However, the main problem of the discipline lies not in the disagreements. In recent years, some philosophy scholars have proposed to reform the current philosophy textbooks, applying System Theory, Control Theory and Information Theory. In 1984, in answer to the call from the Central Committee of the Party, the Foreign Economic Theory Research Association organised seminars to encourage its members to learn reasonable elements from Western economic theories and practice so as to contribute to establishing an economic theory of socialism with Chinese characteristics. The above examples show that under the

14 [The title of the document recording the debate that had taken place in 81 BC, compiled some twenty or thirty years later.]

rapid development of science and technology, many disciplines are, to different extents, facing challenges at present and will continue to do so in the future. What is the situation of researchers of the history of Chinese economic thought? Most people tend to "look backward": it seems that only the economic concepts that came into being before the May Fourth Movement in 1919 can be regarded as Chinese economic thought. Few people are aware of the systemisation of those concepts from 1919 to 1949. They fail to face reality, let alone to prepare for the future. Some even consider that to apply conventional economic categories and terminology in modern China as analytical tools is the Western system, unnecessary comparative analysis and "modernisation of ancient thought". It is essential to portray the glorious heritage of economic thought in ancient and modern China. Yet, it is unwise to take this as the only task, for history keeps moving forward. As long as China continues to develop, it will have its own history of economic thought and its own professional researchers. If we limit the development of this discipline to systemising economic thought in ancient and modern China, the next generation will not be able to adapt to the requirements of the periods when they are in their middle and older age. The characteristics of this discipline determine that the next generation of researchers is required not only to be equipped with the ability to inherit our ancient economic heritage but also with some basic knowledge to organise the achievements of Chinese economic theories that may spring up now and in the near future. Time is pressing, so that the tendency only to look backward should be reversed as early as possible.

Due to this long-standing "backward-looking" tendency, many people are misled into thinking that they are able to study Chinese economic thought with knowledge of Chinese economic history and ancient Chinese alone, which proves to be a one-sided and even wrong idea. Actually, a researcher of the history of Chinese economic thought probably should have the basic knowledge that would be required for the study of any branch of the history of Chinese intellectual thought. But let us be more specific. First, as our research is under the guidance of Marxism, it is necessary to master the knowledge of Marxist Philosophy and Political Economy. In addition, because history of Chinese economic thought is a discipline that proves to be quite theoretical, researchers of this discipline need to have a better command of Marxist Philosophy and Political Economy than students of other disciplines in the history of Chinese intellectual thought. Second, studying the history of Chinese economic thought requires a command of the history of Western economic theories in order to avoid ignorance and short-sighted viewpoints. Moreover, without understanding bourgeois economics to a certain degree, it will certainly be difficult to organise the achievements of the economic thought that developed after the May Fourth Movement. Third, history of economic thought has developed into a discipline so that the research should cover not only ancient Chinese economic thought but also relevant contemporary economic thought. Last but not least, the researchers of this discipline, in addition to having basic knowledge of Chinese and foreign economic history, as well as ancient Chinese, should aim at some degree of mastery over English and advanced mathematics, for most Western economists in modern times can hardly write a paper without involving mathematics. There are many papers on economic thought by Chinese scholars of history in the early twentieth century but the phenomenon becomes rare after 1960s. It is predicted that in the near future, works in this discipline will all be written by professional economists. Researchers in other disciplines will not be able to have a hand in it. This is the general trend we observe in different countries in the world. What many people have imagined, that those who acquire a basic knowledge of Chinese economic history and ancient Chinese are thereby qualified to engage in the study of history of Chinese economic thought, is quite misleading. Just consider that under the rapid development of the social economy and science and technology, it will take about two decades for the emergence of many Chinese theoretical economists, econometricians, statisticians and economists in sub-branches of the discipline. Will it be possible to organise the theoretical achievements of these new economists just by virtue of the basic knowledge of the above-mentioned two subjects? If a scholar is so limited in capability, can he be called a professional researcher in the history of Chinese economic thought? The situation is pressing. It is quite necessary to raise for consideration the challenges that will befall this discipline in the near future.

2 On the major fields and significance of the study of the history of ancient Chinese economic thought[1]

Wu Baosan

It is common that scholars who study the history of Chinese economic thought have to answer one fundamental question: what is the significance of the subject? To be more critical, the question is whether ancient Chinese society, which spanned over 2,000 years, produced economic theories that are worthy of research. On the surface, this question has been answered by several published accounts of the History of Chinese Economic Thought and has therefore become an anachronism. However, in reality the question is still haunting the economics community. Although the question has been partly addressed, with some confusion removed, there has not been sufficient explanation and evidence to give a complete answer. In my view, scholars who study the history of Chinese economic thought should continue to make diligent effort to further explore the subject, reveal the historical facts with objectivity and deepen their understanding through analysis. Accordingly, they can make due contribution to promote Chinese traditional culture and to enrich the study of world economic thought. It will require strenuous attempts and several generations' work to accomplish this task. This study is undertaken in the hope of making a meagre contribution to the enterprise.

Fundamental questions should not receive arbitrary answers. Instead, they should be resolved with care and deliberation, thorough investigation and multi-angled explanation. By doing this, conclusions that can withstand scrutiny may be reached. Starting from this point, I propose to discuss two questions. One is how to treat the study of the history of Chinese economic thought. The other is how to evaluate this subject. The second question is more crucial and requires more attention. The first question will be discussed as follows.

1

It could be highly reasonable for scholars to ask how we should treat the subject of the history of ancient Chinese economic thought. There are two reasons for

1 Originally published as "论中国古代经济思想史研究主要方面及其意义" ("On the major fields and significance of the study of the history of ancient Chinese economic thought"), *Research in Chinese Economic History*, 1991, Issue 1 pp. 65–75.

that. First, China had no research work published domestically in this area before the 1920s. In 1911, Chen Huanzhang published his celebrated work, *The Economic Principles of Confucius and His School*. However, it was published in the USA, only in an English version, and was therefore unknown to many Chinese students and scholars. Second, specialised research on the history of Chinese economic thought only has a history of fifty years if we start from Gan Naiguang's concise study, *The History of Pre-Qin Economic Thought*, published in 1926. In contrast, the first ever book focused on this area, written by Jérôme-Adolphe Blanqui,[2] was published in 1837–1838. In this sense, China lagged behind Europe by nearly 100 years. Besides, this type of research only started growing in China in the 1980s. However, since we are comparing the history of Chinese economic thought with the history of Western economic thought, the question also arises of why the first works on the history of European economic thought did not emerge until 1837. Thus, the review of the development of the history of European economic thought can offer us useful insights.

Like other disciplines, the history of economic theory, or the history of economic thought, became an independent subject only after it gained the ability to reveal its inner logic within the research realm through the constant accumulation of knowledge and ongoing research. It took several generations to reach such a stage. Then, the subject blended its theoretical features with its observability and its verifiability. Economics emerged as an independent science when the feudal system in Western Europe collapsed and the capitalist system appeared. This happened after commodity production and exchange became well developed, specifically during the period between the fifteenth and seventeenth centuries. This period also witnessed the inception of the theory of mercantilism, which represented the interest of commercial capital and had a sharp focus on foreign trade policy. According to Marx, "mercantilism is the first school which explores the modern production mode from a theoretical perspective".[3] Prior to mercantilism, natural economy was the predominant economy in ancient Greece, ancient Rome and feudal society during the medieval period. Within those societies, economic relationships were simple and any discussion of economic issues was mostly an extension of discussion within the philosophical or political realms. Economic issues were rarely studied as an independent subject. This was also the case in ancient China.

We can see that it was more than 200 years between the birth of mercantilism and the advent of the first work on the history of European economic thought, namely the book written by Blanqui. In view of this, we can understand that works focused on history of European economic thought appeared after the period of mercantilism and after other schools had sprung up as a result of

---

2 Blanqui, J.A., *Histoire de l'économie politique en Europe depuis les anciens jusqu'a nos jours*. [Published in English in 1880 as *History of Political Economy in Europe*. tr. E.J. Leonard, New York: Putnam.]
3 Karl Marx and Frederick Engels, *Collected Works* vol. 25, Beijing: People's Publishing House, p. 376.

capitalist development. Those schools include the Physiocrats represented by Francois Quesnay and Classical Economics as inaugurated by Adam Smith, with more advanced theoretical systems developed by David Ricardo in Britain and Simonde de Sismondi in France. Since economics, as an independent science, had evolved into an increasingly sophisticated subject, it is necessary to study its development from an objective point of view. The concepts of modern economic thought originate from older ideas and this justifies the need to study the history and development of economic thought. As the economies of Europe and the United States underwent drastic changes and developments, many different schools of economic thought sprang up and coexisted with each other. This then led to the flourishing of economic thought. As a result, economics was established as a subject with many branches. Before the First World War, the sub-areas within economics, such as industrial economics, labour economics, agricultural economics and finance, had not come into being. At the same time, the history of economic thought turned into a major course for study and degree-oriented exams in French universities. After the Second World War, despite the change of circumstances, the subject of the history of economic thought still maintained its important status within economic science and new works in the subject were published regularly. We can clearly see its importance in economics.

In China, since capitalist industry and commerce developed at a slow pace, economic thought had long not been able to break free from the feudalism-based framework with its focus on natural economy. It was not until China opened its door to Western capitalist powers in the mid-nineteenth century that theoretical works appeared on modern modes of production. From the mid-nineteenth century to the early twentieth century, the academic focus had been on the introduction of Western economic theories: the study of the history of Chinese economic thought was not on the agenda. Then, in the 1920s, Sun Yatsen's National Revolutionary Theory stimulated many intellectuals to explore various means to revitalise China in its political and economic aspects. Scholars began to study the history of Chinese economic thought in order to "prepare for the creation of new economic thought in China".[4] From this perspective, we can say that the development of the history of Chinese economic thought in the late 1950s stemmed from the aspiration of scholars to help establish Chinese socialist economic theory and to enrich the understanding of the previously neglected history of ancient Chinese economic thought.

Some foreign scholars have also recognised the neglect of ancient Chinese economic thought and argued for its study. For example, Russian sinologist Shi Taiyin remarked that

> the curricula and teaching practice of the history of economic thought, so far have attached no significance to China and other oriental countries.... The

---

4 Tang Qingzeng, Preface to *The History of Chinese Economic Thought*, vol. 1, Shanghai: Commercial Press, 1936.

study has only been confined to the formation of the economic thought within the European continent; the study on the history of world economic thought should be revolutionised and it is necessary to include oriental countries into the research topic[5]

In other words, the general works on the history of economic thought were histories only of European and North American economic thought, and economic thought from various age-old cultures in the world was excluded. At the same time, some Western intellectuals have shown a strong interest in studying the history of ancient Chinese economic thought. Joseph Schumpeter, one of the most famous economists of modern times, once said,

> More than anywhere else we might expect to find such traces [of analytic effort] in ancient China, the home of the oldest literary culture of which we know. We find in fact a highly developed public administration that deal currently with agrarian, commercial, and financial problems.... Moreover, there were methods of monetary management and of exchange control that seem to presuppose a certain amount of analysis. The phenomenon incident to the recurrent inflations were no doubt observed and discussed by men much superior to us in cultural refinement.[6]

Western economists have no doubt about China's long history and splendid culture. But they also have very limited knowledge of ancient Chinese economic thought due to their inability to read historical works in the original language and the paucity of studies on the subject that have been translated into a Western language. Moreover, there are problems with the works that have been translated. Chen Huanzhang's contributions apply modern economic concepts in an overly rigid manner and lack scientific analysis. Li Zhaoyi has published in French, but his ideas lack profundity and are not well-known. Recently, the book *A Concise History of Chinese Economic Thought*, written by Hu Jichuang, has been published in English.[7] This book fills previous gaps and enables foreigners to understand more about the key content and development of Chinese economic thought. In the past, Western economists believed that although ancient Chinese economic thought was rich, many policies and proposals lacked scientific analysis. For instance, H.C. Tyler wrote: "in Eastern countries nothing can be

---

5 В.М. us Теии ГуаНb-пз, *ИниесслелоВаНйэйэ JiepeBoд*, 1959.
6 Schumpeter, J.A., *A History of Economic Analysis*, 1954, London: George Allen & Unwin, p. 55. [Schumpeter went on to say,

> But no piece of reasoning on strictly economic topics has come down to us that can be called "scientific" within our meaning of the term.... There may have been analytic work, the records of which failed to survive. But there is reason to suppose that there was not much of it.

(Ibid.)]

7 Hu Jichuang, *A Concise History of Chinese Economic Thought*, Beijing: Foreign Languages Press, 1988.

compared to the good start of economic analysis from the medieval monks in the Western countries".[8] To refute this argument one cannot rely on confronting words. Instead, we must rely on research and thorough study. This is one of the goals that my work hopes to achieve.

In general, the discipline of the history of Chinese economic thought attracts attention from home and abroad. This discipline has a rich ancient literature and is also an essential part of the general history of world economic thought. Despite a late start due to the historical conditions outlined above, the discipline of the history of Chinese economic thought will increasingly expand in its research scope and depth, and will show its significance as the Chinese economy develops further and economic research continues to expand. In the following section we will discuss the content and the significance of Chinese economic thought taking pre-Qin thought as our case study.

2

The economic thought of different historical periods and different scholars roughly covers three aspects. The first is the philosophy used as the foundation or the starting point for the economic thought. The second is the ideas, propositions and policies regarding various economic issues. The third is the analysis of the internal and external relations of economic phenomena and issues. The economic theories established by great economists always consist of all three aspects. Adam Smith's economic theory is the most notable example. His theory uses moral philosophy as its philosophical base and also includes theoretical analysis on the contributing factors of the capitalist economic system and the various relationships within the system. Moreover, it provides solutions from the perspective of economic liberalism. But not all economists clearly present all three aspects of economic thought. An extreme example is that many mathematical economists only give an analysis of the internal and external relations for explaining economic phenomena and they neither shed any light on the ideas on which their theories are based nor make any policy recommendations. But even in this kind of extreme example it is not hard to figure out the foundational theory and the indicative policy recommendations based on the assumptions and the mechanism of different relations. Generally speaking, it is a common phenomenon that economists only focus on one or two aspects and ignore the others. That is the case in modern times and was even more so in ancient times. This does not prevent us from discussing economic thought in terms of those three aspects. We think that all three aspects are important. Ancient Chinese economic thought is mostly presented in the form of philosophical and political ideas and usually lacks economic analysis. Therefore, apart from making a special effort to explain the economic-philosophical ideas and other policy-based ideas, we should seek to explore the economic analysis contained in those ideas and discuss its significance. Now I would like to give a brief explanation of all three

8 Tyler, H.C. "The Oriental Economic Thought", *American Economic Review*, May 1956.

aspects in pre-Qin economic thought and their significance. I will deal with the basic ideas or philosophical ideas first, as they are the starting point of economic thought.

There is no division within the ancient discipline. The ancient thinkers always study a subject from the viewpoint of the origin of the universe and social system, which is referred to as heaven and humanity, and the relationship between nature and man. In modern terms, the discipline starts from the areas of philosophy, politics and ethics, and only discusses generalities within these areas. Economic issues were merely part of their discussions or regarded as one of the specific topics for discussion. The great classical thinkers from China and from other countries are first acknowledged as philosophers, educators or politicians, and they are rarely described as economists even though their theories are rich in economic ideas. Plato initiates an impressive discussion of the division of labour in his *Utopia*. Aristotle expounds his well-known monetary theory only as specific issues within his works on ethics and political science. The following part will show that ancient Chinese economic thought emerged in a similar pattern.

It is important to note that although the pattern reflected in the relations between ancient philosophy, politics, ethics and economic thought is undoubtedly subject to the low level of scientific development at the time, the economic thought has an inherent and inevitable link with philosophical and political thought. The existence of a particular economic system and particular economic problems requires thinkers to jump out of the framework of politics and ethics and put aside the interests of different classes in order to provide useful explanations as well as seek philosophical insights from areas including the relations between nature and man. At the same time, the thought regarding the state and the political system, of moral standards that distinguish good from evil, justice and injustice, and the relationship between nature and man, all inevitably relate to the stance of thinkers of different schools regarding economic issues and the economic system. These stances can also refer to their attitude, support or opposition, towards economic systems and economic issues during their periods. As a result, economics emerged under historical circumstances. In fact, the forces and counter-forces shown in the above two aspects exist both in ancient and modern economic thought. As we know, ancient economic thought was secondary to the subjects of philosophy, politics and ethics. On the surface, this relationship has its uniqueness. However, if we examine the essential relations between the economic thought and those dominant subjects, we can find that the relationship has existed ever since those ancient times. However, in ancient times economic thought did not grow into an independent discipline. This in turn further accentuated its subsidiary characteristic. Therefore, it is necessary to discuss the foundational ideas from philosophy, politics, ethics and other basic ideas when studying the ancient world economy. This necessity is greater when a certain theory becomes an important part of the traditional culture of the country, and its impact on modern economic development turns into the next important issue to study. We now take Confucianism and Daoism as examples.

Confucianism dominated Chinese feudal society for more than 2,000 years. All famous Confucian thinkers, including Confucius himself, are known as philosophers, political thinkers and ethical thinkers. They are not recognised as specialist economists. We should focus on the philosophy and political ideas on which Confucian economic thought was based and explore the special significance of those philosophical and political ideas in studying economic issues. During the past one or two decades, several parts of East Asia, such as South Korea, Singapore, Hong Kong, and Taiwan, Province of China, have developed very rapidly. Confucianism is a dominant culture in all these areas. Under these circumstances, two questions have been raised. One is whether traditional culture, especially Confucianism, has positive or negative impacts on economic development; the other is how the impact is demonstrated. On the surface, these issues seem purely related to philosophy, politics and ethics, but traditional culture undoubtedly covers economic activities and also the economic thought contained in those activities. Indeed, those economic thoughts are embodied in Confucian philosophy and its political and ethical thinking. Therefore, to discuss the relations between Confucianism and economic development one must study which economic ideas from Confucianism can play a positive role in economic development, and the foundational philosophical, political and ethical theories.

In general, the philosophical, political and ethical ideas of Confucius are embodied in his views on "Propriety" and "Benevolence". Propriety relates to behaviour consistent with the feudal patriarchal hierarchy at that time. Confucius repeatedly praises propriety and condemns overstepping etiquette because he thinks that the patriarchal hierarchy of feudal ethics should be maintained. He also proposes the concept of "righteousness". Specifically, any conduct that can meet the various standards of the ethical system of patriarchal feudalism can also fulfil the standard of "righteousness". "Benevolence" is a core virtue in the system of moral standards. The system promotes the practice of "Propriety" and "Benevolence" and includes ideas like duty to parents, love for brothers, loyalty to the king and forgiveness for the transgressions of others. Broadly speaking, we should love other people and think of them from our own perspective.

Confucius's philosophy and political ethics have undoubtedly been reflected in his analysis of some significant economic issues. Thus, Confucianism holds that in order to implement good governance and ensure a peaceful life for the people, rulers should have the qualities of "dignity, generosity, trust, diligence and virtuousness": "If one is courteous, one is not treated with rudeness; if one is tolerant, one wins over the multitude; if one is of good faith, others give one responsibility; if one is diligent, one obtains results; and if one is kind, one is competent to command others."[9] The five virtues of Confucianism fall into the category of Benevolence, and generosity and virtuousness become guiding ideas for addressing economic issues. With this idea as the guiding principle, Confucius discussed people-oriented ideas at length, such as "valuing the people" ("the people should have food, and the rites of mourning and sacrifice should be

9 *Analects*, XVII.5.

observed"[10]), "benefiting the people" ("[benefit] the people on the basis of what the people will really find beneficial"[11]), "enriching the people" ("if the people are rich, the government will be also rich"[12]), "feeding people" ("providing for the needs of the people"[13]), and "bringing salvation to the multitude".[14] Such injunctions were all applications of the principles of "generosity" and "virtuousness". Indeed, those ideas have been reflected in the economic policies promoted by Confucius, such as lifting prohibitions and reducing taxes.

In the realm of political ideas, Mencius further developed Confucius's theory of Benevolence by introducing the concept of Benevolent Government which advocated the primacy of the people over government itself. In terms of ethical ideas, Mencius advances Confucius's ideas by infusing the concept of "Benevolence and Righteousness" with more profound and structured content.

The theory of "Benevolence and Righteousness" had a great impact on intellectuals from different schools of thought during the Warring States period, becoming a prominent subject of the time. In the Han dynasty, Confucianism was the only school of thought espoused by governments. Throughout Chinese feudal society, Confucianism was embraced by dynastic rulers and held a dominant position in the sphere of culture and education. There are two reasons why the theory of Benevolence had such a long-lasting effect. One is that its ideas could be adapted to different times. Such ideas included loyalty, duty to parents, virtuousness and righteousness, which were designed to maintain social order. A second reason is that the ideas possessed some universal characteristics shared by all periods throughout Chinese history. For example, the economic thought embodied in the theory of Benevolence contains some elements of democracy by encompassing "love for other people", "benefiting the people" and "enriching the people", which are intended to promote a socially harmonious community development. When we are considering the relationship between Chinese traditional culture and economic development, it is necessary to quote those common thoughts in Confucius's theory of Benevolence and the economic policy with its insights on democracy. If it is the case that Confucius's theories have a positive impact on economic modernisation, then an in-depth study of the theory of Benevolence and of Confucius's economic thought would be called for.

Moreover, we should investigate further Confucius's idea of "benefiting the people" and whether it amounts to a laissez-faire ideology. Zhu Jiazhen has argued that Confucius's policy of lifting prohibitions was different from European ideas of laissez-faire and free competition.[15] This discussion is highly

---

10 Ibid., XX.1.
11 Ibid., XX.2.
12 [Or, as rendered by Arthur Waley in *The Analects* (London: Everyman, 2000), "When the Hundred Families [i.e. all the people] enjoy plenty, the prince necessarily shares in that plenty." Ibid., XII.9.]
13 Ibid., V.16.
14 Ibid., VI.30.
15 "Research on Confucius's Economic Thought" in *Discussion of Chinese Economic Thought*, Beijing: People's Press, 1985.

pertinent as it is important to distinguish between the two different types of ideas. It may also be added that Confucius's theories of "lifting prohibitions" and "benefiting the people" are based on the idea of benevolence. Although there is no doubt that the idea of benevolence requires that sufficient attention should be given to personal accomplishment, the highest goal is to unite the family and conduct good governance. In this respect, Confucius believes that the home is the cell of society, but the country stands above the home as a political organisation representing a region, and individuals belong to both their homes and their countries. The home and country are both holistic and an entirety, and both have their own purpose and mission. The individuals are part of the entirety and cannot be separated from it. Therefore, Confucius and Confucian thought regarding economic policy, such as "employing people at the proper seasons" and "light tax", always proceed from the overall purpose of pursuing the interest of the country rather than the interest of the individual.

Confucian thought also denies the use of personal interest as a symbol of the whole society's interest. For example, Confucius regards some ideas, such as setting six trade barricades, as non-benevolence (Chapter 4th Year of King Wen, *Zuo's Commentary*) and promotes the idea of scrapping the government's exclusive rights on developing resources in mountainous and water areas (Chapter 7th Wu Yi Jie[16]). Others example can be found from Mencius, who advocates that "government should inspect the goods but not levy tax at customs pass", and "government should not levy any tax in the market". Those proposals are conducive to facilitating the businessman's trade activities and farmers' firewood collection and fishing. However, the Confucian idea of benevolence is strikingly different from laissez-faire ideas. The latter are based on the abolition of personal dependence relations of the feudal system and the adoption of a free market in the domestic sphere on the basis of egoism and utilitarianism. Understanding the economic ideas of Confucius from a laissez-faire perspective will not only result in the incorrect understanding of Confucius's economic thought but also lead to the wrong conclusion of the discussion on the relations between modern economic development and the economic thought of Confucius. This is also the reason why we stress that when studying the economic ideas of ancient thinkers, especially if our interest is the impact of economic thought on current economic development, we should study the philosophy behind the economic ideas.

Now let us consider Daoist philosophy and its relationship with economic thought. The Daoist school of thought did not accept the unequal status within the ritual hierarchy described by the Propriety theories, or the practices of delivering punishment, granting rewards and imposing prohibitions. Daoists believed

16 From *Kongzi jia yu* ("The School Sayings of Confucius"). ["The School Saying of Confucius" is purportedly a record of the words and deeds of Confucius and his students. Some scholars claim that the book was written in the Han dynasty, others argue that it was compiled earlier by Confucius's grandson, and others aver that it has no relation to the "historical Confucius" whatsoever. There is no scholarly consensus.]

that human society and nature are equally subject to the control of the original Dao. Dao referred to the original form of all things in the universe, including human activities, and Dao indicates that everything develops naturally.[17] From this perspective, individual activities and governance should be carried out with respect for "inner rules". Thus, this school of thought advocates that individuals should "look to the simple, reduce self-love, curb desire",[18] and not be bothered by the material world. By doing this, the school contends that one can achieve great physical and mental freedom and spend one's life in a state of contentment. In terms of country governance, rulers should avoid too much intervention.[19] With regard to any human intervention, the Daoist advocates complete respect for the inner rules of things, and regards "small country with a small population" as the ideal model of society. Those ideas are the essential part of all Daoist economic thought.

The question of how to understand Daoist philosophy through the ages has evoked many debates and led to different conclusions. Different interpretations of Daoism will generate different views on Daoist economic thought. For example, Tang Qingzeng's argument that Zhuangzi's theories only focus on the past but ignore the present needs to be revised.[20] Nevertheless, the study of economic thought from the standpoint of philosophy is an even greater necessity in the case of Daoism than for other philosophically informed positions. British scientist Joseph Needham discusses Daoism's view on "knowledge" and part of his argument can be used as an example to explain this issue.[21] Needham notes that the works of Laozi and Zhuangzi contain many statements referring to anti-knowledge, anti-benevolence and anti-righteousness, anti-technique and anti-study. Therefore, he thinks that Daoism shows approval of eradicating knowledge and desires. The textual examples he uses are as follows: "get rid of wisdom, the people are better off a hundred times";[22]

> If rulers give up the highest knowledge, the people will benefit a hundred times more. If rulers abandon the principles of benevolence and righteousness, the people's filial piety will be restored. If rulers abandon opportunistic practices and desires for profits, thieves will cease to exist."[23]

"Someday there will be a great awakening when we know that all this is a great dream. Yet the stupid believe they are awake ... Confucius and you are both

---

17 *Daodejing*, 25 (from *Laozi: Daodejing*, E. Ryden, tr., Oxford: Oxford University Press, 2008).
18 *Daodejing*, 19.
19 Ibid., 63.
20 See the first and the fourth section of Chapter 4 in Tang Qingzeng's *History of Chinese Economic Thought*, first half volume, 1937.
21 Joseph Needham, *Science and Civilization in China*, vol. 2 (English version. Cambridge: Cambridge University Press, 1956, pp. 86–89).
22 *Daodejing* 19.
23 [A paraphrase of *Daodejing* 3.]

dreaming!"[24] How should we understand these words? Daoists believe that within any body of "knowledge" there are divisions between truth and falsity. The knowledge taught by popular sciences, such as sagely wisdom, benevolence, righteousness and skills, can only instil people with greed, give them the motive to become thieves, and preoccupy them with pedantic means of distinguishing between different levels in the social hierarchy. Such learning is not true or real knowledge. Real knowledge requires one to understand Dao and "Nature". So-called knowledge related to the patriarchal feudal hierarchy is false knowledge and must be discarded. Only then can true knowledge be acquired.

For example, in his description of a chariot builder who is chopping wood, Zhuangzi wrote that he works at a perfect pace with good skills and deep understanding of his work and fully masters the skills of wood chopping for chariot construction. Zhuangzi has another description, this time of a skilled butcher. With the knowledge of an ox's physiological structure and based on the natural texture of its meat, the butcher splits the ox and dissects it skilfully and therefore shows complete mastery of the relevant skills. These examples illustrate the point that the knowledge inherited in the world, which is obtained from observation and experience, is true knowledge. This is consistent with Dao's basic idea of following the inner rules of things.

As a further illustration, Laozi advocated "no wants" or "less wants". The word "wants" here points to the unnecessary greed that goes beyond the inner rule of things. From Laozi's perspective, the greed within the patriarchal feudal society is the main source of social instability. So he advocated that this greed should be removed or constrained to the minimal level: one should attempt to live a life of simplicity and modesty. Apparently, Laozi does not oppose the wants that meet the "natural" needs of people. Accordingly, he put forward the "Rule of the Saint" for governance, according to which rulers should ensure that the people have enough food and other necessities that are the basic requirements for a healthy life. Beyond that, any desires were deemed a material disturbance to life.

As another example, the Doctrine of Inaction [*wu-wei*] has come to be regarded as retrogressive and negative. But that view is based on ideas from Confucius and other schools. For the Daoist, the doctrine contains much positivity. The "inaction" constructed by the Daoist indicates that one should follow the rules of nature and respect the original forms of things. It is not an injunction to promote inertia. Rather, it is an injunction not to distort the original form of things for one's own benefit. For example, the Daoist objects to the ethical standards of Confucianism and to Legalism's idea of enforcing harsh law and severe punishment. Laozi did talk about country governance but he suggested that in order to conduct good country governance and to love the people, the ruler, "Generates and does not possess them ['the myriad things']; Acts and does not

---

24 "Discussion on Making All Things Equal", in *Zhuangzi: Basic Writings* (hereafter *Zhuangzi*) (B. Watson, tr., New York: Columbia University Press, 2003) p. 43.

rely on them; Grows and does not lord over them".[25] The ruler should follow the words of the Sage: "I do not act yet the people act of themselves; I appreciate examining yet the people are correct of themselves; I do not interfere yet the people become rich of themselves; I long to be without longing, yet the people are lumpen of themselves."[26] When discussing the failure of country governance, Zhuangzi makes the following observation: "What disturbs the regular method of Heaven comes into collision with the nature of things, prevents the accomplishment of the mysterious operations of Heaven, scatters the herds of animals, makes the birds sing at night, is calamitous to vegetation, and disastrous to inspects – all this is owing, I conceive, to the error of governing men".[27] Commenting on a related passage in *Zhuangzi*,[28] Joseph Needham remarked, "Bearing in mind what mankind knows today about soil conservation and natural protection, and all the experience we have gained as to the proper relations between pure and applied science, this passage of Zhuangzi seems as profound and prophetic as any he ever wrote."[29] This statement also shows that the Daoist inaction doctrine is positive and aims to benefit humankind. Therefore, using Daoist philosophy to illustrate the economic thought of Daoism is an absolute necessity. Daoism is an independent school and its economic thought deserves attention and further investigation.

Incidentally, the Daoist economic thought on "inaction" contains the ideas of economic individualism, equality and democracy, and laissez-faire. But this strand of economic thought is based on the premise of simple social interaction within a "small country with small population" and is intended to maintain social order and encourage individual freedom within people's minds and bodies. Indeed, in traditional Chinese academic thought, Confucianism and Daoism have had the greatest impact. Daoism, although the lesser influence historically, possesses the quality of being critical and encouraging equality and democracy as well as free thinking. It played a positive role in the Emperor Wen-Jing period of the Han dynasty and exerted influence during peasants' uprisings in different dynasties. Moreover, it inspired many great thinkers in Chinese history when they were establishing their own thought. These are historical facts that warrant thorough consideration. As such, when we discuss the relationship between

---

25 *Daodejing*, 51.
26 Ibid., 57.
27 *Zhuangzi*, *"Zai Yao"* ("Letting Be and Exercising Forbearance")
28

> [What you are asking about is the material basis of things; what you desire to control can only be the scattered fragments of these things (which have been destroyed by your previous interference). According to your government of the world, the vapours of the clouds, before they were collected, would descend in rain; the herbs and trees would shed their leaves before they became yellow; and the light of the sun and moon would hasten to extinction.
> *Zhuagnzi, "Zai Yao"* ("Letting Be and Exercising Forbearance")]

29 Joseph Needham, *Science and Civilization in China*, vol. 2, p. 99.

traditional culture and current modernisation it is of great significance to delve into the economic thought and philosophy of Daoism.

Here I conclude the discussion of the necessity of studying the underlying philosophy of economic thought. It should be noted that this necessity is mostly reflected when founder thinkers try to establish a new school. Later thinkers from the same school merely inherit the ideas of basic philosophy that their founders adopted.

3

Thinkers of the pre-Qin period were mostly scholars who aspired to serve their government. Though Daoists had the intention of living in seclusion, they did not exclude political issues from their conversations. When discussing government affairs and politics they alluded to various economic problems and measures. In particular, in the Spring and Autumn and Warring States periods the society underwent dramatic changes. Various important economic issues were brought to the attention of those thinkers who were expected to provide explanations and solutions. As such, many famous thinkers sprang up along with various theories. The curtain was lifted on an era with splendid academic cultures and different and competing schools of thought and theories. In the past 2,000 years, those thoughts and theories, undoubtedly including economic thought, have become an important part of Chinese traditional culture and their influence remains with us today. Chinese academic thought originated from the pre-Qin era. There is a saying that the river starts from its source and that one cannot locate the river without finding the source. Therefore, as with studying academic thought in other fields, studying pre-Qin economic thought has more than purely historical significance. Pre-Qin academic thought is rich and profound and the economic thought contained in it includes both normative and empirical content. We will now provide several prominent examples to illustrate the contribution of pre-Qin thinkers in terms of both normative and empirical content. Here, we need to note that normative and empirical economic thought are often not sharply separated in ancient writings. But we may still distinguish between them even though this may be a difficult task. In addition, in ancient times, compared with normative economic ideas and propositions, there was a relative dearth of empirical economic discourse. But, although rare, it did exist. The situation was caused by the fact that economic thought at that time had not evolved into an independent subject, either in Eastern or Western societies.

Shi (referring to food production) and *Huo* (referring to handicraft production) are two early Chinese economic concepts, and they are the main topics relating to the economic plan of the country and people's livelihood. *Shi* and *Huo* have exerted the most long-lasting influence on Chinese society. These two concepts and their related policies first appeared in the chapter *Hong Fan* of the book *Shang Shu* ("The History of the Former Han Dynasty") in the Western Zhou dynasty. Based on historical accounts, after King Wu defeated the Shang state, a Shang minister, Qizi, said to King Wu that Heaven gave Da Yu[30] nine different grand methods of ruling the country. Among the nine grand methods, the third type is referred to as a set of "Eight Policies". According to the listing within the Eight Policies, the first one is *Shi* and the second is *Huo*. Specifically, in terms of ruling the country, in the third class rule known as a set of "Eight Policies", the most important one is food production and the second is handicraft production. These two simple concepts accurately describe the two most important economic policies for an agricultural country where natural economy prevails. After that, thinkers from different dynasties tended to focus on these two policies when discussing economic issues. Starting from the *History of the Former Han Dynasty* (*Han Shu*), books of historical records throughout different dynasties all have one large volume named "*Shi* and *Huo*", which contain statistics on *Shi* and *Huo* and related suggestions, propositions and legislation from different thinkers and politicians. Even nowadays, the guiding principles of Chinese economic policy still attach an important status to *Shi*. The notions of *Shi* and *Huo* and their related policy claims indicate that the two ideas fall into the "macro" category, namely they are national-policy-oriented. We can see that thinkers and politicians from the Spring and Autumn period and the Warring States period followed these two guiding concepts to conduct copious discussion of economic issues.

Confucius regarded *Shi* as the first and foremost issue for ruling a country. His student Zi Gong once asked him about how to govern a country. In response, Confucius said that three things were necessary, "sufficient food, sufficient weapons, and the confidence [trust] of the common people".[31] It is obvious that Confucius thinks "sufficient food" should be given the top priority.[32] Confucius probed this issue deeper. "Sufficient food" is a matter of production, and in feudal society land was owned by lords and landlords. Those lords and landlords mainly charged the farmers labour rent or natural rent to share their production. Confucius pointed out that besides "sufficient food" there existed another issue regarding how much rent farmers should give to feudal lords. In feudal society, rent depends on both land fertility and excessive expropriation beyond land rents based on extra-economic coercion. When Jikangzi intended to levy a heavy military tax, Confucius expressed his proposition of "light tax" to his student Ranqiu.[33] Confucius's meaning was that government should levy a light tax on farmers in order to boost their initiative: only by this means can a society achieve the goal of "sufficient food". This stance of Confucius is demonstrated more clearly in the dialogue between Duke Ai and Confucius's student, You Ruo, who explained to the duke the benefits of lower taxation in the following terms: "When the people enjoy plenty, the prince necessarily shares in that plenty. But

---

30 [One of the legendary sage-kings.]
31 *Analects*, XII.7.
32 [More accurately, "sufficient food" is to be given a higher priority than "sufficient weapons", but "trust" is accorded the highest priority of the three.]
33 *Zuo Zhuan* (Spring and Autumn Annals). Chapter on 11th year of Duke Ai's period.

when the people have not enough for their needs, the prince cannot expect to have enough for his needs."[34] This indicates that if the tax rate is reasonable, farmers will be encouraged to raise production and the government will gain sufficient tax. Otherwise, when the excessive exploitation of the government leads to the decrease or even dissolution of sources of tax revenue, the government will end up with a small tax revenue.

Confucius's "light tax" theory is an important part of his thought of "enriching the people" and has further developed and deepened the idea of carrying out the policy of "giving food the top priority". Confucius draws a connection between production and distribution and examines the reaction of distribution on production, which is one of his considerable contributions to early Chinese economic thought. In addition, those ideas have been inherited by the later Confucian school and hold an important place in subsequent Chinese economic thought. Incidentally, Tang Qingzeng notes that Quesnay, the head of the Physiocratic School, wrote in the foreword to the draft of his Economic Table that "if farmers of the country are poor, the country will be poor; if farmers of the country are rich, the country will be rich". Tang thinks that Quesnay's words are influenced by Confucius's idea that "When the people enjoy plenty, the prince necessarily shares in that plenty. But when the people have not enough for their needs, the prince cannot expect to have enough for his needs."[35] This influence claimed by Tang Qingzeng could become a subject to study. However, given Quesnay's admiration for Confucianism and the similarity between his words and Confucius's, it is evident that the two schools share some common features.[36]

Sun Wu, the great strategist of Confucius's period, once analysed the decisive economic factors in determining whether a regime can survive. In 1973, the book *Wu Wen*, dating from the Han dynasty, was unearthed in a tomb at Yinque Mountain, Linyi, Shandong Province. This book records a dialogue between King Helu and Sun Wu in which King Helu asks Sun Wu which one of the six most powerful governors in Jin State, namely Fan, Zhi, Zhong Hang, Han, Wei and Zhao, will be cast out first. Sun Wu responds as follows: the basic unit of land measurement (the *mu*) adopted by Fan and Zhong Hang are both smaller than that adopted by Zhi, but the tax Fan and Zhong Hang levy on each unit is the same as that of Zhi; therefore, Fan and Zhong Hang will be the first two to be cast out. Likewise, the basic unit in land measurement adopted by Zhi is smaller than that of Han and Wei, but the tax Zhi levies on each unit is the same as that of Han and Wei; therefore, Zhi will be eliminated after Fan and Zhong Hang. Again, the basic unit of land measurement adopted by Han and Wei is smaller than that of Zhao, but the tax Han and Wei levy on each unit is higher than that

---

34 *Analects* XII.9.

35 Tang Qingzeng, the first and the fourth section of Chapter 4 in his *History of Chinese Economic Thought*, 1937, p. 365.

36 See "The research on the impact of Chinese ancient economic thought on French Physiocratic School" *Researches in Chinese Economic History*, 1989(1). [See also Tan Min, this volume.]

of Zhao; therefore, Han and Wei will follow Zhi's exit. With the largest basic unit of land measurement and the lightest tax per unit, Zhao will "eventually control Jin State".[37]

Sun Wu judges the fate of the six governors from the perspective of agricultural production. He thinks that whether agricultural production will boom or decline will be determined by two factors: the unit area and the tax per unit. Suppose that tax rate of the land controlled by the six governors is the same but the land measurement systems differ. For instance, Fan and Zhong Hang define *mu* as an area 160 measured steps wide and long; Han and Wei define one *mu* as an area 200 measured steps wide and long; while for Zhao, *mu* represents an area of 240 measured steps. Due to the different land measurement systems, the production per *mu* in lands belonging to the governors will be different. Even when the tax rate per *mu* is the same, the actual tax burden can vary to a large degree – the smaller (or larger) the area represented by one *mu*, the heavier (or lighter) the tax burden will be. The different systems will have a different impact on farmers' incentive to produce. As a result, the production on the land with a small *mu* will decrease while the production on land with a large *mu* will thrive. This contributes to a chronological sequence where five governors are removed at different times and one survives to the end.

Sun Wu's analysis uses abstract scientific methods and holds a high theoretical significance. By passing over other details, he identifies two decisive factors which can be regarded as two independent variables in the contraction or expansion of agriculture. He puts the six governors in the same position and, based on different circumstances of the two variables, he observes the differences in the state of agricultural production in the six areas under the control of the six governors. He finds that different results will occur in response to different assumptions about the two variables. When conducting empirical study, one needs to consider how producers react to the complex factors which affect production. But, in Sun Wu's analysis he leaves out other factors and obtains critical results based only on the decisive ones. This analysis contains both the policy of "putting food as top priority", and Confucius's ideas of light tax and enriching the people. Moreover, it also introduces the new element of the land measurement system to the discussion. Indeed, this analysis not only made significant progress in the method of analysis, but also raised the analysis to a high level which includes determinacy and has a quantitative base. From this, we have full reason to acknowledge Sun Wu as a remarkable quantitative analyst in the economic field, which is a rarity in the ancient world.

Sun Wu's analysis of the survival or demise of the six governors and the sequences of those occurrences has been largely borne out by historical facts. Sun Wu has talked about the land measurement system of the land controlled by the Governor Zhao, which defines one *mu* as an area with 240 measured steps in

---

37 Chapter Yi Wen of *Sun Zi Art of War*, compiled by Han Tomb Group of Yinque Mountain, Cultural Relics Publishing House, 1976.

length and width. This system later became the blueprint of Shang Yang's reforms in the Qin state.

Thinkers of the pre-Qin period established many *Shi*-oriented or agriculture-oriented economic theories and we will not go to the length of listing them all here. Rather, we confine our attention to one other Confucian scholar, Xunzi, from the Warring States period.

Xunzi constructed his theory of enriching the country by absorbing different ideas, such as Confucius's theory of light tax, Guan Zhong's idea of levying differential taxes based on the fertility of land, Mencius's ideas of *chan* (perpetual property), Mo Di's theory of frugal consumption and Shang Yang's idea of "agriculture first and commerce second". Xunzi's economic theories made contributions in the following aspects.

First, he points out a dilemma between limited resources and endless wants and considers this as the fundamental reason for social-economic problems: "If men are of equal power and station and have the same likes and dislikes, then there will not be enough goods to supply their wants and they will inevitably quarrel. Quarrelling must lead to disorder".[38] This idea, the starting point and cornerstone of modern Western economic theory, was therefore expressed 2,000 years ago by Xunzi.

Second, he also put forward a concept of "demand", that is, "pursuit of wants". He thought that "wants" could not be self-satisfied and that under the feudal hierarchy system one can seek only to satisfy "demand". In addition, one should pursue demand only within certain boundaries marked by the principles of courtesy and righteousness (the king "established the rules for people to perform courtesy and execute righteousness, so as to satisfy their wants and fulfil their demands").

Third, based on the feudal hierarchy system, Xunzi introduces the theory of social division of labour among the four classes of scholars, farmers, artisans and merchants, and also the theory that each social class should focus on its own work. He regards those two theories as the basis for increasing wealth and circulation of property in society. Compared with Mencius and Guan Zhong, Xunzi sheds more light on the social division theory and labour division theory, a contribution based on a scientific attitude reflected in his belief in "knowing the rules of nature and utilising them"

Fourth, by inheriting the theories of "light tax" from other thinkers, Xunzi introduced the theory of "enriching the country". It includes the following two ideas. First, when the people are rich, the country can be rich. Second, the ruler should realise that a country and its people should become rich in tandem. This theory of "enriching the country" is also directed against Legalism's theory of "gathering wealth for the country". The latter is fraught with many dangers, such as the problem of enforcing strict laws at the expense of "kindness", as pointed out by the scholar Sima Qian. In contrast, Xunzi advocated "supporting the

---

38 *Xunzi*, "The Regulations of a King" in *Xunzi: Basic Writings* (hereafter *Xunzi*) (B. Watson tr., New York: Colombia University Press, 2003).

people". This is reflected in his proposals that goods should be inspected but not taxed at customs passes and in markets, mountain and water resources should not be taxed, and land tax should reflect differences in fertility and distance to market.[39] In his view, adoption of his policies would stimulate the efforts of farmers, artisans and merchants and thus increase production. This will lead to an increase of tax for the government which will be conducive to the formation of a rich country. Xunzi also put forward two new concepts. First, that production is the foundation of wealth and the source of the supply of goods. Second, that the government's tax revenue is the end form of wealth and originates from supply. This theory is Xunzi's contribution to the modern theory of public finance and is still useful today.

Fifth, Xunzi believes that the problem of "more wants and less resources" can be addressed in a feudal society by adopting appropriate policy measures, such as the division of labour, the development of production and the imposition of light taxes. He argues that "even though a king's wants cannot be eradicated, the wants only need to be largely fulfilled not fully fulfilled; even though a door-keeper's wants cannot be fully removed, he can still restrain his demands".[40] Put another way, Xunzi thinks that people in all different classes can make their "wants" and "demands" satisfied under the feudal system, where "treating people based on their social classes and ages with due courtesy" is still the prevalent idea. This completes the system of economic theory constructed by Xunzi in pursuit of "enriching the country". Compared with other pre-Qin thinkers, Xunzi's writing on "enriching the country" exhibited a more systematic and focused nature, thereby lifting the study of economic phenomena to a new level.

The economic thought of different thinkers considered above was largely directed to enriching the country and benefiting the people. For Confucianism, the country is the extension of the family. The individual exists in the family and in the country. The country has its own purpose and missions, such as social harmony and national unity. Individuals exist to accomplish those goals. To understand individuals' activities, we need to examine the relationship between individuals and the country, not just individuals' own activities. The purpose and existence of the whole country cannot be broken down into individual purposes. From this basic point, thinkers suggested macroeconomic policies such as *Shi* and *Huo* and "enriching the country and the people at the same time". These thinkers did not maintain that the policy ideas are an aggregation of many individual independent economic activities. Therefore, most ideas from the pre-Qin

39 Ibid.
40 [As rendered by Watson:

Even a lowly gate-keeper cannot keep from having desires, for they are the inseparable attributes of the basic nature. On the other hand, even the Son of Heaven cannot completely satisfy all his desires. But although one cannot satisfy all his desires, he can come close to satisfying them, and although one cannot do away with all desires, he can control the search for satisfaction.

(*Xunzi*, "Rectifying Names", p. 156)]

period would be described as type of macroeconomic thought. Even the ideas of "supporting the people" and "enriching the people" are not based on an analysis of how individual farmers become rich through their own individual economic activities. Instead, those ideas examine the relationship between the individual and the country. Therefore, we cannot detect any discourse on individual economy or microeconomic behaviour. However, this does not mean that there are no microeconomic ideas in pre-Qin thought. On the contrary, microeconomic ideas do exist, but are rarely seen. We will try to give some examples.

We can find the most prominent examples from the area of business operations. Sima Qian referred to the principle of "choosing the right timing" adopted by Bai Gui, a famous businessman who lived in the early Warring States period. Sima Qian conveys Bai Gui's modus operandi thus: "When the year is good and the harvest plentiful, I buy up grain and sell silk and lacquer; when [silkworm] cocoons are on the market, I buy up raw silk and sell grain". Sima Qian also reported that when Bai Gui "saw a good opportunity, he pounced on it like a fierce animal or a bird of prey".[41] Another businessman, Fan Li (Lord Zhu), who was originally a politician and later became a great dealer, is said by Sima Qian to have adopted various techniques for "accumulating wealth": maintaining product quality, not overstocking working capital, not dealing with the transaction of goods that are hard to store and easy to corrode, and not being tempted by a high selling price. Besides, one should know the price fluctuation according to the supply level. When the price of the goods is high one should sell those goods directly; when the price is low one should increase purchases immediately. Products and goods should be circulated constantly just like flowing water. This is also part of the principle of "choosing the right timing"[42] In Sima Qian's writings, a principle of "coping with scarcity" is also mentioned:

> When there is a drought, that is the time to start laying away a stock of boats; and when there is a flood, that is the time to start buying up carts. This is the principle behind the use of goods.[43]

"Choosing the right timing" and "coping with scarcity" are two principles that have been passed down to later generations. They are the microeconomic foundations for business activity. Issues such as seasonal patterns contained in the launch of an individual commodity, the general laws of price fluctuations, the circulation principle for commodities and currency, were to become important theoretical issues.

We can also find a trace of microeconomic analysis in the agricultural area. For example, the chapter "Cheng Ma" in *Guanzi* provides an incisive analysis on how to raise a small farmer's incentive to produce. According to the argument,

41 "The Biographies of the Money-Makers" in B. Watson (tr.) *Records of the Grand Historian, Han Dynasty II* (New York: Columbia University Press, 1993), p. 439.
42 Ibid., pp. 436–437.
43 Ibid.

farmers should pay only a fair amount of tax and every household should be responsible for its own operation:

> People will notice the difference between day and night, understand the time limitation and feel the threat of hunger. Therefore, they will sleep early and rise early. Besides, the whole family, including father and sons, will be concerned about production and will work hard with contentment without being seized by tiredness. Therefore, the people will not turn into villains. In this situation, both land resources and human resources will be endless. However, if the people are not informed about the importance of time, they will not understand it, and if they are not instructed by reason, they will not work hard. When the land is divided into different parts and the people work on their own plots, they will understand the need to work and be good men.

This analysis of the small farmer economy is very thorough and still has relevance today.

In short, with the pre-Qin period as its emerging stage, rich economic thought was developed in Chinese feudal society. In addition to economic philosophy and policy insights, the economic thought of pre-Qin writers contained some brilliant examples of economic analysis. Studies in this area are not only necessary to carry forward our traditional culture but also to enrich our understanding of world economic thought in ancient times. The analysis offered here serves only as an initial and preliminary study on which much remains to be built.

3 *Fu Guo Xue* and the "economics" of ancient China[1]

Zhao Jing

In modern China, many people regard economics as an imported subject. Even some Chinese economists hold the view that China has never had a decent economic heritage in its long history and consider the economic achievement of ancient Chinese people as something that "deserves no attention".[2] It is natural for foreigners to be unfamiliar with the heritage of Chinese economics when the Chinese themselves are also unfamiliar with it.

Is there any economic heritage in ancient China? What is the characteristic of China's economic heritage? How to evaluate its achievements? This article attempts to provide some suggestions for answering these questions.

The ancient Chinese understanding of "economy" and "economics"

The words "economy" and "economic" were long in existence in ancient China. In the fourth century AD people used the word "economy",[3] and reached a basic consensus on its meaning. In the Eastern Jin dynasty (founded in AD 317) Emperor Yuan released an imperial decree to praise and honour Minister Ji Zhan: "loyal, noble, refined and honest as well as concerned and knowledgeable about the economy".[4] Ge Hong, the well-known divine during the same period, also said: "Study of economic policy is the task of Confucian scholars".[5] In the Sui and Tang dynasty, it became more common to use the term "economy".[6] The

---

1 Originally published as "中国古代的"经济学"与富国学" ("Fu Guo Xue and the 'Economics' of Ancient China"), in "赵靖文集" (Collected Writings of Zhao Jing). Beijing: Beijing University Publishing House, 2001, pp. 471–489.
2 Zhao Lanping, *Modern European Economics*, Preface. Shanghai: Commercial Press, 1933.
3 经济 (*Jingji*).
4 *The Book of Jin Dynasty* (written between AD 644 and 646), *Biography of Ji Zhan*. Chinese for the sentence: 瞻忠亮雅正, 识局经济。 [*The Book of Jin Dynasty*, ed. Fang Xuanling *et al.*, Beijing: Zhonghua Book Company, 1974]
5 *Baopuzi*. Main Part. Root of Understanding (抱朴子内篇明本). Chinese for the sentence: 经世济俗之略, 儒者之务也。 [*Baopuzi* "Zhong Shuo", Ge Hong, Beijing: Zhonghua Book Company, 1980.]
6 经济.

renowned Sui dynasty scholar, Wang Tong, was famous for his expertise in "economic methods".[7] Many well-known ministers in the early Tang dynasty, such as Fang Xuanling and Wei Zheng, were his disciples. It was said that "his family were proficient at economic methods for generations".[8] The name of the Emperor Tai of the Tang dynasty was Li Shimin, and the words *shi min* （世民） mean "manage the society and bring comfort to common people".[9] The term "economics"[10] had also come into being in the Tang dynasty. Yan Wei, the poet in middle Tang dynasty, wrote "Ask the teacher about economics".[11]

After the Tang dynasty, terms such as "economy" and "economics" were commonly used. Moreover, various books named "economy" or "statecraft" emerged one after another, such as *Selected Writings on Economics*[12] *by Teng Gong in the Song dynasty, Economic Papers* by Li Shizhan in the Yuan dynasty and *Economic Categories* by Li Qi in the Ming dynasty. In both the Ming and Qing dynasties, there were people who were devoted to compiling documents and works specialising in the "economic methods" of their time and edited voluminous books on this specific topic, such as *Works on Economics of Ming Dynasty* and *Works on Economics of Qing Dynasty*. In the Qing dynasty, "economics" was emphasised by scholar-bureaucrats who were concerned about the national interest and people's livelihood, and the subject was taken as symbolising the opposition to a complicated and impractical style of learning. The theory of "economy" was more prevalent after the middle of the Qing dynasty, and presented a trend of coexistence with orthodoxy, such as "argumentation", "textual research" and "prose and verse" doctrines.

However, "economics" or "the theory of economy" mentioned by people in ancient China was not the same as economics in the modern sense. In ancient times, "economy" referred to *Jing Shi Ji Wu*[13] *and Jing Guo Ji Min*,[14] meaning "administrate people well and ensure national security, rule the country and bring peace to the world". "Economics" or "the theory of economy" referred to the related knowledge and learning of national governance, which included not only financial and economic aspects but also politics, law, military studies, geography, construction and so-called "foreign knowledge" as well.

Viewed in terms of economics in the modern sense, "economics" in ancient China was not real economics at all. Indeed, from the perspective of modern economics, the vast majority of material accumulated from Chinese ancient "economics" may seem irrelevant and deserving of little attention.

---

7 经济之道 (*Jingji Zhi Dao*).
8 *Zhong Shuo*, Volume 6.
9 *Old Book of Tang, Record of Tai Emperor*. [*Old Book of Tang, Record of Tai Emperor*, ed. Liu Xu, Beijing: Zhonghua Book Company, 1975.]
10 经济学 (*Jingjixue*).
11 "Meeting Gentlemen at Tian Temple in Autumn", *Poetry of Tang Dynasty*, Volume 263. [*Poetry of Tang Dynasty*, Cao Yin *et al.*, Beijing: Zhonghua Book Company, 1999.]
12 经济文衡.
13 经世济物.
14 经国济民.

However, saying that Chinese ancient "economics" was not economics in the modern sense does not mean that people in ancient China did not undertake research in this field, or that there was little economic content in China's cultural heritage, or that China's economic legacy was of insufficient and shallow content and therefore unworthy of serious consideration.

Economics is merely the social-economic life reflected in people's minds. As long as people live in any period and region that contains economic life, they will always encounter various conflicts and problems. In order to solve these conflicts and problems, people will continually put forward ideas or opinions which often produce arguments and disputes. In order to advocate their own ideas and opinions while refuting those of others, people must resort to theory, which results in a variety of theoretical viewpoints. The ideas and opinions proposed to solve the conflicts and problems in real economic life, as well as the theoretical viewpoints put forward to explain and demonstrate these ideas and opinions, constitute the economic thought of a particular time and place. Along with the development and changes of economic life, economic thought has also been developed and improved. Economics was born when economic thought developed into an independent science.

Economic life is the most basic social life of human beings. People in any region, any country or any time cannot live without economic life, and ancient China was no exception. Besides, China is a country with long history, vast territory and large population. All levels of political power, especially the central government, have played an important role in China's social-economic life. Taking into consideration these conditions, compared with other countries and regions in the same period the complexity and diversity of ancient China's economic life was unique. Solving problems of society and economic life in ancient China was bound to generate a variety of ideas and opinions, evoke arguments and debates, and finally produce different economic perspectives and doctrines. Consequently, there was not only research and exploration in the field of economics in ancient China but a rich and colourful heritage in this area. The economic legacy of ancient China is an important part of China's cultural heritage and its achievements can be compared favourably with other components of China's cultural heritage such as philosophy, history, literature and art. However, in ancient China, economics was not researched within the scope of "economics", but mainly under the name of country-enrichment. The economic heritage of ancient China mostly took the form of *Fu Guo Xue*.[15]

"Economics" of ancient China left voluminous books and documents for posterity and preserved a wealth of materials on many subjects. It is meaningful to explore, organise and study this information. However, it is impossible to search for the economic heritage of ancient China from "economics" or "statecraft". We should seek it from *Fu Guo Xue*.

---

15 富国学.

The formation of *Fu Guo Xue*

Research on the economy always starts from wealth. Wealth in ancient China was discussed from three different perspectives. The first was from the perspective of the whole country and community, namely "country enriching"; the second was from the perspective of common people, which was the so-called "people enriching" issue; the third was from the perspective of private family or the "family enriching" issue. Even before the Spring and Autumn period, the concepts of "riches" and "wealth" had emerged[16] although they were the subject of little academic and theoretical discussion. It seems likely that it was during the Spring and Autumn period that the study and discussion of wealth issues from the above three perspectives really began.

As a task that attracted people's attention and concern, "country-enrichment" was proposed in the context of the great power rivalry that took place in the Spring and Autumn period. Since the eastward relocation of the capital by King Ping of Zhou,[17] the royal family suffered an increasing decline. In the Western Zhou dynasty, the power of producing ritual music and ordering wars was transferred from the Son of Heaven (Emperor) to the feudal lords.[18] Some powerful vassal states fought fiercely against each other for the purpose of establishing dominance, which generated so-called "Five Powerful Chiefs" in the Spring and Autumn period. Strong military power is essential for hegemony, but it is impossible to establish strong military power without solid economic strength. Thus, the policy of "making the country rich and its military force efficient" had become the "kingcraft" for nations in the Spring and Autumn period, especially for those with qualified hegemony. The theoretical study or *Fu Guo Xue* also started at this time.

In the Spring and Autumn period it was Duke Huan of Qi's chief adviser, Guan Zhong, who first implemented the policy of becoming rich and mighty and put forward several theoretical viewpoints to achieve the target. It is said that Guan Zhong enriched the state of Qi and strengthened its military force by trade and wealth accumulation.[19] It is mentioned in *Guanzi* that: "If grain is plentiful, the state will prosper. If the state prospers, its armed forces will be strong. If the armed forces are strong, they will be victorious in battle [and] the state's territory will expand."[20] Here it is clearly recognised that wealth accumulation (in the form of grain) and country-enrichment is the premise of military strengthening

16 In ancient China, riches and wealth were seldom used as one term. Sometimes the word "riches" was used and sometimes the word "wealth" was used; in theoretical discussions, "wealth" was more commonly used.

17 In 770 BC, the capital of Hao Jing, which is the region Xi'an and Xian Yang of middle China now, was replaced by the new capital of Luo Yi, which is the region of Luo Yang at present. Luo Yang is to the east of Xi'an.

18 *Analects*, XVI.2.

19 Sima Qian, *Records of the Grand Historian*, "The Biographies of the Money-makers", B. Watson (tr.), New York: Columbia University Press, 1993, p. 435.

20 *Guanzi*, "Zhi Guo" ("Maintaining the State in Good Order"). W. Allyn Rickett, *Guanzi* vol. 2. (Princeton: Princeton University Press, 1998).

and that invincible military force is based on invincible wealth. *Guanzi* was compiled by later writers rather than Guan Zhong himself, but it included some description and statements of Guan Zhong's thought. Taking the above argument as an example, it was consistent with Guan Zhong's understanding of the relationship between country-enrichment and military strengthening.

The term of *Fu Guo* in ancient China was divided into broad and narrow senses. The narrow sense referred to increasing the state's fiscal revenues and reserves by enriching the national treasury. The broad sense referred to increasing the total national wealth of the whole country, which can be called "country-enrichment".

Although Guan Zhong was the first to advocate country-enrichment, he never gave any clear explanation of its meaning. He associated country-enrichment with military strengthening, which apparently meant to take the former as the financial basis for the latter. That is to say, his idea of country-enrichment must involve enriching the national treasury. However, Guan Zhong was a great statesman with strategic vision and he knew that it was not acceptable to enrich the national treasury and increase the state's fiscal revenues by relying solely on fiscal means of exploiting common people. Under the circumstance that the people's wealth did not increase, it was not only of limited use to rely on increasing tax collection or other fiscal means, it would also arouse people's dissatisfaction. Therefore, while promoting country-enrichment, Guan Zhong also laid stress on people-enrichment, claiming that people-enrichment was the premise of state governance and dominance. He implemented a series of measures to make people rich such as "do not take up people's time", "do not plunder animals", "lead people to make use of forest and lakes according to their seasonal features and minimise the harm to their whole productivity" and "do not levy tax on businessmen".[21]

Guan Zhong also recognised that struggling for hegemony against other vassal states must be based on internal stability and consolidation. National strength would be dissipated in internal friction if most people lived in poor conditions, and the country would end up being unstable and unconsolidated. The immortal words, "When the granaries are full, [the people] will know propriety and moderation. When their clothing and food are adequate, they will know the distinction between honour and shame",[22] fully express an understanding of the relationship between state-enrichment and people-enrichment as well as the relationship between state consolidation and people's security.

It was obvious that the reason for Guan Zhong to advocate state- and people-enrichment was not just for military strengthening but also state consolidation. His idea of enriching the country and the people not only influenced the thought of the generations immediately following but was also the origin of ideas about "world prosperity and stability"[23] for future generations.

21 *History of the State of Qi from Guoyu*, ed. Zuo Qiuming, Shanghai: Shanghai Guji Press, 1978 (The History of States from the eleventh century BC to 476 BC).

22 *Guanzi*, "*Qing Zhong Jia*" ("*Qing Zhong* Economic Policies: A").

23 *Xin Shu, Shu Ning.*

At the end of the Spring and Autumn period, Confucius further developed the thought of enriching people from the perspective of state governing and national security. He considered people-enrichment as the basic guiding principle of state governing. From his point of view, the governors should not only enrich people's material life but should also teach and guide them in the spiritual sphere, the former being the prerequisite for the latter.[24] Confucius and some of his students repeatedly expressed their thoughts on people-enrichment in terms of "people satisfaction" and "civilians' satisfaction".

You Ruo, one of Confucius's students, used the concept of "satisfaction of the emperor" when opposing the proposal of increasing taxes by Duke Ai of Lu. You Ruo is reported as saying: "When the people enjoy plenty, the prince necessarily shares in that plenty. But when the people have not enough for their needs, the prince cannot expect to have enough for his needs."[25] Meeting the needs of the prince here means the narrow sense of state-enrichment, while meeting the needs of the people means people-enrichment. It is said that these two famous remarks of You Ruo were the earliest theoretical illustration of the mutual relationship between people-enrichment and narrow sense of state-enrichment (enrichment of national treasury) in ancient China.

During the Warring States period, the issue of country-enrichment and military strengthening had become the topic that was debated heatedly by politicians and ideologists. Not only the kings and their subordinates of the seven vassal states (the Seven Powers in the Warring State Period) who were striving for the way of enrichment, but also the variety of academic schools in "contention of a hundred schools of thought"[26] were concerned with this issue.[27]

It was Legalism which stood most strongly for state-enrichment and military strengthening. Legalists proposed to eliminate the battles for hegemony among vassal states by establishing a unified "empire". Hence they regarded a strong military as the most important state policy and contended that the most effective way to govern the country was to "unify the people and fight together".[28] They wished to put all human and material resources together for the annexation battles among vassal states. They understood clearly that it was unrealistic to launch frequent large-scale annexation battles without solid economic strength.

24
> When the Master went to Wei, Ran You drove his carriage. "How dense is the population!" exclaimed the Master. "When the people have multiplied, what more should be done for them?" asked Ran You. "Enrich them," Confucius replied. "And when they have been enriched, what more should be done for them?" "Instruct [educate] them," he replied.
> (*Analects*, XIII.9)

25 *Analects*, XII.9.

26 During the Spring and Autumn Period (770–476 BC) and the Warring States Period (475–221 BC), many different schools of thought emerged. They eagerly discussed and debated with one another and formed the so-called period of "contention of a hundred schools of thought".

27 "Related" here means different attitudes towards the issue of country-enrichment and military strengthening, which contain both the optimistic and the pessimistic.

28 *Book of the Lord of Shang* (c.359–338 BC) "Suan Di". [*Book of the Lord of Shang*, ed. Shang Yang, Beijing: Zhonghua Book Company, 2011.]

The Shang School of Legalism believed explicitly that without a rich country and abundant economic strength, "one cannot keep one's own territory in annexation battles".[29] Therefore, they considered state-enrichment as the basis and guarantee of strong military strength. However, in the relationship between stat-enrichment and military strengthening they always regarded the latter as the decisive and overwhelming priority. They believed that the purpose of state-enrichment was only for military strength and must be subordinate to its needs. This was the most prominent feature of Legalism's understanding of state-enrichment.

In order to make state-enrichment subordinate to military strengthening, the government must put the wealth into military uses as far as possible, while this wealth should be first centralised in the hands of government. Therefore, the state-enrichment proposed by Legalism obviously bore the meaning of national treasury enrichment. They insisted that "People should turn over all their food to the state without hoarding at home",[30] which would involve collecting all grain and wealth surplus to people's basic requirements.

However, the amount of surplus grain and wealth would depend ultimately on total national wealth. Increasing the total national wealth could only rely on production. In ancient society, when people lived mainly on agriculture, it was most important to increase agricultural production. Therefore, Legalism promoted "enriching the country by agriculture"[31] and considered the implementation of "strengthening the country by emphasising agriculture and war" (耕战) as the central policy of state-enrichment.[32]

In addition, although Legalism vigorously promoted state-enrichment rather than people-enrichment, it was also recognised that excessive poverty and unstable social security were not conducive to the unification of power for foreign wars. That people in one country should not be too rich or too poor was considered by them as the ideal situation. To achieve this target they claimed to promote a policy of "making poor people rich while making rich people poor".[33] "Making poor people rich" meant providing fields and houses for landless poor people and enabling them to maintain their family livelihood and afford taxes and corvée to the country; "making rich people poor" meant that the state treasury would appropriate all wealth beyond what was required to maintain people's basic life in order to meet the needs of war.

The policy and theory of state-enrichment that served for operating the country were vehemently opposed by Mencius Confucianism, which was the largest school of Confucianism. Mencius Confucianism inherited Confucius's belief in teaching people morality. They thought highly of benevolent govern-

---

29 "Agriculture and Battle", ibid.
30 "Persuading People", ibid.
31 *Han Feizi*, "The Five Vermin".
32 The country of Qin established two basic policies: one was to develop agriculture and the other was to enlarge territory by conquest. These two policies supported each other, and all the resources in the country were to be mobilised to these ends.
33 "Persuading People", *Book of the Lord of Shang*.

ment and kingcraft, regarded the dictatorship advocated by Legalism as incompatible with their position, and spared no effort to attack the Legalist system. Mencius condemned the state-enrichment policy of Legalism as enrichment of tyranny[34] and described Legalists as "despotic rulers and tyrannical officials".[35] While attacking Legalism's proposal of state-enrichment, Mencius actively promoted a people-enrichment policy and believed that benevolence on the part of the ruler can "make people rich".[36] He considered people-enrichment as the basis of teaching people and improving their moral standards. He not only preached the importance of enriching people for state governing but presented the highest ideal of people-enrichment – that is, being "fully sufficient".[37] He explained "fully sufficient" as making food for each family "as plentiful as water and fire", and exhorted that in "governing the Empire", the wise ruler "tries to make food as plentiful as water and fire", adding, "When that happens, how can there be any among his people who are not benevolent".[38]

For the means of people-enrichment, Mencius proposed land management and lightening taxes.[39] Light taxation was naturally tit for tat with "treasury tribute" advocated by Legalism, while "land management" was basically the same as Legalism's policy of "enriching country by agriculture" and "making full use of land". This shows that the seemingly incompatible propositions of Legalism's "state-enrichment" and Mencius Confucianism's "people-enrichment" both contained the requirement of increasing total national wealth by developing social production (principally agricultural production at that time).

This common point made it possible under certain conditions to integrate Legalism's policy of state-enrichment with Mencius Confucianism's policy of people-enrichment. In the late Warring States period, "Sun Confucianism",[40] affected deeply by Legalism, finally achieved this integration.

Under the banner of "state-enrichment", Xunzi, the great master of Sun Confucianism, made a relatively comprehensive discussion on the formation of national wealth, distribution and redistribution, the division of labour, exchange, consumption and accumulation, as well as the role of national power in realising state-enrichment and people-enrichment.

Xunzi defined "state-enrichment" as "wealth for both governors and people" and "satisfying the whole world". "Wealth for governors" referred to the enrichment of the national treasury, while "wealth for people" meant sufficiency for each family. The state-enrichment policy of Xunzi included both the narrow

---

34 *Mencius*, VI.B.9. [tr. D.C. Lau, *Mencius*, London: Penguin Classics, 2004).

35 Ibid., III.A.3.

36 *Mencius*, VII.A.23.

37 [Or "more than sufficient" in the sense of "more than enough", according to the D.C. Lau translation.]

38 *Mencius* VII.A.23.

39 Ibid., VII.A. 22–23.

40 It was Han Feizi (born *c.*280, died 233 BC), regarded as perhaps the greatest of ancient China's Legalist philosophers, who termed Mencius's school of Confucianism as "Mencius Confucianism" and Xun Kuang's school as "Sun Confucianism".

sense of state-enrichment, namely enrichment of the national treasury, and people-enrichment. He required both to be realised in a simultaneous and coordinated way. The definition of state-enrichment proposed by Xunzi had therefore unified people-enrichment and national treasury enrichment.

It was only the growth of national wealth that could achieve people-enrichment and national treasury enrichment at the same time, because people's wealth and state revenue are components of national wealth as well as the results of distribution and redistribution of national wealth. It is impossible to achieve "wealth for both governors and people" at the same time if national wealth itself is invariable. Xunzi emphasised repeatedly that the source of wealth was "field and county" as well as all sorts of industries people engaged in. Only by fertilising the land and organising agriculture, industry, and commerce, can we achieve a "huge and wealthy domain".[41] In this way, Xunzi unified the broad sense of state-enrichment and the narrow sense of state-enrichment and people-enrichment within the scope of *Fu Guo*. People-enrichment and national wealth enrichment became the integral components of *Fu Guo Xue* ever since, and the way to deal with the two parts and their mutual relationship became integral to the study of *Fu Guo Xue*, which was henceforth gradually to dominate China's macroeconomic research.

After the period of Xunzi, research on all aspects of China's economics achieved significant development basically within the framework of *Fu Guo Xue*. Although *Fu Guo Xue* in ancient China had not formed an independent science, it had considerable depth in theoretical research on many issues and formed some intrinsic and organic links among its components.

After the formation of *Fu Guo Xue*, research on people-enrichment (*Fu Min Xue*) disappeared. Some basic theoretical issues related to national treasury enrichment, such as the relationship between economics and finance, the role of finance in macro-control and the tax burden limits, had all been included in the scope of *Fu Guo Xue*, while some concrete and specific issues relating to national treasury enrichment, such as budget, tax forms and treasury management, continued to exist in the form of the "Theory of Handling Money" (理财学).

Family-enrichment

Fu Guo Xue naturally contained the requirement of personal and family wealth, while people-enrichment considered the issue from a "macro" perspective rather than talking about private wealth from a "micro" perspective. The latter belonged to the area of family-enrichment as distinct from people-enrichment. At first, most ideologists and politicians who were concerned about state-enrichment and family-enrichment were unwilling to undertake intensive study of family-enrichment, to which some of them held an obviously negative attitude.

Confucius advocated not only enriching and satisfying people, but also mentioned the issue of family-enrichment as well: "wealth and eminence are what

41 See, in particular, *Xunzi*, "The Regulations of a King".

everyone desires."[42] "Desires", which proposes questions from a personal perspective, belong to the issue of family-enrichment. However, Confucius always talked about family-enrichment issues from the standpoint of the "gentleman"; that is, from the noble's perspective. He believed that "gentlemen" who pursued family-enrichment were likely to incite competition from other "gentlemen" and thus jeopardise the internal balance of material interests within the nobility; moreover, their behaviour could provoke resentment and resistance on the part of the people by amassing wealth through the exercise of power to the detriment of social stability. Therefore, he stressed that the pursuit of family-enrichment should have a limit, which was the standard of wealth prescribed for nobles by propriety rules in the Western Zhou dynasty. In his view, family-enrichment should not go beyond propriety rules otherwise it was "disloyal" and would "break the rules". Therefore, after mentioning that "wealth and eminence are what everyone desires", he added: "but if they can only be obtained in an improper way, [one] must relinquish them."[43] "The wealth and eminence obtained through the improper way mean nothing to me."[44] From Confucius, Confucian scholars' discussion of family-enrichment had been absorbed into a strict code of ethics. What people considered on the family-enrichment issue was not its means, measures, or the regularity of the activity itself, but the moral way of enriching the family. Family-enrichment itself is not the goal of economic activity, thus it cannot be an independent subject of academic research. The issue of family-enrichment almost disappeared from the purview of Confucian economic research.

Legalists were extreme nationalists who emphasised that any individual or private economic activities must be subordinated to the national policy of state-enrichment and military strengthening. They recognised that people were unwilling to enrich their families by relying on farming and fighting because agricultural work was the most difficult, while joining the army and fighting was the most dangerous. But they also claimed that only farming and fighting were the most effective professions to realise state-enrichment and military strengthening. If there were professions other than farming and fighting that could enrich the family, people would certainly avoid farming and fighting. Therefore, they advocated all manner of stringent measures to block other ways for enrichment, crack down and restrain other activities, and thus make farming and fighting the only possible ways of enriching the family. This is the theory of "gaining benefit from the only way".[45]

Even for people who engaged in farming and fighting, Legalism proposed to constrain family-enrichment within an extremely low limit. It was mentioned above that Legalism proposed to appropriate people's wealth and food beyond their basis needs. Since there is no surplus wealth for people or accumulated

---

42 *Analects*, IV.5.
43 Ibid.
44 *Analects*, VII.12. [Cf. "riches and honours acquired by unrighteous means are to me like the floating clouds". *Analects* VII.16.]
45 *Book of the Lord Shang*, "Jin Ling".

food in a private family, there would have been little sense in talking about family-enrichment.

Confucians also stressed a restraint on the activity of family-enrichment, in their case from considerations of morality and justice, which undoubtedly set serious obstacles for research in this area. However, morality and justice are only spiritual restrictions and are without mandatory force. Legalism regarded family-enrichment as something contrary to the national policy of state-enrichment and military strengthening and advocated the restriction and suppression of the pursuit of riches by national mandatory force. Legalism was obviously more negative than Confucianism in terms of family-enrichment.

Mohists advocated relatively average positions in wealth possession and material life. They proposed reducing the collection of "jewels, birds, beasts, dogs, and horses" in order "to increase the amount of clothing, houses, weapons ... boats and carts."[46] They also did not hold a positive attitude towards family-enrichment. Daoists believed that the polarisation of wealth would intensify social conflict and cause turmoil: they were not in favour of the pursuit of family-enrichment either. *Laozi* warned that "much hoarding leads to much loss";[47] and "when gold and jade fill the storeroom, none can keep them".[48] *Laozi* strongly advised people to "know what is enough" and "know when to stop",[49] and maintained further that "The Sage does not store".[50]

Those who believed in the *Qing Zhong* ("Light-Heavy") theory held the most extreme attitude towards family-enrichment.[51] They argued that for making the country strong and consolidated it was not only necessary to strengthen military autarchy in the political aspect, it was also necessary to exercise national control and dominance in the economic aspect. In other words: "the rights of bestowal and deprivation lie with the monarch, while the rights of enrichment and impoverishment also rest with monarch."[52] They believed that if the pursuit of family-enrichment was allowed, rich people would dominate and enslave poor people by their wealth, which would undermine the country's right to control and dominate social-economic life."[53] People with more wealth, merchants in particular, have a greater capability to dominate the poor and may also seek economic domination over entire countries. The very existence of merchants was therefore seen as giving rise to the intolerable possibility of "one country with two monarchs or kings."[54]

---

46 *Mozi*, "Moderation in expenditure".
47 *Daodejing*, 44.
48 Ibid., 9.
49 Ibid., 44.
50 Ibid., 81.
51 The *Qing Zhong* theory is mainly represented by a section of chapters in the *Guanzi*. *Guanzi* was not the collection of only one school of thought and the "*Qing Zhing*" chapters were totally different from other part of the book, thus representing a relatively independent contribution.
52 *Guanzi*, "Gue Xu" ("The state's store of grain").
53 Ibid.
54 *Guanzi*, "Qing Zhong Jia" ("*Qing Zhong* Economic policies: A").

In the Spring and Autumn period, as well as Warring States period, it was only the Commercialist School, representing the interests of merchants, who investigated issues of family-enrichment. Among other enquiries, they summarised the merchants' experience of business and proposed various principles relating to market conditions, price variations and supply and demand, and business opportunities. Their discussions of family-enrichment laid the foundations for a new area of enquiry in ancient China, namely, the "Theory of Making Wealth".[55]

The Commercialist School studied the family-enrichment issue only from a "micro", personal profit perspective, without touching upon the significant economic issues that affected the national interest and people's livelihood. Their research and discussion was isolated from the mainstream of economic issues at that time, while their study of family-enrichment issues was not related to state- and people-enrichment.

It was the famous historian Sima Qian in the Western Han dynasty who studied the issues of state-, people- and family-enrichment and attempted to integrate *Fu Guo Xue* with the "Theory of Making Wealth".

Sima Qian held that it is human nature to pursue family-enrichment. People are born with a multiplicity of desires that they seek to satisfy as fully as possible by a variety of means, in particular by the private possession of wealth through family-enrichment behaviour. The desire for family-enrichment was common to all: "The desire for wealth does not need to be taught; it is an integral part of human nature."[56] Regardless of people's status or occupation – whether civilian officials, military officers, saints, hermits, farmers, workers, merchants, doctors, thieves, bandits, gamblers or prostitutes – all "live for seeking wealth and benefit".

Sima Qian considered the wealth obtained by activities such as robbery, grave-robbing, fraud, corruption and bribery as "evil riches" which are invalid and should be subject to state laws and sanctions. Enriching the family by means other than those illegal ones, especially by the economic activities of agriculture, industry, commerce and politics, were legitimate and should not be suppressed or interfered with by the government. He also argued that if one became rich, one would be thought of as capable and moral, whereas poverty would be attended by shame. Sima Qian believed that the polarisation of wealth in society is completely in line with natural phenomena: "Poverty and wealth are not the sort of things that are arbitrarily handed to men or taken away: the clever have a surplus; the stupid never have enough".[57]

Sima Qian not only affirmed the legitimacy of family-enrichment, he also claimed that it was entirely consistent with state-enrichment. He divided the ways of becoming rich into two categories. The first is "deprive and give", which means to deprive some people of their wealth and give it to others. All kinds of "evil riches" and the wealth of nobles and officials gained by high position and salary are said to

---

55 "Making wealth" can also be termed "managing producing" and "managing industry", which means managing the assets and industry of the family.
56 *Historical Records*, "The Biographies of the Money-Makers".
57 Ibid.

fall into this category. The other way is to expand the source of wealth by increasing the wealth-generating base, as identified with the economic activities of agriculture, industry and commerce which are the "source of food and clothes". In Sima Qian's view, "deprive and give" is only to transfer wealth between different people, which cannot lead to an increase in total national wealth. "Deprive and give" can enrich some families but it cannot change the total national wealth of the whole community or the whole country and is not consistent with state-enrichment. But the situation is completely different when enriching families comes from the activities of agriculture, industry and commerce because they are the source of food and clothes. Wealth is undoubtedly generated by these economic activities: "Society obviously must have farmers before it can eat; foresters, fishermen, miners etc. before it can make use of natural resources; craftsmen before it can have manufactured goods; and merchants before they can be distributed."[58] People who engaged in the economic activities of agriculture, forestry and animal husbandry, industry and commerce, extend the source of food and clothes while achieving family-enrichment and thus make a contribution to state-enrichment. Family-enrichment of this form is therefore fully consistent with state-enrichment. In Sima Qian's words, "These four classes [of farmers, artisans, merchants, and "foresters, fishermen, miners, etc."] are the source of the people's clothing and food. When the source is large, there will be plenty for everyone, but when the source is small, there will be scarcity. On the one hand, the state will be enriched, and on the other, powerful families will be enriched."[59]

Sima Qian had negated at one stroke his predecessors' negative and reserved viewpoints that family-enrichment was incompatible with state-enrichment. His single core of family-enrichment and state-enrichment laid a theoretical foundation for the integration of *Fu Guo Xue* and the "Theory of Making Wealth".

If this system of Sima Qian had been generally accepted by people who engaged in economic issues at that time as well as in the future, the economic study of ancient China would have developed into a comprehensive subject on the enrichment of state, people and family, namely *Fu Xue*[60] or *Cai Fu Xue*,[61] including economic research from both "macro" and "micro" perspectives. Unfortunately, the social-economic conditions were not conducive to such a development: the prejudice towards family-enrichment in traditional thought ran too deep.[62] Sima Qian's thought was too advanced to be popular in ancient

58 Ibid.
59 Ibid.
60 富学.
61 财富学.
62 As mentioned above, influential schools of thought such as the Confucian, Mohist, Daoist and Legalist, all held a relatively negative attitude towards the issue of family-enrichment. The later Confucian school, which came to exercise an enduring influence over China's ideology, regarded *Yi* (suitable ways of getting benefit) as more important than *Li* (benefit itself), and taught that the pursuit of happiness must be strictly confined by moral standards. This was to become the dogma of "cherishing *Yi* and despising *Li*". Under this dogma, words or actions to gain wealth and benefit in order to enrich the family were despised and shunned by gentlemen. This tradition formed a strong prejudice among knowledgeable people, which seriously hindered the development of the Theory of Making Wealth.

China. During the following 2,000 years after Sima Qian, China's research in the economic field was basically developed in the framework of *Fu Guo Xue*, while the "Theory of Making Wealth" attracted little attention.

The confusion of modern translators, and the reversion of the name to economics

As the "economics" in ancient China was quite different in content from modern economics, so for a long period of time after China came into contact with economics or political economy from Western countries, "economics" was not considered as its translation.

China's first Western educational institution, the School of Combined Learning (*Tongwenguan*[63]) had begun to offer economic courses in the 1860s. At that time, students trained by School were divided into two categories: eight-year student (who were required to learn foreign language) and five-year student (who were not).The final year for both sets of students included an economics course, but the name of the course was "state-enrichment policy" (Fu Guo Ce[64]) rather than economics. The textbook used by *Tongwenguan* was *A Manual of Political Economy* compiled by the Englishman, Henry Fawcett, which was later translated into Chinese by Wang Fengzao, with its translated name as *Fu Guo Ce*. This name was used for a period of time, with other translated names such as *Fu Guo Yang Min Ce* and *Fu Guo Xue* used subsequently.

The reason for initially translating "Economics" as *Fu Guo Ce* or *Fu Guo Xue* was related to the ancient Chinese practice of subsuming economic research within the scope of "state-enrichment". Until the late nineteenth and early twentieth centuries, translated names like "Theory of Handling Money" (*Li Cai Xue*) and *Ping Zhun Xue*[65] also appeared, but were not widely used.

Yan Fu, who translated a number of Western academic works, claimed to translate Economics in accordance with its original Greek meaning as *Ji-Xue*.[66] This translation was not accepted by Chinese academia, probably because the translated term was unfamiliar. Later, Liang Qichao attempted to use *Sheng-Ji-Xue*[67] as the translated name, but this was also a failure.

It was the Japanese rather than the Chinese who first translated Economics or Political Economy as economics (*Jingjixue*) or political economics (*Zheng Zhi Jingjixue*[68]). In the early Meiji period, the literature department of Kai Cheng School (one of the precursors to Tokyo University) had an economics course for junior students, and the content was no longer "the strategy of administrate affairs and

---

63 同文馆.
64 富国策.
65 *Ping Zhun* (平准) is a measure used by feudal Chinese governments to stabilise prices. Goods are sold when their prices are high and bought when prices are low.
66 "Examples of the Translation of the *Wealth of Nations*". In *Collection of Books Translated by Yan Fu*, Shanghai: Commercial Press, 1931.
67 生计学.
68 政治经济学.

people-enrichment" as in ancient China, but rather modern scientific economics. In the seventh year of the Meiji period (AD 1875), Tokyo University was established and within the following five years the economics course was renamed as "Theory of Managing Finance"[69] and expanded to a "specialism" (major). Soon afterwards, Fawcett's *A Manual of Political Economy* was renamed as *Theory of Managing Finance*, and it was the same with *Principles of Political Economy* by J.S. Mill. During this period, Political Economy was even translated as "Political Theory of Managing Finance". Only subsequently did the translated name of the subject revert to and fix on "Economics".

Affected by Japan, China also gradually used the translated name of "Economics" in the early twentieth century. People who initially used this name were Japanese teachers employed by Chinese schools and Chinese students returning from Japan. After 1906, the translated name of "Economics" was used widely by more and more people, as in *The Essence of Economics* (by Lin Huguang) and *Economics Lectures* (by Wang Shaozeng) published in 1906, *Principles of Economics* (by Li Zuoting) published in 1907, as well as *Principles of Economy* (by Zhu Baoshou) published in 1908. Although other names were still being used, they were not as precise and appropriate as "Economics" (经济学) in comparison.

After the Revolution of 1911, Sun Yatsen made a comparison among a variety of translated names of Economics or Political Economy in modern China and Japan, and pronounced that the translation should be "Economics" (*Jingjixue*[70]). He claimed:

> Economics initially originated in China. Guanzi was an economist in ancient China.... In the following times, the principles related to economy had become a systematic theory, part of which was named as *Fu Guo Xue*, another part as "chrematistics". Neither part is sufficient to interpret the full meaning. Only "economics" comes closest to the original meaning.[71]

Sun Yatsen not only proposed the suggestion of "name rectification" of translated names, but believed that *Fu Guo Xue* in ancient China was actually "Economics" and that Guanzi (Guan Zhong), who first promoted *Fu Guo Xue*, was China's first economist.

The translated name of Economics or Political Economy had been finally determined as "Economics". Once the translated name was established, names like *Fu Guo Xue* and *Fu Guo Ce*, in common use over a long historical period, gradually disappeared.

Although the old names were to disappear, the excellent heritage of *Fu Guo Xue* should never be forgotten. For example, enriching the country must take the development of production and increase in total national wealth as its preconditions; it must deal with the relationship between production and consumption,

69 理财学.
70 经济学.
71 *Complete Works of Sun Yatsen*, Volume 2, Beijing: Zhonghua Book Company, 1982, p. 510.

and strive to "expand capital and use it economically";[72] it should "produce more and consume less" and "produce fast and use slowly";[73] it must coordinate development between the sectors of agriculture, industry and commerce; it should "meet the needs of both country and people"; it must neither be allowed to enrich the national treasury by exploiting people's wealth, nor "meet the national interest through damaging the interest of people"; it should give consideration to both enrichment and balance, and achieve balance on the basis of enrichment; it should make everyone rich rather than poor; and it must ensure that family-enrichment is consistent with state-enrichment and fight against the policy of "deprive and give" as the means of family-enrichment. These features of ancient *Fu Guo Xue*, as well as other treasures of our cultural heritage, must be preserved and carried forward by future generations.

72 *Xunzi*, "A Discussion of Heaven".
73 *The Book of Rites*, "Da Xue" ("The Great Learning"): "There is a great course for the production of wealth. Let the producers be many, and the consumers be few. Let there be activity in the production, and economy in the expenditure. Then the wealth will always be sufficient." [IV.35, Legge edition.]

4 The Chinese origin of Physiocratic economics[1]

Tan Min

In the seventeenth and eighteenth centuries, as modern economics came to be an independent science, an unusual period of cultural exchange between China and European countries, especially France, lasted for almost one and a half centuries. This special historical phenomenon has aroused the attention of both Chinese and foreigners, including scholars specialising in the history of economic thought. From the perspective of economics, the first thing to have been noticed is that French Physiocracy, known for its respect for Chinese culture, came into being under the same particular historical circumstance. Quesnay, the leader of the Physiocratic School, is known as the "European Confucius". Another significant representative figure, Turgot, is also remarkable for his masterpiece, *Reflections on the Formulation and Distribution of Riches*, which is a collection of studies on the problems in China including a preface he wrote for two Chinese young men studying in France. Such examples present us with the question of the relationship between the Physiocratic School and the westward-spread of Chinese culture and make it an essential topic for scholars interested in the foundations of modern economics.

The ideological origin of natural order

The thought of natural order is the philosophical foundation of the system of Physiocracy. The Chinese term *Zhong Nong Zhu Yi* (重农主义) is *physiocratie* in French, originally indicating the rule of nature or, in Du Pont's definition, the "science of natural order". The argument of this paper is that Physiocrats borrowed heavily from external thought, particularly from the ancient Chinese thought that had come to be known in Europe at the time.

The concept of natural order proposed by the Physiocrats has several fundamental aspects. First of all, the concept aims to reveal the natural laws or universal rules that dominate human society which admittedly has its root in the traditional Western concept of natural law. However, the concepts of *Tian Di Zhi Dao* (天地之道, "the doctrine of Heaven and Earth"), *Tian Xing You Chang*

1 Originally published as "重农学派经济学说的中国渊源" ("The Chinese Origin of Physiocratic Economics"), *Economic Research Journal*, 1990 Issue 6, pp. 66–76.

(天行有常, "nature is the true law"), *Tian Li* (天理, "justice of nature") or *Wan Wu Zhi Li* (万物之理, "the reason of all things") that are commonly seen in ancient China also connote the cultural tradition of worship for universal rules. Those Chinese-style thoughts of universal rules in particular were disseminated by the Western missionaries who had operated in China and thus had great influence on contemporary intellectual circles in Europe. The Physiocratic School is a typical example of a positive influence by China. Quesnay pointed out that the ancient Chinese empire was "erudite and cultivated" and surpassed "the most cultivated country in Europe" in an "astonishing and admirable" way, precisely because "the Chinese constitution was founded upon the explicit and unchangeable law";[2] the "explicit and unchangeable law", according to his understanding of China's basic law, is the "natural law" which is different from various kinds of artificial laws laid down by man. In his view, all laws in China – including "written laws" and tax law that combined ethics and politics, civil law and criminal law which set up different levels of supervising systems, and official law containing rules for rewards and punishment – must embody and ensure the implementation of natural laws, so "the governing institutions of China were built on the basis of natural laws".[3] It was therefore recognised that universal rules and natural laws were part of the independent ideological systems of China and of Western countries. Chinese traditional thought thereby presented itself as a worthy object of study for the Physiocratic School.

Second, the Physiocratic concept of natural order ascribes the order to the creation of god, which may appear to be a purely Western conception. However, in words such as *Tian* (天, "Heaven") and *Shang Di* (上帝, "celestial ruler") from ancient Chinese books and records, the Physiocratic School found the classical argument that natural order is explained by theology. Hence they advised the ruler of France not to let personal will dominate but learn from the Chinese emperors to "follow the will of god" and pay homage to the Chinese philosophy of divine providence. They also took up the explanation in Chinese philosophy that the role of god in the natural order only lies in the creation of basic natural rules at the "very beginning" of human society; that is, as soon as natural rules were established, the role of god becomes unimportant and the only thing that matters is how to know and obey the rules. This latter understanding actually departs from the track of traditional Western religion and restricts the decisive role of god. Among the connotations of natural order, the one that emphasises god's status as creator is the most typical feature of the original Western concept of natural law. The Physiocratic School added some ingredients from Chinese culture to the Western conception.

Third, the concept of natural order appeals to the reason of people, holding that the highest or the fundamental rule of social and natural order "manifests

---

2 Quesnay, *Despotism in China* Foreword and Section 1 of Chapter 1. See *Countries on the European Continent in 17th and 18th Century* Part 4, translated by Gu Xiegao *et al.*, Beijing: Commercial Press, 1986, pp. 72–73.

3 L.A. Maverick, *China: A Model For Europe* (San Antonio, Texas: Paul Anderson Company, 1946), pp. 225, 186, 190–191.

itself through the glory of wisdom which is gained from education and the study of nature".[4] Chinese scholarship in philosophy has proved fully that China was the one of the "intellectual sources during the age of reason"[5] in eighteenth century Europe. Furthermore, in the case of the Physiocratic School, when Quesnay was exploring China's "natural laws" he had recognised that the Chinese were guided by "the glory of reason" and made a compliment to the study of natural rules in China by praising it as "reaching the highest level of perfection", so that China should "be placed above all the other countries".[6] He also introduced the education system of ancient China into the theory of natural order, holding that "except China, no countries have ever attached any import-ance to the necessity of this facility which could be the basis of governance"; therefore, "a solid and prosperous government should follow the example of the Chinese empire, making profound study and long-term popularised education the fundamental natural laws of its social system and the major objective of governance".[7] The point of view that national education has significant meaning for studying and obeying the natural laws has no counterpart in traditional Euro-pean thought, so some Western scholars believe the inclusion of education in the thought of natural order "obviously has taken China's education as its reference."[8]

Fourth, the Physiocratic position brings the so-called "moral laws" or "moral order", as well as the "laws of objects", into the category of natural order. Ques-nay's inclusion of moral laws was once regarded as a revolutionary and creative supposition which differs significantly from traditional Western theories. However, it actually agrees with the Confucian moral theory that was introduced from China. As the "Confucius of Europe", Quesnay made himself a distinctive figure in that he introduced the exploration of objective laws into the field of social science, starting with the field of economic science and including the com-plete and systematic moral theory of the Confucian school. As the moral law and order here mentioned indicate, human society, just like the physical world, has eternal natural laws as distinct from artificial laws that can vary with time and space. This perspective comes mainly from Confucian moral theory.

Fifth, the position on natural order reveals an organic integrity in which various elements are interdependent. Modern scholars believed that it set up the position of the Physiocratic School as the "pioneer of organic sociologists"[9]; when the theory of social organism was applied to the economic area it became

4 *Anthology of Quesnay's Economic Writings* (魁奈经济著作选集), tr. Wu Feidan *et al.*, Beijing: Commercial Press, 1981, pp. 400, 404, 406.

5 Zhu Qianzhi, *The Influence of Chinese Philosophy on Europe*, Fuzhou: Fujian People's Publish-ing House, 1985. p. 367.

6 Maverick, *China: A Model For Europe*, pp. 225, 186, 190–191.

7 *Anthology of Quesnay's Economic Writings* (魁奈经济著作选集), pp. 404, 400, 406.

8 G.F. Hudson, *Europe and China* (London: Edward Arnold & Co., 1931), p. 326.

9 C. Gide and C. Rist, *A History of Economic Doctrines* (Volume 1), Beijing: Commercial Press, 1986. p. 17.

Quesnay's economic organism theory which was of "real originality".[10] According to textual research conducted by European experts, the organism theory was something new that had emerged in the West after the seventeenth century. But this is to ignore the fact that "organic materialism" or "organic naturalism" had been a feature of traditional Chinese thought.[11] Several Western natural scientists have admitted the dissemination of the ancient Chinese organism theory in the West and its influence thereupon, or affirmed that such a trend in modern natural science could find its precursor in ancient Chinese civilisation. In fact, in the field of social science the Physiocratic School had applied the organism theory to the analysis of social-economic phenomenon in a creative way, which could be traced back to the organism theory of ancient China, and showed its originality either from the diachronic perspective embodying the heritage of thinkers of older generations in Europe or the synchronic point of view involving the influence from foreign countries in the eighteenth century.

Finally, the concept of natural order aims at obtaining the highest welfare. There is certainly continuity between this idea and the traditional Western theory of natural law but it also shares a similarity with the objective of "ruling the country and pacifying all" proposed in Chinese Confucian theories. In particular, the objective of ruling the country and pacifying all China that had been advocated by the Confucians should be established upon the knowledge of the laws of objects; just as the Chinese idiom said, *Ge Wu Zhi Zhi* (格物致知, "to study natural phenomena is to attain knowledge"). This latter perspective agrees entirely with the view of the Physiocratic School that stresses knowledge of and obedience to natural laws as the means of attaining the highest welfare: an agreement that is not accidental.

Thus, it can be inferred that the thought of natural order proposed by the Physiocratic School is closely related to ancient Chinese theories and that the relationship between them is even closer than the relationship with the traditional Western concept of natural law. Of the basic connotations of natural order, those that are inspired by Western history of natural law can find the same or similar content in ancient Chinese theories. However, some important connotations such as moral order and organism theory are unique and common in ancient Chinese theories but are scarcely seen in traditional Western thought. Besides, in those connotations of which the reference can be taken from both China and Western countries, the Physiocratic School seems to have had a bias towards Chinese sources. This is because, on the one hand, "European scholars had a bias towards Chinese culture, and threw the ancient Greek aside";[12] and, on the other hand, under the impact of the dissemination of Chinese culture, the Physiocratic School in particular adopted a critical attitude towards traditional European culture. For example, Quesnay extolled the *Analects* of Confucius as "excelling

10 H. Higgs, *The Physiocrats* (New York: The Langland Press, 1952), p. 46.
11 J. Needham, "The Communication History of Science Between China and the West" (中国与西方在科学史上的交往), from Pan Jixing, *Anthology of Joseph Needham*, Shenyang: Liaoning Science and Technology Press, 1986, p. 162.
12 Zhu Qianzhi, *The Influence of Chinese Philosophy on Europe*, p. 185.

the words of the seven sages of Greece"[13] and his followers held that "the Republic of Greece never had any idea of the law of order".[14] These are typical arguments of the Physiocratic School.

The above-mentioned arguments may be unfamiliar to the modern scholar, yet they were admitted by the Physiocrats 200 years ago. The most typical part rests not only in Quesnay's clear recognition of his respect for "the political system and moral system of the vast Chinese empire built upon science and natural rules" but also in his opinion that "the Chinese theories can be regarded as the exemplification for every nation" and his demonstration, with China as the example, that "the laws that build the natural order are eternal and indestructible".[15] In this way, Quesnay himself provides eloquent testimony for the conclusions reached above.

The mystery of the Economic Table (*tableau economique*)

Here, the mysterious origin of the thoughts in the Economic Table will be studied. Quesnay said nothing about the source of inspiration when creating the table but the opinions of his followers and his opponents revealed something worth noticing. Those opinions seem complicated and confusing, and some of them contain only a few words, but still they provide valuable evidence for further study. Three representative arguments will be chosen for further analysis.

The first argument is represented by Quesnay's contemporary, Clair, who published *Da Yu and Confucius* in 1769. He mentioned in his book that to "sum up the thoughts of different schools incorporated in the studies and works of the Chinese legislators, their opinions with eternality and excellence have no equivalence in Europe or anywhere else in the current world." Here, "opinions with eternality and excellence" refer to "the basic law of natural order". In his view, the principle of natural order was not found in Europe until 1759[16] with the appearance of a "genius who applies this principle" in France, namely Quesnay, whose application took the form of the Economic Table. Also, "the Economic Table can be used as a touchstone for every social system in future".[17] And, according to later generations, Quesnay's Economic Table "has provided images" for the law of natural order discovered by the Chinese;[18] and, "Chinese thought have been systematised in the Economic Table".[19]

13 Adolf Reichwein, *China and Europe: Intellectual and Artistic Contacts in the 18th Century*, Beijing: Commercial Press, 1962, p. 93.
14 Gide and Rist, *A History of Economic Doctrines* (Volume 1), p. 65, note 77.
15 *Anthology of Quesnay's Economic Writings* (魁奈经济著作选集), pp. 395–396.
16 Clair might not see the first edition of Quesnay's Economic Table in 1758, so here it refers to the 1759 edition.
17 后藤末雄 *The Dissemination of Chinese Thought in France*, Japanese version, 1956, pp. 388, 389.
18 L.A. Maverick, "The Chinese and the Physiocrats", *Economic History*, Vol. 4, No. 15, p. 317.
19 后藤末雄, *The Dissemination of Chinese Thought in France*, Japanese version, 1956, pp. 388, 389.

When Clair stressed that the Economic Table revealed the "core of nature" or the "real nature" that had been hidden by man for so long, he meant "the natural laws that ensure the reproduction and continuity of expenditure of human society".[20] He believed the basic law of natural order had been mastered by "Chinese legislators" for a long time and had endued their "opinions with eternality and excellence"; thus, although Quesnay created the Economic Table to demonstrate specifically the principles of natural order and was to that extent a "genius", he was actually following in the steps of the Chinese ancients. As has been mentioned above, the thought of natural order of the Physiocratic School did absorb several essential factors from traditional Chinese culture. Therefore, Clair connected the production of the Economic Table directly with the enlightenment of the Chinese concepts through the basic link of the principle of natural order, which is of historical authenticity and by no means a concocted story.

The second argument comes from those supporters and critics of the Physiocratic School at that time who compared the Economic Table to the sixty-four divinatory trigrams in *The Book of Changes* (*I Ching* [or *Zhouyi*]). Supporters praised the Economic Table by saying, "the table resolves the principles of economics clearly with only a few words, just like Fu Xi's sixty-four divinatory trigrams clearly expounding the essence of philosophy".[21] Critics also compared the Economic Table with the trigrams in *The Book of Changes* to demonstrate that the table was like "the *Book of Changes* comprised of sixty-four divinatory trigrams using linking lines to indicate the change of every factor", criticising them as "incomprehensible".[22] This argument has such a wide influence that when Oncken was sorting and editing Quesnay's works in economics and philosophy, he specifically pointed out that the structure of the Economic Table imitated "the sixty-four divinatory trigrams of Fu Xi", and even regarded Quesnay's Economic Table as the accomplishment of Confucius's unfinished work.[23] Some other modern scholars also believe that Quesnay's Economic Table "was inspired by the *Book of Changes* and Fu Xi's sixty-four divinatory trigrams".[24]

When the *Book of Changes* was introduced to Europe, this ancient and mysterious Eastern classic at once attracted Western scholars and was called "the oldest memento of science that has been preserved in the universe".[25] Quesnay was one of the many Western admirers of the *Book of Changes*. He claimed that Chinese scholars showed "the highest respect" towards the *Book of Changes*, whose author Fu Xi was "the father of knowledge and good governance"; he attributed the achievement of resolving the "mysterious lines" in the *Book of*

---

20 *Anthology of Quesnay's Economic Writings* (魁奈经济著作选集), p. 245.
21 Zhu Qianzhi, *The Influence of Chinese Philosophy on Europe*, p. 317.
22 Higgs, *The Physiocrats*, pp. 149, 150.
23 Zhu Qianzhi, *The Influence of Chinese Philosophy on Europe*, p. 317.
24 L. Einaudi, *Francois Quesnay et la Physiocratie* (Paris: Institut national d'études démographiques,1958), p. 168.
25 Gottfried Wilhelm Leibniz: "Lettre à M.de Rèmond sur la théologie naturelle des Chinois", *Study on Chinese Philosophy*, 1982, No, 1.

Changes to Confucius,[26] showing his admiration towards the ancient Chinese "saints" and their works.

The reasons why Quesnay valued the *Book of Changes* so much start with its revelation of "the mystery that is significant to the country's governance". The *Book of Changes* stresses "simplicity", i.e. managing complexity with simplicity and mastering the universal law of change to control different kinds of complexity, which to Quesnay's was the very "mystery" of the book. At the same time, the *Book of Changes* took the stance of the unified organism theory that all things in the universe are interdependent and interacted. The whole universe was studied macroscopically with a view to understanding the knowledge of "the reason of all things" and thus usually adopted the method of comprehensive analysis that goes beyond the isolated study of individuals. The *Book of Changes* also stresses that all things in the universe should keep in agreement and harmony with each other, which is termed *Tai He* (太和, "the most harmonious state"), manifesting itself specifically in the form of a conversation and balance between *Yin* and *Yang* in the change of hexagrams and lines in the graphs. Together with the concepts of *Zhong Xing* and *Zhong Dao* (中行 and 中道, both meaning "moderation") that are frequently mentioned in the *Book of Changes*, these ideas constitute the unique ideology of balance in ancient China. Therefore, the important contributions of Quesnay's Economic Table that have been praised by the later economists, such as the principle of managing complexity with simplicity, a macroscopic or comprehensive analytical method, balance theory, the description of the organic system of the entire economic life, and so on, can all find parallels in the *Book of Changes*. In contrast, these ideas stand clearly apart from the economic views expressed in ancient Greece and ancient Rome, which are confined to specific economic problems. Besides, it seems obvious that it was the *Book of Changes*, with its explanation of different kinds of trigram, which must have inspired Quesnay to use the graphic form to describe social-economic activities. Indeed, so much was admitted by both his followers and critics at the time.

The third argument for the Chinese influence holds that the Economic Table is related to Chinese hieroglyphs. Quesnay himself compared his Economic Table to "the hieroglyph of arithmetic".[27] His followers pointed out more specifically that the formulae in the table were "as precise as the ancient Chinese characters".[28] The nineteenth century critics often took the saw-tooth-shaped lines in the Table as "incomprehensible hieroglyphs".[29] As with many contemporary European scholars, Quesnay's followers likened the Chinese hieroglyph to scientific functions, especially of a mathematical nature, thus providing a link with the mathematical method of the Economic Table. The suggestion that

26 Quesnay, "Despotism in China" Chapter 2, from Maverick, *China: A Model For Europe*, pp. 180–187.

27 W.A. Eltis, "Francois Quesnay", *Oxford Economic Papers*, Vol. 27, No. 2, p. 190.

28 Gide and Rist, *A History of Economic Doctrines* (Volume 1), p. 51, note 4.

29 J. St. Lewinski, *The Founders of Political Economics* (London: P.S. King, 1931), p. 51.

the precision of the Economic Table was influenced by the mathematical perception of Chinese characters may seem incredible now, but it was less so in the historical context of the cultural exchange between China and the West. Besides, modern scholars still perceive the Chinese hieroglyph as "the quality of 'mathematics' in language";[30] furthermore, the hexagrams and lines of the *Book of Changes* which were regarded as the origin of Chinese characters at that time can be summarised in terms of a complicated and precise mathematical structure.[31] All things considered, it seems reasonable to suggest that the origin of the Economic Table may have been related to the Chinese hieroglyph.

Regardless of the specific content in the relation between ancient Chinese thought and the Economic Table, the mere fact that people frequently mentioned and valued the relation is enough to indicate that the westward-spread of Chinese culture was undoubtedly a major influence. But, as time passed, Westerners gradually effaced the special imprint that the cultural exchange between China and the West had left upon the creation of the Table. So, when they traced its intellectual origin they remained firmly rooted in a traditional Western perspective.

In fact, current works in the history of economic thought put forward several Western-centric views on the intellectual origin of the Economic Table, none of them totally convincing. For example, it has been suggested that the circulation concept of the Economic Table was inspired by the blood circulation in the human body discovered by European biologists. However, there are many facts to prove that the circulation concept also came from traditional Chinese culture, which was richer in terms of the importance of its position in people's minds, the extensiveness of its application and the precision of its expression, including the direct application of the simile of abstract circulation concept and blood circulation to the analysis of economic activities. Given the richness of the circulation concept in Chinese culture, and its dissemination in Europe, Quesnay may well have drawn on Chinese culture in this area.

It has also been argued that Physiocratic principles should be traced to earlier European thought such as Cantillon's analysis of the circulation process of social income and Boisguillebert's thoughts on the balance of the whole. However, two things should be pointed out. First, these pioneers all lived in the seventeenth and eighteenth centuries when Chinese ideas were entering Europe, and where the theories and views of Cantillon and Boisguillebert came from is still to be explored. Second, it was inevitable for Quesnay, the "Confucius of Europe", to maintain certain Western traditions, but this did not prevent him from borrowing ideas from the East to create the principles of the Economic Table.

30 Joseph Needham, *A History of Science and Technology of China*, Beijing: Science and Technology Press, 1975, p. 71.
31 Dong Guangbi, *The Mathematic Structure of Yi Gram* (易图的数学结构), Shanghai: Shanghai People's Publishing House, 1987.

Laissez-faire and the theory of "governing by doing nothing that is against nature" in ancient China

The Physiocrats derived economic liberalism from the concept of natural order, coming up with the famous slogan of "laissez-faire" which is quite close to the governing principles of "going with the benefit of the people and benefit them" and "doing everything by doing nothing" based on the concept of "going with the natural laws" or "emulating nature" in ancient China. The various connotations of the slogan of "laissez-faire", such as the concept of self-interest of naturalism, the principle of free course of trade, anti-government interference, and the major function of the government as knowing, obeying and imparting to the civilians the laws of natural order, can all find their counterparts in traditional Chinese thought with its emphasis on "governing by doing nothing that is against nature", "to follow the example of the good", "to govern by virtue", and "a man of virtue does nothing". The principle of laissez-faire and the concept of "governing by doing nothing that is against nature" agree with each other in many important respects. It is therefore unsurprising that both Chinese and Western scholars have related laissez-faire to the concept of "doing nothing" in ancient China when analysing the origin of Physiocratic theories, and have shown that the Physiocrats had a profound understanding of the Chinese culture that was disseminated to the West at that time.

What is especially noteworthy is that when the Physiocrats advocated laissez-faire they held the "open-minded" autocratic monarchy in China as an ideal model. Quesnay once described the open-mindedness of the Chinese autocratic monarchy as follows: "the governing system in China is built upon the basis of the natural laws", so the common acknowledgement of and emphasis on the natural laws hindered the Chinese emperors from evildoing and encouraged them to administrate legally and perform good deeds, making "this authority turn into the rulers' gospel and the subjects' worship of rule"; the Chinese emperors were sons of God and the main successors of God's great image on Earth, so they were full of virtue, tended to confess, loved the people like a Father, executed and obeyed the "explicit and unchangeable law" themselves; while the tyrants of each dynasty, who ever wanted to abolish the law, would finally be overruled by the law and removed from power by the people; the bases of the empire's religion, law and education were ethical precepts, upon which the sacred and stable relations between the monarch and his subjects had been built; the custom of encouraging remonstration set up restrictions on the absolute power of the monarch, and "perhaps there were no other countries allowing remonstrations with the monarch as freely as in China"; the supervisory systems at each level in China also "has no rivals in respect of its form"; because the Chinese aristocratic class except the Confucius family was not hereditary, the officers of each level could only be selected through imperial examinations in which their performance and ability would be taken into account, and they were well learned, with only one function of protecting and educating the people (and so on).[32] Moreover, in his works about China, Quesnay took many pages to analyse and dispute, point by point, Montesquieu's criticism of Chinese autocracy,[33] considering himself as a publicist and protector of the Chinese autocratic system.

It is noteworthy that Quesnay deduced his economic standards directly from the Chinese political system. In his opinion, since the Chinese autocracy was built upon the basis of natural laws and restricted by different rules, ethical precepts, the remonstration system, and imperial examinations, the Chinese autocracy could only perform "silent governance". Here, "silent governance" embodies the laissez-faire principle that the Physiocrats advocated strenuously. Quesnay further explained that,

> it may be hard to believe that the Chinese emperors indeed have so much time to handle the affairs of such a vast empire in person ... and miraculous order is still preserved there. Various laws are exercised so perfectly in dealing with all kinds of difficulties, that two hours would be enough for him to fulfil all his duties every day.[34]

In this way, he expressed his keen appreciation of the "silent governance" of China.

Quesnay's understanding is backed up by many popular views in ancient China. For example, "Getting up to work at sunrise and stopping work at sunset, digging a well for water and ploughing the land for food, I earn my own living without any help or guidance of the emperors";[35] "govern by virtue, then gain the whole world's submission by doing nothing";[36] "Heaven sees with the eyes of its people. Heaven hears with the ears of its people".[37] These and other sayings all reflect the state of laissez-faire under the typical open-minded autocratic monarchy which is unique to China and has no manifestation in the West. So, it can be inferred that the advocacy of laissez-faire by Quesnay and the Physiocratic School is closely related to the principle of "governing by doing nothing that is against nature" of the Chinese open-minded autocratic monarchy. Quesnay extolled the virtues of the open-minded autocracy in China and attempted to create an ideal model applicable to European countries, especially France, from a large amount of information about China. Therefore, he repeatedly declared that "the law of China should be compared with the natural laws that are the basis of a prosperous government" and made "the governance principles imparted and conducted as a science in China" the norm against which to

---

32 Quesnay, "Despotism in China", Chapters 1–7.
33 Ibid., Chapter 7, Section 1.
34 Quesnay, "Despotism in China", Chapter 5, from Maverick, *China: A Model For Europe*, p. 228.
35 Huangpu Mi, "Plough Land (击壤歌), Emperor Age (帝王世纪)", Beijing: Zhonghua Book Company, 1964.
36 Zhu Xi, "Governance" (为政), Commentary on *Analects* (论语集注) Vol. 1, Jinan: Qilü Press, 1992.
37 *Mencius*, V.A.5.

check and establish "the natural basis of a good governance".[38] Here he expressed his political ideal and clearly demonstrated the harmony between laissez-faire and open-minded autocracy.

In short, regardless of its correctness, the co-practice of laissez-faire and open-minded autocracy offers important evidence of Quesnay's acceptance of Chinese thought. The open-minded autocracy had been a traditional idea in China for thousands of years, while the thought of the West, especially after the Renaissance, was always against autocracy. Hence this view held by Quesnay was of a purely Chinese nature.

Physiocratic theory and the emphasis on agriculture in traditional Chinese thought

Among all the cultural knowledge that the Physiocrats learned from the Chinese empire, the thought of emphasising agriculture was one of the most precious to them. The reports about China in European intellectual circles of the time were full of knowledge on this point. Particularly, the many reports of China's agriculture which were circulated by missionaries who had operated in China had a significant influence on the French Physiocrats.

Quesnay once said that a kingdom in Europe (meaning France) had not recognised the importance of agriculture or the prepaid wealth of cultivation; "in contrast, agriculture is always esteemed as important in China, and people living on agriculture always gain extra attention from the emperors". Hence, when he talked about the "fundamental law" of China, he devoted a chapter to agriculture in which he sketched the contours of a typical agricultural country obeying the principle of natural order. In his words, "in whatever age, no one can deny that the country (referring to China) is the most beautiful, prosperous, and the most populous kingdom known to us."[39]

When investigating the agricultural affairs of China, Quesnay especially appreciated the positive support that the emperors of each dynasty had given to agriculture. He called the "law of the dynasty", which was established for the prosperity of agriculture by Yao and Shun in ancient legend, the "relics of science and wisdom left by them"[40] under the influence of which later emperors respected the trades of crop-planting and mulberry-raising, urged local officials to attach importance to agriculture, and selected the outstanding peasants as the eighth rank officials possessing noble reputation and equivalent privileges.[41] Among the specific measures of emphasising agriculture, the Physiocrats showed the deepest interest in the Chinese emperors' *Jitian* (籍田, "ploughing the farmland in person"). So, in Mirabeau's fourth edition of *Agricultural Philosophy*, which was finished under the supervision of Quesnay, the

38 Maverick, *China: A Model For Europe*, pp. 111, 138.
39 Ibid., pp. 204, 206.
40 *Countries on the European Continent in 17th and 18th Century*, tr. Gu Xiegao *et al.*, p. 80.
41 Maverick, *China: A Model For Europe*, pp. 197, 206.

cover of the first chapter was a specially designed illustration of Chinese emperors ploughing land together with ordinary people.[42] As later generations have realised, the message conveyed by the illustrations is as follows: the Chinese emperor

> as the Son of Heaven, represents the "natural order", i.e. the "the divine providence"; as an emperor who encourages the development of agriculture, he solemnly holds the plough once every year. His civilians actually are governed by themselves, i.e. the emperor rules them through conventions and etiquettes[43]

Quesnay urged Louis XV and his Crown Prince to emulate the Chinese emperors and conduct *Jitian* themselves: an unmistakable case of the influence of ancient Chinese thought on Physiocracy.

The influence of Chinese thought is further evidenced in the net product theory of the Physiocrats. The ancient Chinese scholars always regarded agricultural production as the root of enriching the country and the people, which is demonstrated in sayings like "the country would be impoverished if agriculture is harmed", "a powerful country cannot be made without agriculture as its root", and "the root is restored and hence the people would be rich", "the trade of agriculture is the best way to get rich". Here, the principal yardstick to measure the country's prosperity is whether its agriculture is damaged or supported and enhanced, implying that only agricultural production can generate a surplus to enrich the country, as in the Physiocratic net product theory. During the Ming dynasty in particular, when the missionaries to China were at their most active, many Chinese scholars proposed different kinds of theoretical bases to explain and advocate the importance of agriculture. For example, it was contended that agriculture is an industry that "can produce what the heaven and the earth have not provided", being the only production sector that actually creates wealth, while the other economic sectors only take the wealth created by agriculture but cannot create wealth; getting rich through agriculture was believed to be an activity that "gains resources from the heaven", different from the other sectors which "gain resources from people"; both the "manufacture" of industry and the "goods distribution" of commerce only perform the distributive function of transferring wealth, but "industry and commerce originate in agriculture" and neither can be the origin of wealth.[44] Obviously, Quesnay's "net product" theory was built upon the very basis of the similar theories and opinions in ancient Chinese thought.

The West had never had the concept of "net product", so when Mirabeau, a faithful follower of Quesnay, claimed "the discovery of net product should be owed to the respectable European Confucius; and it will change the pattern of

---

42 Einaudi, *Francois Quesnay et la Physiocratie*, p. 263.
43 Gide and Rist, *A History of Economic Doctrines* (Volume 1), p. 39.
44 Zhuang Yuanchen 《叔苴子内外篇》（《丛书集成》版）, 外篇卷一 and Xu Guangqi 《拟上安边御房疏》, from 《皇明经世文编》 Vol. 490.

the world one day",[45] he can be interpreted as providing a hint about the relation between the establishment of "net product" theory and the traditional Chinese thought represented by Confucius. Another contemporary of Quesnay also said to him, "What you are advocating, that agriculture is the only origin of wealth, is the theory that has already been established by Socrates, Fu Xi, Yao, Shun and Confucius."[46] This may be taken as tantamount to an admission that ancient Chinese thought was a major source of inspiration for the "net product" theory.

Under the influence of the common emphasis on agriculture, the Physiocratic School and the Chinese ancients showed many similarities in their attitudes towards industry and commerce. First of all, the Physiocratic School divided society into three classes, namely, the trades of agriculture, industry and commerce, which is similar to the traditional division of social classes in China. Quesnay mentioned that the civilian class of China "includes peasants, merchants and craftsmen" among which "the peasants rank the first class, followed by the merchants";[47] and, "in China, the status of peasants is higher than those of the merchants or craftsmen".[48] Through the contrast, Quesnay pointed out that France had not realised the importance of agriculture.

Second, the Physiocratic School applied nearly the same simile as the Chinese concept of *Ben Mo* (本末, "root and branches"). The theoretical basis and even the language used by Quesnay and Mirabeau in their discussion of the dependency between industry and commerce (the branches) and agriculture (the root), can all find their prototypes in the ancient Chinese representation of agriculture as the root and industry and commerce as the branches.

Third, the Physiocratic School took the example of China to illustrate the point that although industry and commerce are secondary to agriculture, their social and economic functions cannot be denied. Quesnay mentioned Shen Nong's contribution of "promoting the trade and establishing the markets" after his succession to the throne[49] and listed "removal of the inveteracy and restoration of commercial credit" as one of the most important political achievements of Confucius when he was in the position of senior official in the state of Lu. Moreover, Quesnay praised lavishly the commerce of China for its "considerable prosperity", saying that the whole of Europe could not rival China in commerce, where "the whole empire is like a huge market". He not only admired China for its prosperous commerce but also defended China against the allegation that Chinese businessmen were deceitful, holding that fraud would not be tolerated "in such a civilised country as China". These compliments and comments in defence of China came out of his understanding of the indispensable economic

45 Gide and Rist, *A History of Economic Doctrines* (Volume 1).

46 Reichwein, *China and Europe: Intellectual and Artistic Contacts in the 18th Century*, pp. 94–95.

47 *Countries on the European Continent in 17th and 18th Century*, tr. Gu Xiegao *et al.*, pp. 88, 90.

48 Maverick, *China: A Model For Europe*, p. 205.

49 [Shen Nong is the second of the mythical emperors, said to have been born in the twenty-eighth century BC. With the head of a bull and the body of a man, he is also referred to as Yandi, or Emperor Yan.]

function of "agriculture-based commerce" in the practical examples of China. This idea also represents the trend of attitudes towards industry and commerce since the Ming and Qing dynasties.

Finally, the Physiocrats placed stress on Chinese policies and practices in the area of foreign trade. Quesnay paid particular attention to the reasons why China's foreign trade was "quite limited". The first reason was that "the Chinese find all the daily necessaries at home (and the large population guarantees a domestic market that can consume all the goods)". Second, because domestic business was prosperous, the Chinese seldom attempted to expand markets abroad. Third, except for the businessmen, "foreign trade probably did more harm than good to the prosperity of the country" because "some praiseworthy countries were corrupted by the contamination of foreign trade". In other words, China had done the right thing by insisting on "quite limited" foreign trade activities in order to be free from harm and retain prosperity. Quesnay then used the fact that China was prosperous but had "quite limited" foreign trade activities as a powerful weapon to attack mercantilism and to refute the popular idea in Europe which held that wealth was produced in the domain of circulation and was therefore enhanced by foreign trade.[50]

It must be admitted, however, that the Physiocratic theory of Quesnay and the ancient Chinese thought of emphasising agriculture are different in at least one fundamental respect. The former "in fact declared the establishment of the capitalist production system upon the ruins of feudalism";[51] the latter was totally feudal and had at most acquired a few capitalist trappings by the time of the Ming and Qing dynasties. Nonetheless, the ancient Chinese thought of emphasising agriculture had great influence upon Quesnay's Physiocracy. Any scholar who has abandoned the prejudice of euro-centrism will not be blind to this fact.

Taxation and finance

The westward-spread of ancient Chinese thought on taxation gave impetus to tax reform in France. One of the notable examples is that Vauban, the pioneer of the Physiocratic School, advocated the Chinese-style tithe. As to the later Physiocratic School, the flat-tax policy created by Quesnay was also to some degree influenced by the ancient Chinese tax system.

First, when Quesnay described the tax system of China, he especially mentioned the "solid foundation" of the tax law, i.e. the restriction of the natural order on the tax. In his opinion, no country except China had paid any attention to this foundation.[52] Therefore, when he emphasised that a flat land tax "follows

---

50 Maverick, *China: A Model For Europe*, pp. 208, 209, 211.
51 Karl Marx, *Theories of Surplus Value*, Vol. 1, Beijing: Publishing House, 1975, p. 28.
52 Quesnay, "Despotism in China", Chapter 8, from *Anthology of Quesnay's Economic Writings* (魁奈经济著作选集), pp. 400, 404.

the instruction of natural order" and "taxes in all the other forms are in violation of the natural order",[53] he took the tax system in China as his example.

Second, Quesnay pointed out that the tax system of China was mainly land tax which was levied on the basis of the area and the degree of fertility of the land, and that all the taxes were paid by the landowners and should not be imposed on the tenant farmers.[54] He used these features of the Chinese tax system as the theoretical basis for the flat land tax. Therefore, he summarised the Chinese tax system as follows: in an agricultural country, the total amount of tax needed by the country is no more than "part of the surplus product after deducting the labour cost and other expenses" of the landowners.[55] It thus becomes quite clear that the single land tax of Quesnay takes the taxation theory and practice of China as its exemplar.

Third, Quesnay's objection to taxes on non-landowners, including tenant farmers, industrialists and merchants, may also be regarded as of Chinese origin. When he argued that the taxes should not be imposed on the tenant farmers, he repeatedly pointed out that in China "there is no tax levied on the cultivated land of the tenant farmers" and that "no tenant farmers need to pay taxes in China".[56] His negative attitude towards the taxation of commodities is also said to have been "based on the opinions of the Chinese". As he argued, the view (which he endorsed) that taxation of commodities and the poll tax would inevitably cause a shift in the burden of taxation and thereby do harm to national production "is the fundamental principle that the Chinese have followed to pursue a peaceful life for thousands of years; however, the correctness of the conclusion that the Chinese people have drawn from the theory is hardly convincing for the Europeans".[57]

Finally, of other tax principles mentioned frequently by Quesnay some were clearly inspired by Chinese precedents. For example, he was against the taxation of farming and required that taxes should be levied "according to the rules" and in an "orderly" way,[58] as they were in China. All the taxes levied by the emperors were publicised to let every taxpayer know how much tax he should pay.[59] Another example is that when Quesnay argued for simplifying the taxation institutions to save costs, he paid much attention to the reputed "simplicity" of the Chinese tax system, especially the fact that "levying taxes is completed in an orderly way without too many special officials".[60] In addition, his thought on a rational tax burden, reflected in the idea that "a fixed proportion exists between the national revenue and the land income",[61] was also drawn from Chinese tax principles.

53 *Anthology of Quesnay's Economic Writings* (魁奈经济著作选集), pp. 343, 314.
54 Maverick, *China: A Model For Europe*, p. 200.
55 *Anthology of Quesnay's Economic Writings* (魁奈经济著作选集), pp. 411, 412–413.
56 Maverick, *China: A Model For Europe*, pp. 220, 221.
57 *Anthology of Quesnay's Economic Writings* (魁奈经济著作选集), pp. 411, 412–413.
58 Quesnay, "Grains", from *Anthology of Quesnay's Economic Writings* (魁奈经济著作选集), pp. 56, 77.
59 Maverick, *China: A Model For Europe*, pp. 36, 18, 30–31.
60 Maverick, *China: A Model For Europe*, pp. 221–224.
61 *Anthology of Quesnay's Economic Writings* (魁奈经济著作选集), p. 411.

The above-mentioned points are mostly from Quesnay's description of the Chinese tax system, indicating that his theory of a single land tax owed much to ancient Chinese thought.

The Physiocrats also attached great importance to the Chinese finance expenditure system. Quesnay elaborated on the expenditure principles according to the "ancient principles of the Chinese government" and incorporated several of those principles into the general norms he set up for the economic governance of agricultural countries.[62] Under the title of "the final accounts of the total social wealth", he wrote about how China resolved the final accounts of the expenditure of the national revenue through knowledge that was "suitable to lead people through the glory of reason, making the government totally subject to the indestructible natural laws that set up the foundation of the social system".[63] In short, Quesnay took China as the exemplar in all financial expenditure matters and tried to discover the general financial norms that French rulers should follow from Chinese thought and practice so as to resolve the critical domestic financial crisis at the time.

Conclusion

The economic theories of the Physiocrats were influenced significantly by ancient Chinese economic thought. Among the Physiocratic theories, some are totally inspired by Chinese thought, some take the Chinese views as their principal but not exclusive inspiration, some adopt the examples of China to enhance or enrich the original arguments of the Physiocrats or add examples from China to support similar Western traditions, and others just "ask the spirits for help"[64] from ancient Chinese traditional culture. All these cases prove just how eager the Physiocrats were to learn from Chinese culture. Before the seventeenth century, the development of economic thought in ancient China had always been in the front rank of global accomplishment. China's rich and glorious achievements in economic thought were therefore a major source of knowledge for the Physiocrats, far more so than traditional Western thought. Hence, we can assert that ancient Chinese thought was a significant intellectual inspiration for the economic theories of the Physiocrats. Marx once pointed out that the Physiocrats are "the real founder of modern political economy"[65] and that "the Physiocratic system provides the first systematic understanding of capitalist production".[66] Given its importance to the development of Physiocratic thought, it may be concluded that ancient Chinese economic thought should be celebrated not only as a glorious achievement in its own right, but also as one of the main intellectual origins of modern political economy.

62 Maverick, *China: A Model For Europe*, pp. 221–224.
63 *Anthology of Quesnay's Economic Writings* (魁奈经济著作选集), pp. 418–420.
64 Karl Marx, "18th Brumaire of Louis Bonaparte", from *The Complete Works of Marx and Engels*, Vol. 8, Beijing: People's Publishing House, 1961, p. 121.
65 Marx, *Theories of Surplus Value*, p. 15.
66 Karl Marx, *Das Kapital*, Vol. 2, Beijing: People's Publishing House, 1975, p. 399.

5   On *Guanzi Qing Zhong*[1]

Ye Shichang

1

Guanzi Qing Zhong ("Master Guang Zhong's Theory of Weighing and Balancing Economic Forces") occupies a very important position in the history of Chinese economic thought. However, there is no settled opinion on the understanding and evaluation of the work. In this paper I will offer my own views on these matters.

What type of economic theory is contained in *Guanzi Qing Zhong*? As we know, two capital forms existed in a pre-capitalist society, commercial capital and usury capital. During the Warring States period, China's commercial capital already enjoyed a certain level of development and its economic laws were known to the people of the time. *Guanzi Qing Zhong* contained an argument on the laws of commercial capital. The commercial capital with which it dealt was not of a general form but was managed by a feudal state representing the interests and benefits of the ruling class. Therefore, we can say that the book was a work on the laws of state commercial capital at the early stage of feudal society.

State commercial capital was combined with the super-economic coercive power of the feudal regime. Its economic activities can be summarised as "integrating, ordering and commercial management", which is termed "weighing and balancing" in the ancient essay. As it could be applicable for control of commodity circulation, depending on the political power, its role is far more than that of general commercial capital.

On behalf of the feudal landlord class, the author(s) of the work created a theory of commodity management for the benefit of the feudal state. Nonetheless, in its economic thought there existed two kinds of contradiction, each representing its own interests and benefits. In order to maintain the stability of the feudal order, the participation of landlords and merchants in the circulation process had to be appropriately restricted, and the range of price fluctuations had to be controlled through the regulation of commodity circulation. At the same time, price fluctuations were required in order to maximise revenue for the

1 Originally published as "论《管子·轻重》" ("On *Guanzi Qing Zhong*"), *Economic Research Journal*, 1965 Issue 1, pp. 56–61.

feudal state. Both of these conflicting objectives were reflected in the book although the latter was treated as the more important concern. It is no exaggeration to say that *Guanzi Qing Zhong* was actually an economic theory for the feudal state's pursuit of maximum commercial profit.

Aimed at the circulation process, *Guanzi Qing Zhong* studied the laws of commercial capital activity, which was similar to the concern of later mercantilism and arguably led to similar conclusions. However, mercantilism belongs to a period of primitive capital accumulation with monetary gain as the sole objective. *Guanzi Qing Zhong* also argued that "A state will not stand firm if it cannot attract wealth and people from around the world". But, living in an historical period when natural economy was dominant, the author of the book did not give priority to monetary pursuit and he did not believe that there would be any difference in the roles of foreign trade and domestic trade for the purpose of increasing the state's wealth.

2

The author(s) of *Guanzi Qing Zhong* expounded a theory of exchange value. Some scholars have argued that the book did not discuss value,[2] but this view is mistaken. It was recognised that the following factors might determine the exchange value of a commodity.

1   Output volume: the more, the cheaper.
2   Crop harvest: the poorer, the more expensive.[3]
3   Seasonal effects on exchange value.[4]
4   Level of urgency of administrative orders.
5   Whether hoarded or stored.[5]

The above factors together imply that exchange value is determined by the quantity of commodity including the connection between output supply and demand. *Guanzi* could see only the surface of commodity circulation, not the intrinsic value of the commodity.[6] As a result, the exchange value of the commodity was taken as the commodity's value.

Based on such a value theory, *Guanzi* set up a "light-heavy" commodity weighting theory. On one hand, this theory indicated recognition of the contributing factors to the oscillations of commodity prices. On the other, it was taken

2 See Hu Jichuang, *The History of Chinese Economic Thought*, Shanghai People's Publishing House, 1962, Vol. I p. 505.
3 *Guanzi* "Guo Xu" ("The State's Store of Grain").
4 *Guanzi Qi Chen Qi Zhu. Selective Readings of the Thinkers*, Volume V, Beijing: Book Company, 1954, p. 287. This classic is not from *Qing Zhong* but is related to the theory on value, hence cited.
5 *Guanzi* "Guo Xu" ("The State's Store of Grain").
6 [The author evidently means "intrinsic value" in the Marxian sense of "value".]

to imply that a feudal state should enforce a "light-heavy" weighting policy in order to control such oscillations.

For pursuit of commercial profits, *Guanzi Qing Zhong* argued against stability of commodity prices, the argument being that only by allowing unstable commodity price fluctuations could a feudal state's business management gain and secure profits.[7] But this did not reflect an appreciation of the objective law "to make the commodity prices move evenly up and down around a central point".[8] In fact, there was no comprehension of a centre for price fluctuations, and certainly not of a centre that was achieved by means of balance.

The author(s) of *Guanzi Qing Zhong* believed the state's "orders" may alter commodity prices. Thus:

> when the prince levies special taxes and other demands on the people, if his order says that payment must be made in full within 10 days, the prices for property and goods will fall by 10 per cent ... but if the order is issued in the morning and payment must be made in full that night, prices will fall by 90 per cent.[9]

That is, an excessively short duration in the taxation deadline might affect a commodity's price. If the tax was on a sum of money and a short duration was imposed, the peasants might choose to trade their farm produce hastily for money in order to meet the taxation demand, which would then lead to a reduction of the prices of their produce. In general, the shorter the deadline for tax payment, the lower the prices the traders would offer. For a most serious case, 90 per cent of the value of the items might be lost.

Because of the importance of "order" in the state, *Guanzi Qing Zhong* proposed to tax the common people on their produce in accordance with the orders from the government rather that attempting to collect taxes within a very short deadline.[10] In line with these orders, the commodity weighting relation was altered for the sake of the maximum business profits. Through intentional management of fluctuations in commodity prices and the practice of speculation and profiteering, the feudal state tried to control both the currency and the supply and price of grain. Such fraudulent ways of business were often described in the *Qing Zhong* chapters.

Guanzi Qing Zhong also established public finance theory based on the weighting policy. The main purpose was to advise the ruling class to exploit the people "without their notice and reasoning, below the surface". Some scholars suggest that *Guanzi*'s financial proposition was to exempt or reduce taxes. However, as a matter of fact, the proposal was for a policy of heavy taxation in the disguise of light taxation!

---

7 *Guanzi*, "Qing Zhong Yi" ("Qing Zhong Economic Policies: B").
8 Hu Jichuang, *The History of Chinese Economic Thought*, Vol. I, p. 346.
9 *Guanzi*, "Guo Xu" ("The State's Store of Grain").
10 Ibid.

The book also contained discussion of the economic relations between states. The opinion expressed was that a state would not become strong unless it could gather wealth from other states.[11] While trading with its foreign partners, the state should make full use of the treasure obtained from other states;[12] otherwise, such trade could result in national subjugation.[13] The measure to gather together all the wealth from all the states was, therefore, dual weighting of careful storage and giving priority to circulation. In the trade with foreign business owners, if prices were doubled in the state, grain might flow into the state. Otherwise, the state's grain might flow out to other states.[14] A domestic high-price policy was therefore necessary for the state to import foreign items.

Indeed, it was maintained that an increase of commodity prices can attract imports of a foreign commodity. To a certain extent, such a proposition is consistent with the law of commodity circulation. But the theory does appear somewhat absurd: it completely ignored the role of the law of value and suggests that commodity prices could be sustained eternally at a high level, whereas a price divorced from value[15] could be maintained only under particular conditions and would fall following the inflow of commodities in large quantity.

Guanzi tried to apply the weighting technique to foreign trade in order to secure huge profits from state-managed foreign trade. At the same time, it exaggerated the role of economic struggle and believed that an economic blockade alone could result in the surrender of a neighbouring state.

3

Guanzi also discussed currency. It was maintained that currency was an outcome of an ancestral king's subjective will (such arguments left a far-reaching influence on later generations) and that the currency itself, whether in the form of pearl, jade, gold, knife-shaped coin or cloth material, had no determinate value at all. Concerning the function of currency, "gold knife or cloth currency"[16] was deemed to be "a universal and intermediary way for the people in business";[17] that is, it was a means of currency circulation as well as the medium of commodity exchange.[18] The function of currency as a measure of value was beyond the author(s)' comprehension. Other functions, such as a store of value and means of international payment, were mentioned but not analysed.

The relationships between currency and value in commodity exchange were summarised as follows.

11 *Guanzi*, "Qing Zhong Jia" ("Qing Zhong Economic Policies: A").
12 *Guanzi*, "Di Shu" ("Methods for Exploiting the Earth").
13 *Guanzi*, "Qing Zhong Yi" ("Qing Zhong Economic Policies: B").
14 *Guanzi*, "Shan Zhi Shu" ("The Best Methods for Ensuring Fiscal Control").
15 ["Value" in the Marxian sense.]
16 *Guanzi*, "Guo Xu" ("The State's Store of Grain").
17 *Guanzi*, "Qing Zhong Yi" ("Qing Zhong Economic Policies: B").
18 *Guanzi*, "Kui Du" ("Calculations and Measures").

1   The relationship between money and goods in general: when money is "heavy" then goods will be "light" (cheap in terms of money); and when money is "light" then goods will be "heavy" (dear in terms of money).[19]

2   The relationship between grain and goods in general: when grain is "heavy", goods in general will be "light" (cheap in terms of grain); and when grain is "light", goods in general will be "heavy" (dear in terms of grain).[20]

3   The relationship between money and grain: when grain is "heavy", money is "light" (cheap in terms of grain); and when grain is "light", money is "heavy" (dear in terms of grain). Currency is in reverse proportion to grain.[21]

The above relationships reflect the mutual "weighting" relations between items in exchange. As a result, an increase in the exchange capacity of one item may lead to decrease in the capacity of the other and vice versa.

Owing to grain having been selected from all commodities as a major item for exchange, corresponding to currency and other commodities, several commentators have been misled in their interpretations. For instance, Liang Qichao defined grain as a material currency in use at the time and regarded metal currency merely as a "paper" currency.[22] Guo Moruo also took grain as the standard currency, suggesting that the actual currency was regarded as supplementary to grain.[23] Such definitions or assertions are not consistent with the original implications of the book, in terms of which the currency was genuine whereas grain was regarded as a commodity of consequence. In some cases, grain played the role of means of payment. *Guanzi* listed grain as a factor because of its importance. The feudal state put the currency under control and thus a context of "reverse correlation in weighting the values of currency and all commodities" (the more/less valuable the currency, the less/more valuable the commodities) took shape under certain conditions. That was not enough, as the state still needed to control grain and then complete control of commodity circulation, also shaping the situation of "reverse correlation in weighting the values of grain and currency". The grain could be of great significance, as recognised in the book: "with the king's possession of grains and gold currency ... unification and expansion of the territory can be definitely fulfilled".[24] We should not conclude that grain played the practical role of a currency simply because it was used as a reference item for commodity exchange.

Guanzi also posited that "grain alone will determine whether things are expensive or cheap"[25] and advocated changing of various commodities' prices along with the change in the purchasing power in currency, which can be seen

19 *Guanzi*, "Shan Zhi Shu" ("The Best Methods for Ensuring Fiscal Control").
20 *Guanzi*, "Cheng Ma Shu" ("The Art of Fiscal Management").
21 *Guanzi*, "Shan Zhi Shu" ("The Best Methods for Ensuring Fiscal Control").
22 Liang Qichao, *Biography of Guanzi*, Shanghai: Zhonghua Book Company, 1936, p. 61.
23 Guo Moruo, *Collection of Guanzi with Notes*, Book II, Beijing: Science Press, 1956, p. 1137.
24 *Guanzi Qi Chen Qi Zhu: Selective Readings of the Thinkers*, vol. V, p. 371.
25 *Guanzi*, "Cheng Ma Shu" ("The Art of Fiscal Management").

from the "correlation between commodities and currency". Only grain was separately considered in terms of its "own" value, high or low. If a state stocked up grain in an attempt to increase its price, then relative to all other commodities the "grain would be more valuable"; likewise, if the state sold grain and lowered its price, the "grain would be less valuable than the commodities". Making use of the three variables – currency, grain and all other commodities, which formed a complicated correlation of weighting – the ruling class could gain enormous profits. This complies fully with the "control of both grain and currency for balance and stability".

Close attention was paid to reserves of grain, currency capital and regional distribution. Thus, a prince "sees to it that in every city of ten thousand households there are certain to be stores amounting to ten thousand *zhong* of grain and ten million strings of cash."[26] *Guanzi* goes on to say that "a state with ten thousand vehicles must have a stock of currency of the same value".[27] The currency and the grain storage were to be used for "replenishing current stock and selling afterward" or payment for "supply of implements and readiness for relief and of loans from the stock to the people".

Guanzi also advocated that the state should establish a money supply and control "the circulation of money throughout the country".[28] But why distribute the currency so widely? This point has also been misunderstood. Beginning with Liang Qichao, it has been claimed that the currency demand in *Guanzi Qing Zhong* referred to the necessary amount of currency in circulation assuming knowledge of "the need of the exact amount of currency for the entire country and therefore the demand for casting the currency".[29] Such interpretations have never been criticised and have been taken as given in the work of subsequent scholars.

In fact, the "casting and distributing of public currency all over the country" was for calculation of the need for currency capital and credit funds and consequently for the control of commodities and grain nationwide. The amount of the currency for the purchase of grain could be calculated on the basis of the soil fertility levels of different places in the country and therefore the grain yield. Did the amount of currency required happen to be that in circulation? Definitely not. The amount of currency for the purchase of grain was not the sum of the commodity circulation nationwide. In addition, it would be impossible for *Guanzi Qing Zhong* to have posited a demand for currency circulation in conformity with commodity circulation. Such a viewpoint is belied by the weighting theory, which implies the inadaptability between commodity circulation and currency circulation. The assumption that *Guanzi*'s knowledge was sufficient to calculate the necessary amount of currency circulation is to exaggerate the level of

26 *Guanzi*, "Guo Xu" ("The State's Store of Grain").
27 Ibid.
28 *Guanzi*, "Shan Zhi Shu" ("Methods for Ensuring Fiscal Control").
29 Liang Qichao, *Biography of Guanzi*, p. 58.

economic thought at the time. The amount of currency in need was actually that of currency for the state's commercial capital in a particular period.

The author(s) of the book advocated distributing the currency across the country to meet the state's commercial capital activities. Currency capital was to be distributed widely within the country to meet political objectives, something that would be unimaginable for privately owned commercial capital.

4

Guanzi Qing Zhong also reflects the rampant prevalence of usury capital during the Warring States period. In the Qi state, rich creditors could lend currency and cash at interest ranging from 20 per cent to 100 per cent.[30] The prevailing usury capital activities forced local peasants into bankruptcy. As a result, the country became poorer and the army weaker. *Guanzi* therefore suggested restricting or even extinguishing usury capital by means of repayment on the debtors' behalf, or alternatively by the state offering credit to private borrowers.

The measure of repayment on the debtors' behalf also had to depend on the weighting strategy so that the debtors' credit burden could be lightened or removed with only a small additional cost to the state finances. That could be somewhat insubstantial, and in the context of serious, bred-in-the-bone feudal problems of the society, adoption of some policies of the ruling class alone would not be an ideal solution. The author(s) even thought that if the creditors' social status was upgraded, they would willingly abandon the practice of usury exploitation. This proposition, absurd as it was, indicated the authorial standpoint as being on the side of the creditors.

The alternative was for the state to provide credit either in currency or in kind in order to alleviate farming or living difficulties. It would meet the pressing needs of the poverty-stricken peasants. However, the proposal to lend the state's credit was actually a way of cruel usury exploitation. It was a deceptive policy of "collection of interest with no trace of plunder".

The repayment of the state's credit would take place after the harvest. Regardless of whether loans had been advanced in currency or in kind, repayment was calculated at rates that would be adjusted for any fall in crop prices. Although no interest was charged on the surface, in reality the state could make substantial profits. Therefore, the role of credit discussed in the book was to ensure that peasants "do not waste their efforts and the state does not lose its opportunity for profit".[31] In other words, the producers could maintain their reproductive conditions for farming (at least a simple reproduction) and meanwhile the feudal state could monopolise the benefits of usury credit. Then the revenue from the credit might become the commodity capital of the state's commercial capital. The two types of capital were therefore closely bound to each other.

30 *Guanzi*, "Qing Zhong Ding" ("Qing Zhong Economic Policies: D").
31 *Guanzi*, "Guo Xu" ("The State's Store of Grain").

5

Guanzi Qing Zhong is very rich in content. The above discussion has presented only a brief outline of the book's main themes, although it provides an indication of the major propositions. Four observations can be made by way of a conclusion.

First, *Guanzi Qing Zhong* studied China's early circulation process during the feudal period. Although it mentioned how to stimulate grain production through the increase of grain prices, the study of this aspect was generally isolated from the production process and failed to appreciate the relationship between production and circulation by magnifying the independence of the circulation process.

Second, with regard to circulation alone, the book gave the earliest and most comprehensive theoretical outline of commodity circulation in feudal society. There is no other comparable treatment in ancient Chinese economic thought.

Third, the book did not separate general commercial and usury capital from the state's commercial and usury capital. Political power was therefore an integral part of the theory.

Fourth, the role of the state's commercial and usury capital was to ruthlessly exploit the common working people. Whatever the theoretical achievements of the book may have been, this aspect should not be overlooked in coming to an overall evaluation.

6 A comparison between Confucian and Daoist economic philosophies in the pre-Qin era[1]

Tang Renwu

Among the various schools of thought in the pre-Qin period, the most famous and influential were Confucianism and Daoism. Over more than 2,000 years, what influenced the society and the will of the people of China most were two books: *Analects of Confucius*, and *Laozi*, the central sutra of Daoism. Since the Qin dynasty (221–207 BC), numerous schools of thought came into being, vying with each other, such as Confucianism, Mohism, Daoism, Legalism, the Logicians, Yin-Yang, and so on. Yet, in terms of ideological fundamentals, there are two schools only: "In the pre-Qin period, the opposition of various schools of thought was chiefly the opposition between Confucianism and Daoism".[2] Hence, in the study of China's ancient economic thought, as long as we compare the similarities and differences between Confucianism and Daoism we can basically grasp the key features of the intellectual development and the main propositions contained within it.

Opposition between Confucianism and Daoism in philosophic thinking

Both Confucianism and Daoism originated from the Spring and Autumn and Warring States periods when Chinese society was in a stage of profound transformation. *Han Zhi* (*Records of the Han Dynasty*) reports: "Both schools of thought arose out of a time in which kingcraft became weaker, the vassals were vying with each other to govern the country, and there was great dissent among the rulers." In the course of a long historical development, Confucianism and Daoism grew into mutually opposing systems of philosophy owing to their different views on the universe and society. According to Dr Joseph Needham,

---

1 Originally published as "先秦儒道思想比较" ("A Comparison of the Economic Thought of Confucianism and Daoism in the Pre-Qin Period") in "中外经济思想比较研究" (*A Comparative Study of Chinese and Foreign Economic Thought*), Shanxi: Shanxi People's Publishing House, 1996, pp. 58–95.

2 Jin Chunfeng, *History of Ideology in the Han Dynasty*, Beijing, China Press of Social Sciences, 2006, p. 618.

Daoism is a negative ideological system whereas Confucianism is a positive one.[3]

Confucian philosophy, with political ethics as its main concern, is essentially based on "the way of humankind". Confucius seldom talked about the way of Heaven, his thinking lacked a systematic epistemology and it was not rich in dialectic ideas.[4] We may say that Confucian philosophy is concerned with human existence in a practical sense. Taking the "way of humankind" as the core, Confucians have made use of a number of categories in "life philosophy" such as "benevolence", "justice", "propriety", "wisdom", "credibility", "golden mean", "filial piety" and so on. Since "rejecting all other schools, and respecting only Confucianism" in the Han dynasty, Confucianism has dominated and determined the whole of Chinese traditional philosophy. On the other hand, Daoist philosophy, with metaphysics and epistemology as its main body, is based on the "Way of Heaven" characterised by "the natural way of inaction"; it regards Heaven, Earth and Humankind as one, taking the whole universe as one entirety and ruling out the existence God or Heaven as personal figures. *Laozi* says: "Dao (Way) has feelings and credibility, but has no action and form"; "Humankind follows the Earth, the Earth follows the Heaven, the Heaven follows Dao, and Dao follows Nature". Hence, the Daoist "Way of Heaven" is a repudiation and challenge to the Confucian "way of humankind". *Laozi* says: "The way of Heaven is to lose the surplus to complement the shortage. But the way of humankind is just the opposite: it loses the shortage to complement the surplus";[5] when "the Great Way is lost, there are benevolence and justice";[6] only "by abandoning both benevolence and justice can the people return to filial piety and love".[7]

Daoists have taken "Way of Heaven" as their basic theme and developed a series of philosophical categories such as "Way", "Existence" and "Non-existence". After the Western Han dynasty, because rulers set Confucianism as the only authorised theory, Daoism was suppressed, but this only forced it to develop further. It has been claimed, "Judging from the surface structure, Chinese traditional culture is a political-ethical theory represented by Confucianism; however, judging from the deep structure, it is the philosophical framework

---

3 Joseph Needham, *Science and Civilization in China*, Vol. II p. 6. Science Press and Shanghai Press of Ancient Books, 1990.

4 Chen Guying, "Backbone Position of Taoism in China's History of Philosophy" *Philosophy Research* 1990(1).

5 [Or, as rendered by Ryden (*Laozi: Daodejing*, E. Ryden, tr., Oxford: Oxford University Press, 2008, henceforth *Daodejing*):

> The way of heaven takes from what has too much to provide for what does not have enough. The way of people is, however, not like this: it takes from those who do not have enough to offer to those who have too much.

(Daodejing, 77)]

6 *Daodejing*, 16.

7 Ibid., 19.

of Daoism".[8] Indeed, not only has Daoist ideology supported traditional Chinese culture but its method of intuitive understanding has also constituted the features of Chinese traditional thinking as distinct from Western thinking.[9] Joseph Needham avers, "if there is no Daoism, China would look like a great tree with some deep roots already rotting away."[10] Lu Xun had the saying, "China's root is completely in Daoism".[11] Lü Simian wrote similarly,

> Daoism is actually the guiding ideology of all schools of thinking. All the other schools discuss some part or some aspect of the universe, but Daoism generalises all of them; all the others refer to the functions of the body but Daoism represents the body itself.[12]

With regard to the fundamental opposition between Confucianism and Daoism in philosophical thinking, many arguments have been put. In the chapter "Nine Schools of Thought" in *Liezi* (*List of Schools of Thought*) it is said: "Daoism takes abstract thinking as its essence while Confucianism regards moral education as its tenet. Of the nine schools of thought, these two are the most fundamental". In *Main Ideas of Six Schools of Thought* by Sima Tan of the Western Han dynasty,[13] there are comments on all the major schools, such as Yin-Yang, Confucianism, Mohism, the Logicians, Legalism and Daoism. When referring to Confucianism and Daoism, Sima Tan writes: "Confucianism is broad but lacks profundity, works hard but achieves little, because its principles are hard to follow completely. Yet, its manners of propriety about king and his ministers, father and son, or older and younger, can never be changed". Whereas,

> Daoism makes people focus their mind, behave in a formless way and enrich all things in the universe. It deals with the most fundamental, following the rule of *yin* and *yang*, adopting the benevolence of Confucianism and Mohism, taking in the principles of the Logicians and Legalists, moving with the time, and adapting to changes of things. It is universally applicable to all things and all occasions.

Hegel wrote, "Confucius was only a practical wise man in worldly life, and in his thinking there is no speculative philosophy at all – only some good-natured, tactful and moral lessons, we cannot get anything special from it"; whereas Daoist philosophy "mentions something general, just like Western philosophy at

8 See Zhou Yuyan and Wu Deqin, "Backbone Position of Daoist Thinking in Chinese Traditional Culture", *Philosophy Research*, 1986(9).
9 Joseph Needham, *Science and Civilization in China*, Vol. II p. 68.
10 Ibid., p. 178.
11 See Volume 11 of *Complete Work of Lu Xun*, Beijing: The People's Literature Press, 1981, p. 353.
12 Lü Simian, *Academic Conspectus of Pre-Qin Dynasty*, Beijing: Encyclopedia of China Publishing House, 1985, p. 27.
13 [Father of Sima Qian.]

first."[14] With regard to the *Analects of Confucius* and *Laozi*, Taiwanese scholar Shen Qijun has made a comparison between their fundamental spiritual purposes as follows:

> *Analects of Confucius* contains thousands of words in twenty chapters, but its aim is to guide peoples' conduct and virtue. It discusses the problem of what human life "should be like". In contrast, *Laozi* has five thousand characters. First, it discusses the truth about the formation and evolution of the universe, second, it talks about the truth and purpose of existence and evolution of affairs of human life, third, it deals with the real happiness of life. On the whole, it discusses the real condition of the universe and life, arguing about the problem of what human life "is like".[15]

Western scholar [H.H.] Dubs has a pertinent remark: "Confucianism has always been the philosophy of successful people or those wishing for success. But Daoism is the philosophy of 'losers' or those having tasted the pains of 'success'."[16] Confucianism returns to ethics while Daoism returns to nature.

Whatever position people may hold, either thinking that Confucianism deals with the rules of the world, or believing that Daoism covers the universe, almost all are agreed that Confucianism and Daoism have had the greatest influence in China and have the highest position in China's history of philosophy, exerting the greatest influence over Chinese philosophy of later generations.

Differences between Confucianism and Daoism in economic thinking

Economic thought as a reflection of philosophy can clearly indicate the features of a thinker's philosophical thinking. Confucius, Mencius, Zhuangzi, among others, were great thinkers with profound knowledge, and each of them has built up his economic thought from his main ideology. Just like their different philosophical thinking, all of their economic thought was meant to serve the newly arising landlord class; yet, in analytical method, specific content and other aspects, all of them can be said to belong to two major systems of economic thought with different features applying to each. Generally speaking, Confucians, owing to their strong sense of engagement with the common world, tried their best to counsel rulers on the financing and management of state affairs; hence, their arguments on socioeconomic thought and life are more and the areas covered are relatively few. In contrast, Daoists, owing to the fact that most of them were hermits, typically engaged in deep and subtle thinking; moreover,

---

14 Hegel, *Lectures on History of Philosophy*, Volume I, pp. 119, 127–128, Beijing: Commercial Press, 1997.
15 Shen Qijun, *Influence of Lao Zi: Cultural Crises and Prospect*, Beijing: China Youth Press, pp. 380–381.
16 Quoted from Joseph Needham, *Science and Civilization in China* Vol. II p. 178.

they were usually out of office, so their sayings on economic matters were relatively few.

Totality and the individual

On the whole, Confucian economic thought is based on a philosophy of human life, taking the "way of humankind" as the guiding theme. Confucians used the mode of political ethics to carry out their economic analysis. Taiwanese scholar Mr Hou Jiaju believes that Confucian economic thought is a type of laissez-faire economics.[17] In contrast, Mr Zhu Jiazhen maintains that Confucius's policy to lift prohibitions and benefit the people was different from the individualism upheld by the bourgeois after the eighteenth century in Europe and the free competition resulting from egoism.[18] Mr Wu Baosan further thinks that the policies advocated by Confucius and Mencius are completely different from Western laissez-faire characterised by abolition of the feudalistic personal bondage relation and free competition in the domestic market based on egoism and utilitarianism, and that using the bourgeois idea of laissez-faire to understand Confucian economic thought will lead to a distortion of the latter. We agree that the Western concept of laissez-faire cannot accurately and comprehensively capture the whole picture of Confucian economic thought. As Mr Wu Baosan has argued, Confucian economic thought is "macroeconomic" whereas Daoist thought includes the idea of individual economy. Such a generalisation is very novel and objective and has also cast doubt on the set practice of using Western economic terms inflexibly to account for China's ancient economic thought. Judging from the whole system of Confucian economic thought, it essentially centres on the management of state affairs. It is concerned with how to manage the economy and regulate politics. Most of it is about how to govern a country and the supreme objective lies in governing the family and managing the state. Confucius thinks the family is a cell of society, the state is the political organisation above the family, and the individual should be subject to the family and the state. Both family and state are holistic, and the whole has its own purpose and mission for existence. The individual exists in the whole, incapable of separation from the whole. Hence, all Confucian economic thought and policy, such as "using the people at the proper time", "reducing taxation" and so on, reflect the holistic purpose of serving the state's supreme interest, which is not conceived merely as an aggregate of individual interests. Therefore, Confucianism seldom analyses the status and role of individuals in socioeconomic life.

Daoism is a rare school in ancient China in that it does place stress on individuals. According to this school, both individuals' economic activities and national administration should comply with nature. There should be no artificial

17 Hou Jiaju, *Pre-Qin Confucian Free Economy Thinking*, Taipei: Lianjing Publishing House, 1983.
18 Quoted from Wu Baosan, "Major Aspects of Study of China's Ancient Economic Ideological History and Their Significance", *History of China's Economy* 1991(1).

intervention, individuals should "restrain from selfishness and desires" and "avoid being harmed by material things" so as to achieve the greatest freedom of body and mind and natural longevity. In the management of state affairs, we should "do nothing; keep eventless" and "follow the natural law, without selfish interest".[19] In general, Daoist materialistic philosophy generates a negative attitude towards economic activity.

Confucian thinkers are concerned about national fiscal revenue. Ran Qiu says, "When the people are rich, the king necessarily shares in that plenty; but when the people have not enough for their needs, the king cannot expect to have enough for his needs",[20] which is a typical Confucian viewpoint about public finance. As to the specific rate of tax, all Confucian thinkers advocate a level of 10 per cent. One of Confucius's disciples proposed the idea *che*, which just means "10 per cent taxation". Mencius said very clearly: "People should pay 10 per cent of their wealth to the state as tax"[21] and suggested to Dai Yingzhi that the state should levy a 10 per cent tax "as soon as possible".[22] Xunzi also advocated that "the tax on the fields shall be one-tenth".[23] In order to develop the state economy Confucian thinkers also advocated the following: "abolish custom and market duties";[24] "The mountains, forests, lakes, and fish weirs shall at certain seasons be closed and at others opened for use, but no taxes shall be levied on their resources";[25] and corvée labour should be demanded "only at the proper season".[26] Hence, judging from Confucian thinkers' economic thought, they were all advocates for enriching the state and seldom discussed economic issues from the angle of the individual.

Daoist thinkers hardly engaged in any economic analysis from the standpoint of the state. They seldom put forward any ideas about public finance and taxation. They were not advocates for enriching the state but were purely advocates for valuing the ego. Their economic thought is essentially an analysis from the individual aspect. Yang Zhu argued against the social ranking system on the grounds that it enchained personal freedom. He laid stress on individual life, and advocated "respecting the ego" or "for the ego",[27] saying "If everyone does not lose a single bit of himself and everyone does not benefit the world at all, the world will be perfect."[28] It is recorded that Mencius was disdainful of Yang Zhu's "ego valuing theory", pointing out: "Yang Zhu chooses egoism. Even if

19 See *Laozi* and *Zhuangzi*.
20 *Analects* XII.9.
21 [This does not appear to be a direct quotation. At one point in *Mencius* III.A.3 it does indeed seem that a tax rate of 10 per cent is favoured, but later in that same section a more nuanced position is expressed: "I suggest that in the country the tax should be one in nine ... but in the capital it should be one in ten".]
22 *Mencius* III.B.8.
23 *Xunzi*, "The Regulations of a King".
24 *Mencius* III.B.8.
25 *Xunzi*, "The regulations of a King".
26 *Xunzi*, "Debating Military Affairs".
27 *Mr Lü's Spring and Autumn [Annals]* (c.239 BC). Chapter "Only Choice".
28 *Huainan Zi*, General Teachings [Beijing: Zhonghua Book Company, 2009.]

he could benefit the Empire by pulling out one hair he would not do it."[29] Laozi's "inaction" [*wu-wei*] proposition is also basically for the individual, standing for "no knowledge and no desire" and "keeping away from sages and abandoning wisdom". Zhuangzi also starts from "I", advocating that "I" should have nothing to do with the world, "I" should not need to be responsible for the surrounding world, nor should need to shoulder any obligation or play a part; "I" should only do things according to my "true feelings", namely, I just let things slide, and I only belong to myself. According to the remark by Guo Xiang, Zhuangzi is a person "who does not lose himself for things"[30] and "keeps his ego and refuses to imitate others".[31] So, we can see that Daoist thinkers regard the individual "I" as their subject of study. They think that of all things in the world, the individual's life is the most precious. Hence:

> In the kingdom of value, the individual's independent freedom is the most fundamental and principal value. As far as the individual is concerned, only life and independent freedom are the most fundamental and most valuable and everything else is secondary, trivial, or even dispensable in comparison with them.[32]

Thus, Laozi's and Zhuangzi's Daoism doubt the utility of politics but affirms the value of the individual. Any illusion in society can be eliminated but the individual's wish to exist is a fact that cannot be negated. If the social system has anything that is inconsistent with the individual's wish to exist properly, we should eliminate or control it so as not to let the branches and leaves damage the root. When one reads Daoist works, one finds that their basic tone lies in taking the analysis of the individual as the purpose. As to whether the state is prosperous and strong and how it should be governed, there is little mention.

We may say, therefore, that a main point of contrast between Confucianism and Daoism lies in the difference between "the theory of enriching the state" in the former and "the theory of respecting the individual" in the latter.

On desire

Human desire is the starting point of modern Western economics. Marx points out that when we study the commodity from the social angle, "how much the quantity of desire is will be a question we cannot avoid. Here, we must study the degree of social desire, namely, its weight."[33] Engels remarks, "Ever since the appearance of opposition of social classes, it is people's wicked lust, rapacity

---

29 *Mencius*, VII.A.26.
30 *Zhuangzizhu*, Note on "Heavenly Fate".
31 Ibid. Note on "Yu Sang Cu".
32 Xiao Gongquan, *History of China's Political Thought* (Part I), p. 167. Taipei: Press of Chinese Culture College, 1980.
33 Marx, *Capital*, Volume 3, Beijing: The People's Press, 1st edition, 1953, p. 212.

and desire for power that became the lever for historical development."[34] China's ancient thinkers also paid great attention to desire. Almost all the schools and sects in the pre-Qin period had excellent arguments about desire, with Confucianism standing for modifying and guiding desire and Daoism advocating getting rid of or indulging it.

Confucius's opinion is that everyone has desires: "Riches and honours – these are what men desire.... Poverty and obscurity – these are what men hate".[35] Yet, Confucius's ideas on the satisfaction of desire are informed by moral preaching. For him, "desire" must conform to the Way, meaning that it must conform to social rank. Therefore, his suggestion for solving desire is that a person should "be contented in poverty", "know his fate", should "be happy in poverty" and "have no resentment although poor". To be specific, we should "be thrifty without violating the manners", "spend without damaging justice", should behave like his favourite disciple, Yan Hui:

> A man of quality indeed was Hui! He lived in a squalid alley with a tiny bowlful of rice to eat and a ladleful of water to drink. Other men would not endure such hardships, but Hui did not let his happiness be affected[36]

Mencius expounds his abstinence proposition from the premise that "human nature is kind". He also thinks such things as wealth, nobility and sex are desired by everyone: "beautiful women are ... something every man desires ... wealth is something every man wants ... rank is something every man wants".[37] But Mencius's analysis of desire stops at a shallow level. The moral rules established by Confucius such as benevolence, justice, propriety and so on, accompanied him all his life, becoming his pet phrases. As he says:

> To nourish the mind, there is nothing better than making the desires few. Here is a man whose desires are few; although there may be certain instances in which he is unable to preserve his mind, they will not be great in number. Here is a man whose desires are many; although there may be instances in which he is able to preserve his mind, they will not be great in number.[38]

Xun Kuang absorbed the Daoist materialistic viewpoint of "Way of Heaven and Nature", abandoned the idealistic factor in the "way of humankind" theory of Confucianism, and combined elements from both Confucianism and Daoism to infuse the Confucian idea of desire with new life. Starting from his theory that

---

34 Engels, *Ludwig Feuerbach and the End of Classical German Philosophy*, Beijing: The People's Press, 3rd edition, 1957, p. 27.
35 *Analects*, IV.5.
36 *Analects*, VI.11.
37 *Mencius*, V.A.1.
38 *Mencius*, VII.B.35.

"human nature is bad", Xun Kuang thinks that desires are people's physiological functions: "it is the nature of man that when he is hungry he will desire satisfaction, when he is cold he will seek warmth, and when he is weary he will desire rest."[39] Xun Kuang's analysis of desire starts from the objective fact that people have their physiological functions and seek to meet their desires. First of all, he affirms that "People have desire from birth" and such desire can find expression in every aspect of human economic life:

> the eye's fondness for beautiful forms, the ear's fondness for beautiful sounds, the mouth's fondness for delicious flavours, the mind's fondness for profit, or the body's fondness for pleasure and ease – these are all products of the emotional nature of man

> It is man's emotional nature to love profit and desire gain.[40]

Everyone has various kinds of desire. Such desires develop along with the growth of production and can never be satisfied. As Xun Kuang says, it is human nature that a

> man whose accomplishments are meagre longs for greatness; an ugly man longs for beauty; a man in cramped quarters longs for spaciousness; a poor man longs for wealth; a humble man longs for eminence. Whatever a man lacks in himself he will seek outside[41]

What is to be done? We should not just "get rid of the desire", "forbid the desire" or "reduce the desire" to suppress it artificially. Instead, Xun Kuang suggests a way called "Daoist desire"; that is, use a proper method to regulate and lead it. Such a proper method according to Xun Kuang is like this: seek the desire only after using rational thought to make the correct judgement: "it must ... be the function of the intellect to guide the search for satisfaction". In his view, so long as we engage in rational thinking human desire can reach a nearly perfect satisfaction in our mind: "although one cannot completely satisfy all his desires, he can come close to satisfying them".[42] It is obvious that Xun Kuang's desire theory has reached quite a high level, not inferior to the desire theory of modern bourgeois thinkers. Have not Western bourgeois thinkers often proposed rational thinking to carry out their analysis of desire? What is even more valuable is that Xun Kuang also carried out a reasonable analysis of the relationship between desire and the means of satisfying it. He requires that "desires [should] not overextend the means for their satisfaction, and material goods [should] not

39 *Xunzi*, "Man's Nature is Evil".
40 Ibid.
41 Ibid.
42 Ibid., "Rectifying Names".

fall short of what [is] desired".[43] That is to say, in the relationship between the means to satisfy the desire and the desire itself, we should neither let the desire be restricted by material conditions, nor let material conditions be completely subject to the desire, but should let the two grow together by mutual interaction. Such a "Daoist desire" theory has advanced by a great leap in comparison with the earlier abstinence theory of Confucius and Mencius. Even so, Xun Kuang still cannot shake off the philosophic frame of "way of humankind" of Confucian ethical preaching, and he has also suggested an objective standard – "manners" or "rites" – to restrict desire.

Daoist thinkers put forward their own theories of desire. Laozi's basic philosophical idea is "Way of Heaven and Nature" and "Inaction (*wu-wei*)". According his opinion, Dao generates all things in the universe; it does not possess them, yet it "stewards" them.[44] Dao itself has a "nameless simplicity"; if "kings and lords could possess it [Dao], all beings would transform themselves … Then there is no desire. No desire is serenity, and the world settles of itself".[45] Therefore, his final requirement for human desire is to have no desire at all: the Sage "leads people away from knowing and wanting".[46]

In Laozi's eyes, the natural "Way of Heaven" is regular and without desire; if you have desire, you will fail to comply with nature, will go against the natural law and will make people fall into mental disorder. Only by having no desire can we return to the simple and natural state and conform to nature. Yet, at a time characterised by destruction of the "Way of Heaven", it would be hard to let people keep desire-free. Laozi therefore suggests a flexible way, that is, to lower the requirement a little, to have "few desires". He advocates, "Keep plain and simple, make desires and selfish interests as few as possible" and be "content with one's lot". Thus:

> Too much love will certainly lead to great cost, and too much accumulation of wealth will surely result in great loss. By being content with your lot and knowing where to stop, you can keep your life long.... The greatest guilt lies in desire, the greatest disaster lies in insatiability, and the greatest fault lies in the desire for more; thus, by contentment with what you have, you can always have enough[47]

Laozi regards contentment with one's lot as the important standard determining people's honour or disgrace, existence or death, and weal or woe; he even thinks that contentment can determine one's wealth: "To know what is enough is to be rich".[48] Evidently, although the great philosopher Laozi is noted for his

43 Ibid., "A Discussion of Rites".
44 *Daodejing*, 10.
45 Ibid., 37.
46 Ibid., 3.
47 *Daodejing*, 44, 46.
48 Ibid., 40.

plain dialectical materialism, he cannot avoid disclosing some idealistic elements in his argument about desire.

Another Daoist, Yang Zhu, had a very distinctive theory of desire although he held a negative attitude towards human economic activities. First of all, he admits that the pursuit of material desires is part of human nature and that everyone is alike regardless of their social status.[49] He says: "People are born with desire and greed". How should we satisfy people's desire? Yang Zhu goes to the other extreme to Laozi by advocating indulgence: "Move after our mind, never violate the natural liking", "Drift according to our will, never go against the trend of all things in the world".[50] Evidently, it is another form of expression of the Daoist philosophy of "Way of Heaven and Nature". In Yang's opinion, only by following our inclinations and seeking everything according to our own desire can we really be said to have followed nature and followed all things in the universe. It is a thoroughly free and wanton attitude.

Another great master of Daoism, Zhuang Zhou, pushed Laozi's "No Desire" idea to the extreme. He negates the function of desire completely:

> The True Man breathes with his heels; the mass of men breathe with their throats. Crushed and bound down, they gasp out their words as though they were retching. Deep in their passions and desires, they are shallow in the workings of Heaven.[51]

He advocates getting rid of desire:

> In the age of perfect virtue, men lived in common with birds and beasts, and were on terms of equality with all creatures, as forming one family – how could they know among themselves the distinctions of superior men and small men? Equally without knowledge, they did not leave the path of their natural virtue; equally free from desires, they were in a state of pure simplicity. In that state of pure simplicity, the nature of the people was what it ought to be.[52]

In Zhuang Zhou's opinion, desire is always harmful. Both satisfying and not satisfying the desire will lead to trouble. If you satisfy the desire, "your emotion will get ill"; if you do not satisfy it, "your body will get ill". The only solution is to be rid of desires by living like animals and all things in universe. Only in this way can we keep our nature plain and simple. Not surprisingly, Zhuang Zhou holds a negative attitude to the development of material standards of living, thinking that all such activity is harming people's natural characteristics. This

---

49 *Mr Lü's Spring and Autumn.* Chapter "On Sexual Desire".
50 *Liezi*, Chapter "Yang Zhu".
51 *Zhuangzi*, "The Great and Venerable Teacher".
52 *Zhuangzi*, "Horse's Hoofs".

shows that Zhuang Zhou has expressed in a passive way his discontent with the exploiting class's limitless greed.

In the Confucian and Daoist theories of desire it is on the whole Confucians, and especially Xun Kuang, who advanced the most complete and profound theory. Xun Kuang adopted the concept of "pursuing" the desire, and put forward the theorem that "desire is always greater than supply", which some 2,000 years later was to be the starting point and foundation stone of various Western economic theories. As for Daoism, its "getting rid of desire" or "orgies" (indulging desires) are novel and unique as theorems but they seem to be more in the nature of complaints about something that cannot be helped. Although "getting rid of desire" seems to refer mainly to the elimination of unwarranted and unnatural greed rather than desires that conform to people's natural needs, and therefore has some positive significance in struggling against exploitation and oppression, in theoretical analysis it is not as thorough and detailed as the analysis by Xun Kuang, although it is more profound than the thinking of Confucius and Mencius.

Utopia

In the design of the future ideal society, Confucians and Daoists used their "supernatural" imaginative power under the guidance of their respective philosophies to conjure up two different types of blueprint.

The Confucian "Great Harmony" ideal society is a social ideal transcending the times which clearly shows the desire of Confucians to engage with politics and enter the common world. At the end of the nineteenth century and the beginning of the twentieth century, the Great Harmony blueprint was praised as the "socialism" of ancient China.[53] When many Taiwanese scholars talked about the influence of Confucianism, they said repeatedly that the "Great Harmony" ideal is a fine design for the future of the world.[54]

Judging from the contents of "Great Harmony" ideal society designed by Confucians, we can see Confucian political-ethical philosophy everywhere, as in "Choosing the worthy and the able persons", "Stressing credibility and keeping good terms with others", "Loving the kin", "Caring for children", "Having pity on the orphan and the widow without discrimination", and so on.[55] All such ideas are based on ethics. We can see the importance of moral human relations in Confucianism very clearly. In economic issues, Confucians have put forward an opinion which is incommensurate with its traditional idea but tallies with the viewpoint of Daoist thinkers. First, "All things on earth belong to the public", the emperor's position should not belong to one family, no hereditary system

---

53 See Kang Youwei, *On Great Harmony*, Shanghai: Shanghai Guji Press, 2009, and Sun Yatsen, *Principle of People's Livelihood*, Guangzhou: Guangdong People Press, 2007.
54 See Chen Lifu and other Taiwan scholars' works.
55 All the quotations are from *Li Ji* (*Book of Rites*) Chapter "Li Yun" ("The Conveyance of Rites"), except as noted otherwise.

should be used and the worthy and able people should be chosen as leaders. Second, all means of production and the fruits of labour should be owned by the whole society, everyone should participate in labour, there should be no classes or exploitation, everyone should help each other equally, "the strong can use their strength properly, the young can be governed by adults, all kinds of misfortunate people such as widowers, widows, orphans, childless couples and handicapped persons and so on, can get proper support from the society." It is really a childish and limitlessly nice ideal society, even more perfect than the "Utopia" designed by Plato of ancient Greece in which classes and exploitation still remain. As far as the universality and profundity of its imagination are concerned, we can say that it is a very advanced idea indeed.

In order to make up for their discursive illusion of the Great Harmony society, Confucians suggested two somewhat more practical programmes: the "better-to-do society" and the "well-field system". These two ideas are based on the private ownership of the means of production. The "better-to-do society" is essentially an example of Confucians' praise of a three-generation society. Here there are classes and exploitation, there are different ranks, there is violence and war, there is reward and punishment, and people observe the "courtesy" rules of government. As for the well-field system, it is basically a land programme in which eight families live around a well-shaped field, are friends to each other, often help each other especially in illness, and stay together until death. Evidently, such an idea is a phantasy full of contradictions; it is itself a "Utopia" for Confucians to realise their ideal policy of benevolence.

Unlike the "Great Harmony" ideal society, Daoist thinkers Laozi and Zhuangzi designed a "small country with few people".[56] In this society there is no war and people have a simple and plain lifestyle: they do not ride a cart, do not take a ship, and do not move faraway until death; everyone can eat fine food and wear beautiful clothes, live happily and at ease; neighbouring countries can

---

56

Build a small country with few people, let people use no tools even if there are hundreds of them available, and let people stay permanently without moving even until death. Even though there are ships and carriages, no one will take them. Even though there are weapons, no one will use them. Let people return to the time of tying knots for recording. Let them enjoy their food, appreciate their clothes, like their dwellings, and love their customs. With a neighbouring country close at hand, people are never in contact with each other although they can hear the crowing of cocks and barking of dogs in the other country

(*Daodejing*, 80)

Also:

In the past, there were Emperor Dating and Emperor Rongcheng, then, there were Emperor Zhurong, Emperor Fuxi and Emperor Shen Nong. In those times, the people tied knots for recording things. They enjoyed their food, appreciated their clothes, liked their dwellings, and loved their customs. With a neighbouring country close at hand, people were never in contact with each other although they could hear the crowing of cocks and barking of dogs in the other country

(*Zhuangzi*, Chapter "On Theft")

see each other, can hear the crow of a cock or the yap of a dog in the neighbouring country, but people from different countries never have contact with each other. One can imagine how small such a society is. At most, it can only be called a "family", certainly not a country. It is a social pattern designed by Daoists in order to cope with the morbid social phenomena existing at the time, such as frequent wars and the pursuit of luxury: an attempt to overcome those problems and return to the primitive village-community type of existence that had been eliminated long before. It reflected their state of mind: they yearned for nature, wanted to return to and hide in Mother Nature, shrinking from the tide of socioeconomic development and escaping from struggle. They wished to find a worry-free Holy Land in imagination but were oblivious to its fundamental contradictions: how can people live an enduringly happy life in such a tiny country with few people, without association with foreign countries and without the marriage relationship?

Another Daoist thinker, Xu Xing, put forward the ideal of a society in which "king and people farm together", similar to the "small country with few people" ideal proposed by Laozi and Zhuangzi. We should say that "king and the people farming together" is closer to the economic reality of that time than "small country with few people". Xu Xing designed his ideal society chiefly from a consideration of production and circulation. He proposed that everyone should join labour and work for a living and that barter should be the means of exchange. This ideal, characterised by opposition to exploitation, oppression and a hierarchical system, is only an illusion that can never be realised. Yet, in comparison with the Confucian "well-field" ideal, it is far more practical. It also reflected the Daoist philosophy of returning to the plain life and complying with nature. As such, it was strongly attacked by Mencius.[57]

In comparing the ideal societies of Confucianism and Daoism, Mr Hu Jichuang's comment is very profound. Confucianism is pursuing a future illusion under the cloak of an ancient vestment, so it is forward-looking thought, whereas Daoism is deserting to a primitive "paradise" bearing the wounds of the times, so it is backward-looking thought.[58] The Confucian Great Harmony ideal is a political declaration, showing the ancient working people's longing for the future. In contrast, the Daoist "small country with few people" is a revolt against reality, showing the ancient intellectuals' bewilderment of current politics. The Great Harmony ideal was to have a much more far-reaching influence upon later generations.

Private ownership

In terms of ownership relations, Confucianism and Daoism also oppose each other fundamentally. Confucians think from their "human political-ethical

---

57 *Mencius* III.A.4.
58 Hu Jichuang, *China's Economic Ideological History* Part I, Shanghai: People's Press, 1963, p. 215.

philosophy", chiefly for maintaining the system of the time and for praising the rising landlord class; thus, they laud and support private ownership. Confucius's "Let a ruler be a ruler, a subject a subject, a father a father, and a son a son"[59] aims to use just such an ethical model of the social order of high or low in order to solidify the ownership relations in the economy. Confucius endorses the distinction between poor and rich and requires that poor working people should be satisfied with their fate. In terms of labouring activity he stands for class difference, opposing the idea that officials should engage in productive labour: "The gentleman plans for the Way and does not plan for food".[60] In taxation, he advocates "minimising taxation" which implies that he supports private ownership. Especially, representative Confucian thinkers consider such a society as their ideal "better-to-do society": "Things produced belong to the private",[61] and the proper courtesy and justice are used "to establish the system and rules". Confucius is a supporter of private ownership.

The "Second Sage" Mencius is even clearer in his support for private ownership. The "constant asset theory" is

> the earliest definite theory about institution of private property in Chinese history. It coincides with the ancient Greek philosopher Aristotle's advocacy of the institution of private property, only that the latter argues for it from the viewpoint of "human nature".[62]

Mencius proclaims that if the common people "have constant assets, they will have a constant mind; if they have no constant assets, they will not have a constant mind". The so-called "constant assets" refer to the long-term possession of means of production together with other assets, chief of which are property and land. More specifically, what Mencius means by the common people's "constant assets" are "a five-*mu* residence" and "a hundred-*mu* field". A common family can rely on these "constant assets" to plant mulberry trees and keep hens, pigs and dogs for a living. According to Mencius, only when people have a certain quantity of assets can the society maintain stability and people be educated and practice "good habits". Mencius defends private ownership from the viewpoint of the stabilisation of social order and this was of progressive significance in those days. However, while defending private ownership, Mencius still clings to his political-ethical philosophy. He combines private ownership with "school education and filial piety", thus keeping faith with his "life philosophy".[63]

Although Xun Kuang does not trumpet Mencius's ideas of the "five-*mu* residence" and "hundred-*mu* field", he also supports the private ownership system of the newly arising landlord class. He argues against heavy taxation, advocates

---

59 *Analects*, XII.11.
60 Ibid., XV.32.
61 *Li Ji* (*Book of Rites*) Chapter "Li Yun" (Conveyance of Rites).
62 Hu Jichuang: *China's Economic Ideological History* Part I, p. 23.
63 [See *Mencius* I.A.3, I.A.7, VII.A.22.]

10 per cent tax for farming so as to reserve riches in the common people, and affirms the reasonableness of the distinction between the poor and the rich.

Unlike Confucians, Daoists argue against the private ownership system. According to Yang Zhu, human beings and materials are bestowed by Mother Nature and do not belong to ourselves; hence we should keep our bodies intact and use materials, but we cannot own them. If we were to regard the body and materials as private property it would be the same as appropriating to ourselves those public properties which rightly belong to the world.[64] As he rejects the private ownership of property, he naturally opposes the legacy system as well. He stands for "leaving no property to the offspring". He praises highly Duanmu Shu's practice: Duanmu reserved a little fraction from the "big money" left by his forefathers for supporting himself; as for the rest of it, he first gave some to his relatives, then he gave some to the villagers, then he gave some to the state.[65]

Laozi also opposes private ownership. He stands for "Generate but not possess, do but not rely"[66] which means that people can produce things but should not appropriate them to themselves. In his opinion, the reason why Heaven and Earth can exist forever is that they do not "generate themselves".[67] The reason why a sage can become a sage is just that he takes no account of himself and is therefore "selfless". Zhuangzi and Xu Xing also oppose private ownership. Zhuangzi exhorted: "When you are rich, you should divide your wealth with others"; and, "When all people in the world benefit together, it will be called 'happiness' indeed, and when all people offer to share what they have with others, it will be called 'peace' in the real sense". Xu Xing argues against the establishment of public granaries or governmental storehouses, encourages the people to live independently, and stands for farming together by both the king and the people.

Supporting and lauding private ownership shows Confucians' enterprising spirit to adapt themselves to the tidal current of history and enter the common world aggressively. The opposition of Daoists thinkers to private ownership is not because they have found the evils and shortcomings of private ownership but because they start from their philosophy of the "Way of Heaven and Nature". They take a completely naturalistic attitude and absolutise natural power: humans are products of nature and if we have private property our encumbrances

---

64 *Liezi*, Chapter "Yang Zhu":

> The body is not my private asset. Since I was born, I have to keep it healthy. Materials are not my private property. Since I have possessed them, I have no right to remove them. The body is of course the source of my life, and the materials are my nourishments. Although I have the full body, I should not possess it; although I use the materials, I should not regard them as my possessions. If I regard the materials and the body as my own, I will occupy the body of the world and occupy the things of the world. Then, how can I be called a sage? Let public things belong to the public, and that is what a human should do. That kind of man is the highest virtuous man.

65 Ibid.
66 *Daodejing*, 51.
67 Ibid., 7.

will be increased, so we shall fail to "keep simple and plain" and comply with nature. Hence, they oppose private ownership but their opposition rests only on a passive obedience to nature and they cannot analyse the evil nature of private ownership from the social system itself. Put another way, their opposition reflects their spirit of passively shrinking back from the world. Even so, from the standpoint of ideological history we cannot deny that the Daoist opposition to private property is still a progressive thought in its own way.

Production

Confucians basically hold an affirmative attitude towards the production of wealth. Confucius declares: If "richness might properly be sought, I would surely make them my aim".[68] His student Zi Gong was a man who valued knowledge of production and was active in advocating the utilisation of machinery for purposes of irrigation. Zi Gong said to an old man in Hanyin: "Use wood to make a machine which is heavy in the back and light in the front, can draw water very fast, and we call it '*gao*'". By this lever-type simple machine, people could "water a hundred border checks of field one day. The efficiency is high".[69] The author of *Da Xue* says: "Where there is earth, there is wealth", which shows the author already knew the role of land in wealth creation. The author of *Zhong Yong* (Golden Mean) went further, realising that industrial production can also bring about wealth: "With hundreds of crafts, we can get enough wealth". Mencius invented the term *shigong* (reward according to performance), which associates one person's quantity of reward with one's labour. As for agricultural production, Mencius stands for "farming in the right season" so as to maintain a sufficient supply of grain, fish, wood and so on. He clearly realised the importance of division of work in production, thinking that if we can "exchange products between different trades", we can let each trade benefit. Mencius's attitude towards productive activities is affirmative.

Xun Kuang is even more positive about productive labour. As he points out, one cannot be good at all kinds of skill, therefore, "farmers work in the field, merchants work in the shop, workers work in the workshop, and officials work in the office". As people accumulate experience in different productive processes, different trades came into being: "those working in the field become farmers, those doing woodwork become workers, and those selling things become merchants." No one can "do all things" and "know all things". "In farming, a gentleman is not as good as a farmer. In buying and selling, a gentleman is not as good as a merchant. In woodwork, a gentleman is not as good as a worker". Therefore, Xunzi requires that "Farmers should do farm work, officials should do office work, workers should do craft work, and merchants should do commercial work", so that everyone may have a permanent job, engage in one kind of production, become familiar with one sort of production process and

68 *Analects*, VII.12.
69 *Zhuangzi*, "Heaven and Earth".

improve productive skills.[70] Xun Kuang also stresses "Demand [corvée] labour [of the people] ... only at the proper season";[71] moreover, he suggests encouraging and protecting production and improving production methods so as to raise labour productivity. He therefore advises that feudal rulers should try to protect production and should understand the appropriate timing of various activities:

> The farmers plough in spring, weed in summer, reap in autumn, and store away in winter. Because they do each at the proper season, there is a never-ending supply of grain and the people have more than enough to eat. Because the lakes and rivers are watched over carefully and closed off at the proper time, there is an ever-increasing supply of fish and other water creatures and the people have more than they can use. Because the felling of trees and cutting of brush is done only at the proper time, the hills are never denuded and yet the people have all the wood they can use. These are the measures of the sage king.[72]

Although Confucians support productive labour, their outlook is based entirely on their political-ethical philosophy. Confucius emphasises that production and acquisition of wealth should conform to an ethical standard. He "seldom talks about profit", and introduces the concepts of *junzi* (gentleman) and *xiaoren* (lowly person) which has had a profound influence on people of all ages. He sets *yi* (justice) against *li* (profit), saying, "Gentlemen are clear about justice while lowly persons are clear about profit".[73] That means that people in the ruling class are born with a liking for justice whereas working people engaged in production know only about making profit. Confucius thus opposes the direct participation of officials and intellectuals in agricultural production and all kinds of workmanship activities, thinking these kinds of manual labour should be the duties of *xiaoren* while *junzi* need only to "learn to get the Way". He says,

> The gentleman plans for the Way and does not plan for food. If you plough, hunger is a possible outcome; but if you study, official salary is a possible outcome. So the gentleman is concerned about the Way and is not concerned about poverty.[74]

70
> [As a basis for action, diversity is impractical. Hence the wise man selects one thing and unifies his actions about it. The farmer is well versed in the ways of the fields, but he cannot become a director of agriculture. The merchant is well versed in the ways of the market, but he cannot become a director of commerce. The artisan is well versed in the process of manufacture, but he cannot become a director of crafts. Yet there are men who, though they possess none of these three skills, are still able to fill the offices that direct them.
> (*Xunzi* "Dispelling Obsession", tr. Watson)]

71 Ibid., "Debating Military Affairs".
72 Ibid., "The Regulations of a King".
73 *Analects* IV.15.
74 Ibid., XV.32.

Such an attitude of setting manual labour against mental labour has had an active role in the development of science and culture, but the fact that he classifies people into *junzi* and *xiaoren* shows the reactionary nature of his belittling of productive labour from the ethical viewpoint.

Mencius inherited Confucius's "seldom talk about profit" attitude. When he discusses wealth production from the viewpoint of the state he resolutely opposes giving priority to wealth and profit. He stresses repeatedly that "Benevolence and justice are enough. There is no need to mention profit", adding, "If you put profit before justice, you will try every means to seize profit". In his opinion,

> If the king only thinks how to profit my country, the official only thinks how to profit my family, and common people only think how to profit myself, then those above and those below will be vying with each other for profit and the state will be imperilled.[75]

We can see that Mencius has clearly put ethics ahead of wealth. It is on such a basis that he advances his famous theory of "mental work" as against "manual work":

> people either do mental work or do manual work. Those doing mental work govern others, and those doing manual work are governed by others. The governed provide food for others while the governing eat food supplied by others. That is a common principle in the whole world.[76]

Mencius has further theorised Confucius's *junzi* and *xiaoren* theory, deeming that the natural duty of manual labourers is to labour for, and be exploited by, their "superiors": "there are men in authority and there will be the common people. Without the former, there would be none to rule over the latter; without the later, there would be none to support the former."[77] Mencius classifies productive labour into manual labour and mental labour, which is a faithful reflection of the development of social productive forces at that time. However, Mencius associates mental labour and manual labour with exploiting and being exploited and raises the relationship to the ethical level. This reactionary position was to become the theoretical basis for the ruling class of all ages to exploit and oppress the working people.

Xun Kuang's opinion on productive labour did mark a small advance on the teachings of Confucius and Mencius although he basically accepted their position. He thinks, "Justice and profit exist in all people". But, "when justice overwhelms profit, the world is an orderly one; when profit overwhelms justice, the world is a chaotic one". Xun Kuang has not repeated Mencius's "mental work

75 *Mencius*, I.A.1.
76 Ibid., III.A.4.
77 Ibid., II.A.3.

and manual work" theory, but he continues to use the saying "Gentlemen live by Dao, while mean persons live by strength"; on the same theme: "Gentlemen exist by morality while mean persons exist by strength. Strength is the servant of morality."[78] Xun Kuang therefore reproduces the viewpoints of Confucius and Mencius on *junzi* versus *xiaoren* and "mental work versus manual work".

The Confucian treatment of production is actually a sort of ethical production outlook. Such thinking has influenced Chinese history for thousands of years, becoming a great impediment to the development of a commodity economy.

Daoists usually return to and hide in the countryside, mountains and forest, and labour for themselves; thus, judging from their practice, they are active practitioners of productive labour. Judging from their sayings, they may seem to take a negative attitude but, on our analysis, their negativity is chiefly targeted on the labour that serves and provides the rulers with luxurious consumer products. As for all sorts of productive labour in conformity with the order of nature, Daoists not only take part in it themselves but advocate it actively. Yang Zhu stands for "moving with the heart, not disobeying the trend of nature". That is, so long as we do not go against natural law, any production activity is necessary because "if people do not wear clothes and eat food, there will be no order of king and his ministers". If people wear no clothes and eat no food, the relationship between king and ministers will no longer exist. In his view, the chief reasons why "the people cannot get proper rest" are the following: "first, working for longevity; second, for reputation; third, for status; fourth, for materials".[79] Because people work for materials they are afraid of "penalty". It is obvious that "working for materials" refers to working for wealth for the ruling class. To such productive labour Yang Zhu takes an understandably negative attitude.

Laozi's attitude towards agricultural production that conforms to natural law is quite positive. He clearly regards as undesirable a situation in which "the fields are overrun with darnel" and "granaries are empty", and suggests that "When the world has the Way, trotting horses are used for their dung", meaning that when Dao prevails there will be no need for galloping war-horses, which can be used solely for the purposes of farming.[80] Judging from this, Laozi does not oppose agricultural production. However, as to the handicraft industry and commercial production, Laozi basically holds a negative attitude.

Laozi declares: "When the people have more sharp weapons, then the state is disordered. When others have more cunning and tricks, then strange things arise. When laws and commands are promulgated, then brigands and robbers will be more."[81] Another saying of his is: "Do not value rare things, so the people will not be robbers or thieves".[82] Laozi's opposition to handicraft production and commerce is not something in the general sense but has its own special meaning.

---

78 *Xunzi, passim.*
79 "Lie Zi" Chapter of *Yang Zhu.*
80 *Daodejing*, 53, 46.
81 Ibid., 57.
82 Ibid., 3.

Laozi's philosophy is "Way of Heaven and Nature", laying stress on the natural essence of things, but handicraft production is changing the form and structure of natural things to meet people's needs and is therefore to be avoided. Additionally, handicraft production is undertaken not to provide necessities for the common people but rather luxury goods for the rulers. Laozi opposes the extravagance and luxurious life of the aristocracy and their cruel exploitation of the people. Hence he takes a negative attitude towards production for the rulers' consumption.

Zhuangzi pursues the ideal of standing aloof from worldly affairs, believing that all types of political system are meant to enchain or damage human nature. He takes a nihilistic attitude towards economic activity. Although he thinks that "Weaving to make clothes and farming to make food are virtuous things", and has nothing contemptuous to say about agricultural production, yet he believes all activities of farming, industry and commerce stress the body and spirit and enslave people to things of the world.

> When farmers have no cultivation to do, they will not be able to live and work in peace and contentment; when merchants have no trading to do, they will not feel happy. So long as people have something to be busy about, they will be diligent; so long as artisans have some machinery to operate, they will feel good because of improvement of efficiency.... All these people are bound to their jobs and cannot change for all their life. Thus, their body and spirit keep moving and moving, they have sunken into things and cannot come back all their life. How sad it is!

Especially, he looks down on handicraft production and commercial activities as he believes all such things are damaging human nature or the nature of things. In his opinion, "if we cannot destroy the natural material, how can we make a utensil? If we do not destroy the white jade, how can we make jade-ware? It is the artisan's guilt to break natural materials to make utensils." His attitude to wealth production is that we need not make artificial things, nor need we use more of our strength. Let everything take its natural course. Do not let our body be stressed by materials, do not enslave ourselves to the material life. We should "let our mind wander in simplicity, blend our spirit with the vastness, follow along with things the way they are, and make no room for personal views".[83] Thus, Zhuangzi's attitude to handicraft production and commercial activities shares a similar basis to Laozi's: handicraft industry and commercial activities have violated nature and changed the essentiality of natural matter.

Trading

One of the greatest contrasts between Confucianism and Daoism in economic thought might be considered their outlook on trading. Confucians engage with real life, hence their response to the developing commodity economy of the time was

---

83 *Zhuangzi*, "Fit for Emperors and Kings".

to accept it on their own terms. In contrast, Daoists take an idealistic, passive and escapist attitude to economic life and were basically opposed to the development of the commodity economy. Having determined that commodity exchange and circulation were activities violating natural law they took an evasive attitude and had virtually nothing to say about such phenomena. It would seem that the exchange of commodities was the subject that Daoists wished to discuss the least.

Confucius recognised the existence of different trades in society. Although he belittled manual labour he did not oppose commodity circulation and exchange. One of his disciples, Zi Gong, was a great merchant in the kingdom of Wei, and Confucius's reputation was attributed, to a large extent, to this rich disciple engaged in commodity transactions: it was Zi Gong who basically supplied Confucius with the financial means to travel from state to state. Hence, Confucius understood the importance of commerce and he not only had no objection to it but also held a supporting attitude. He praised highly Zi Gong's great talent in commerce. He also argued against the policy of Zang Wenzhong (a high-ranking official) of "setting six passes" to impede the exchange and circulation of commodities, saying that Zang Wenzhong was not benevolent. Thus we can see that Confucius approves of, or at least does not oppose, free trade. It is also interesting to note that Confucius compared himself to a commodity:

> Zigong said: "Suppose there is a beautiful jade here, does one wrap it up, put it in a box and keep it, or does one try to get a good price and sell it?" The Master said: "Sell it of course, sell it of course! I am one who is waiting for a price [i.e. an offer]".[84]

If he was antagonistic to exchange and circulation of commodities, Confucius would never have used such a comparison. Finally, the *Analects* contain no evidence of Confucius's opposition to the exchange and circulation of commodities.

Mencius is even more unambiguously positive towards the exchange of commodities and among the thinkers in the pre-Qin period his ideas on trade are the most outstanding, save for some comments in the book *Guanzi*. The importance of trading was clarified by Mencius as follows:

> If people cannot trade the surplus of the fruits of their labours to satisfy one another's needs, then the farmer will be left with surplus grain and the woman with surplus cloth. If things are exchanged, you can feed the carpenter and the carriage-maker.[85]

Mencius's argument on exchanging products between different trades is correct.[86] First, he has realised that in a society with division of work it is only by exchange of commodities can people benefit each other. Second, Mencius seems

---

84 *Analects*, IX.13.
85 *Mencius*, III.B.4.
86 Marx, *Capital*, Volume 1, 1953, pp. 441–443.

to have had some vague cognition about something or other hidden in the exchange of commodities:

> That things are unequal is part of their nature. Some are worth twice or five times, ten or a hundred times, even a thousand and ten thousand times, more than others. If you reduce them to the same level, it will only bring confusion to the Empire.[87]

In Mencius's observation that "things are unequal [as] part of their nature" there seems to be a very vague concept of value (it could not have been anything more than a vague concept given the historical circumstances). He seems to have realised that there is something contained in the commodity and that it is just this "something" that makes the prices of different commodities vary by tens, hundreds or even thousands of times.

Third, Mencius opposes "monopoly" in exchange of commodities:

> In antiquity, the market was for the exchange of what one had for what one lacked. The authorities merely supervised it. There was, however, a despicable fellow who always looked for a vantage point and, going up on it, gazed into the distance to the left and to the right in order to secure for himself all the profit there was in the market. The people all thought him despicable, and, as a result, they taxed him. The taxing of traders began with this despicable fellow.[88]

Although Mencius refers only to the monopoly by some "despicable" merchant, completely different from the capitalistic monopoly of modern times, it was Mencius who brought up the concept for the first time in history. Although we have no way to prove Mencius's claim that the levying of tax on commerce began in such a way, we can see his idea of stressing normal exchange and circulation of commodities.

Although Xunzi advocates encouraging agriculture and repressing commerce, he has a clear understanding of the social function and role of commerce. He thinks that it is just because of exchange of commodities that

> farmers do not have to carve or chisel, to fire or forge, and yet they have all the tools and utensils they need; the artisans and merchants do not have to work the fields, and yet they have plenty of vegetables and grain.[89]

Therefore, he suggests that at "barriers and in markets, the officials shall examine the goods but levy no tax"; furthermore, if the law is impartial and

---

87 *Mencius*, III.A.4.
88 Ibid., II.B.10. [Irene Bloom (New York: Columbia University Press, 2009) gives "greedy" in place of "despicable".]
89 *Xunzi*, "The Regulations of a King".

everyone "acts in accordance with the rules and regulations, then wealth and goods will increase and the state will automatically grow rich"[90] Xunzi thinks commerce is indispensable to the domestic social economy. But, even more noteworthy, he also recognised the importance of foreign trade. In his opinion, trading can cause goods to be circulated and people of each industry can obtain commodities needed by them and produced by others. How to trade? Xun Kuang advocates an equal transaction so as to let both vendor and purchaser suffer no loss, namely, "the trader trades one thing for another thing with equal value, so that no one will gain more or suffer a loss". If we were to "trade one for two" there would be "no loss but gain"; on the contrary, if we "trade two for one", there is "no gain but loss".[91] We have no way to tell what Xun Kuang means exactly by "one" or "two". Is it the "value" or the "price"? But at least we can find from his saying "with neither gain nor loss" that he has discovered the "equal nature" of exchange of commodities, just like Aristotle. On such a basis, Xunzi advocates great development of foreign trade as he thinks it can supply what the homeland cannot produce. In his chapter "The Regulations of a King", he depicts a fine prospect in which each country exports various goods to China. However, according to his trading principle that the "trader trades one for one", he has not mentioned whether China paid in currency or in kind for the trade. Evidently, this is a reflection of Xunzi's optimistic spirit of "the entire world is like one family" in his thought on trading.

Contrary to the strongly positive character of the Confucian outlook on trading, Daoists basically take a negative attitude, proposing a self-sufficient life that is faithful to "nature". Yang Zhu advocates "letting all bodies of the world be public, and letting all things of the world be public". When everything is publically owned, of course, there will be no need for exchange. He advocates "valuing the ego", and even if "valuing the ego" requires "luxurious house, beautiful attire and thick taste", he would not propose "seeking from the outside". But this raises a puzzle: how could Yang Zhu get his "luxurious house, beautiful attire and thick taste" *without* "seeking from the outside"? By one person's self-sufficiency it is evident that he cannot reach that state. Even exploitation belongs to "seeking from the outside". Laozi suggests a small state with few people: "although there are ships and carriages, no one should ride them", "people [of neighbouring states] reach old age without meeting each other"[92]: such a picture of life would seem to have no place for the exchange of commodities. Zhuangzi takes a similarly negative attitude towards commodity exchange activities. Evidently, these views derive from the Daoist philosophy of the "Way of Heaven and Nature".

90 Ibid.
91 Ibid., "Rectifying Names".
92 *Daodejing*, 80.

Allocation

In their outlook on wealth allocation, Confucians and Daoists have something in common to the extent that both advocate "sharing evenly", but their emphasis differs. In Confucius's time, the opposition of the poor and the rich had already become a social problem. In his opinion, "If one acts with a view to profit, there will be much resentment".[93] That is, limitlessly seeking wealth will result in resentment among people and social unrest. But poverty will also lead to resentment: "To avoid resentment when one is poor is difficult".[94] Therefore, Confucius's opinion is that in order to maintain social stability we must solve the problem of unfair wealth distribution among people, that is, practice the policy of an "even allocation" among the poor. He says:

> Those having a country or a family do not worry about too little wealth, they only worry about unevenness in the allocation of wealth; they do not worry about too few people, only worry about unrest in the country. If the wealth is allocated evenly, there will be no poverty. If the country is at peace, we shall not feel people are too few. If peace prevails, the country will not be in danger[95]

Here, obviously, what Confucius suggests about allocation among the poor is a viewpoint from the ruling class: an exhortation to allocate the limited wealth among the working people so as to avoid social unrest caused by great disparity between rich and poor. Poor and rich are relative to each other. Wealth is limited. If we allocate it unevenly, letting some people occupy the wealth of others, the other people will look even poorer. Confucius's purpose is to solve the uneven allocation problem among the poor. The ruling class is not within the scope of his proposal. So, with regard to this problem, Confucius has also taken some supplementary measures in ethical preaching. He educates the working people to "be content with poverty", asking the exploited working people to "know their fate", they should be able to "be happy in poverty", "have no resentment although poor".[96] With regard to the exploiting class, they should "be rich but not smug", "rich but good-mannered".[97] In this way, the world will be at peace and the society will maintain its stability.

---

93 *Analects*, IV.12.
94 *Analects*, XIV.10.
95 [The references to "wealth" would appear to be interpolations by the author. For the interpretation of *Analects* XVI.1 see above, p. 10].
96 [These are not direct textual references; rather, they are allusions to the following:

> A man of quality indeed was Hui! He lived in a squalid alley with a tiny bowlful of rice to eat and a ladleful of water to drink. Other men would not endure such hardships, but Hui did not let his happiness be affected. A man of quality indeed was Hui!

> (*Analects*, VI.11).]

97 *Analects*, XVI.5, also XIV.10.

Xunzi's allocation thinking was developed on the basis of Confucius's "equal allocation to eliminate poverty" idea. In Xunzi's opinion, Mother Nature has provided sufficient food for mankind's existence:

> The farmers plough in spring, weed in summer, reap in autumn, and store away in winter. Because they do each at the proper season, there is a never-ending supply of grain and the people have more than enough to eat. Because the lakes and rivers are watched over carefully and closed off at the proper time, there is an ever-increasing supply of fish and other water creatures and the people have more than they can use. Because the felling of trees and cutting of brush is done only at the proper time, the hills are never denuded and yet the people have all the wood they can use[98]

Therefore, he thinks it is virtually impossible for poverty to appear. If it does appear, it is only because of "improper conduct" associated with social breakdown: "Men, once born, must organise themselves into a society. But if they form a society without hierarchical division, then there will be quarrelling ["improper conduct"]. Where there is quarrelling, there will be chaos".[99] Moreover, "Man is born with desires. If his desires are not satisfied for him, he cannot but seek some means to satisfy them himself. If there are no limits or degrees to his seeking, then he will inevitably fall to wrangling with other men. From wrangling comes disorder".[100] He regards the root of the working people's poverty as "improper conduct", and it is improper conduct that leads to social chaos and to even greater poverty. Just like Confucius, then, he associates poverty with social chaos. Hence, Xun Kuang's allocation theory also centres on the problem of "sharing out evenly to eliminate poverty" among the working people. He also affirms the reasonableness of the difference between poor and rich, believing that one of the fundamental ways to keep the order of the world is that there must be "distinctions between rich and poor, eminent and humble".[101] The comparative wealth of the ruling class is essential: if they are not wealthy, society will lose control and chaos will ensue. At the same time, the poverty of the ruled class should be "compensated, by cutting the surplus to make up for the shortage", so as to even the wealth among "the poor". Hence, Xunzi's allocation idea contains two elements: first, we should admit the difference between rich and poor; second, for the ruled class, we should "even the wealth to eliminate poverty". We can see the Xunzi's ideas on allocation are based on the Confucian ethic of social rank and distinction.

Contrary to Confucian ideas about allocation, which were concerned mainly with the condition of working people, the views of Daoists were targeted chiefly on the rich. The key proposition for Daoists is "Even the Wealth". Starting from

98 *Xunzi*, "The Regulations of a King".
99 Ibid.
100 Ibid., "A Discussion of Rites".
101 Ibid.

the "Way of Heaven and Nature", Laozi believes that the natural law is to oppose any surplus ("to lose the surplus to make up for the shortage"). Therefore, we should follow the natural law to "even the riches". In his words: "The way of heaven takes from what has too much to provide for what does not have enough."[102] But how is that to be done? Laozi advises the rich that they should stop seeking wealth artificially, as artificial seeking of wealth violates the natural law according to the way of Heaven. The rich should follow the example of the sage: "The Sage does not store: having done all for others, he has yet still more; having given all to others, he has yet made more".[103] In Laozi's opinion, so long as we can keep to the above principles we shall conform to the natural law and reach the aim of sharing out riches. Hence: "Heaven and earth came down together to send down sweet dew; though none among the people commanded them, they spread it evenly by themselves."[104] Laozi's wish may be regarded as admirable, yet the fact that he uses natural law to explain the distribution of wealth reflects his weakness in solving problems in real life.

Zhuangzi also advocates "sharing out riches" based on the "Way of Heaven and Nature": "When you are rich, you should divide your wealth with others"; "When all people in the world benefit together, it will be called 'happiness' indeed, and when all people offer to share their possessions, it will be called 'peace' in the real sense".[105]

In summary, the difference between Confucian and Daoist thought on matters of distribution may be put as follows. At bottom, the Confucian idea of "sharing out evenly to eliminate poverty" is an anaesthetic to the working people. It is designed to eliminate *relative* poverty from within their ranks so as to reduce "chaos" and leave the social hierarchy intact. It is therefore something that would be welcomed by the ruling class. In sharp contrast, Daoists seek to eliminate disparities of wealth between the rulers and the ruled. Their aim of "sharing out riches to everyone" is a fighting dagger as far as the working people are concerned and as such it became deeply loved by the peasantry.

Consumption

Confucians and Daoists superficially agree about consumption to the extent that both advocate thrift and oppose extravagance. Yet, as in other areas, each school of thinkers has its own distinctive position. As ever, the Confucian outlook is based on its ethical philosophy whereas the Daoist outlook is based on the philosophy of the "Way of Heaven and Nature".

According to Mr Hu Jichuang, Confucius's position on consumption has two main aspects: the general principle is to be content with one's lot, and the specific standard of consumption is to be "thrifty without violating courtesy" and

---

102 *Daodejing*, 77.
103 Ibid., 81.
104 Ibid., 32.
105 *Zhuangzi*, Chapter "Of Heaven and Earth".

"consuming without damaging justice". Evidently, such ideas have a clear ethical character that is closely related to "courtesy" and "justice" and has a typical feature of didacticism. On the whole, these doctrines are directed at the ruling class. The working people have no reliable supply even of clothes and food, so the injunctions to be "thrifty without violating courtesy" and to consume "without damaging justice" would hardly apply to them. As far as they are concerned, the only relevant points from Confucius's teaching are to be content and happy with poverty. In the specific standard of consumption, Confucius, from the point of view of maintaining the feudal order, holds that "If people are extravagant, they will look haughty, but being thrifty can make them stable. Being stable is much better than being haughty". Between "extravagant" and "thrifty", of course, Confucius prefers "thrifty". But he does not advocate unbounded thrift: "thrift" should not violate "courtesy". For example, Yan Zi wore the same fur coat for thirty years and although he was praised by Confucius for his thriftiness he was also deemed to have been *too* thrifty. The thriftiness Confucius advocated should conform to standards of "courtesy" in the rank order of feudal society. When Zi Gong wanted to save sheep for the purpose of sacrificing them to god, Confucius said "You love your sheep more: but I love courtesy more". Of course, "loving courtesy" does not mean extravagance: "In courtesy, it is better to be frugal rather than lavish".[106] In personal living consumption, on the one hand, he requires that a "gentleman avoids seeking to satisfy his appetite to the full when he eats and avoid seeking comfort when he is at home", and even should not be "ashamed of bad clothes and bad food".[107] His disciple Yan Hui "lived in a squalid alley with a tiny bowlful of rice to eat and a ladleful of water to drink ... but Hui did not let his happiness be affected", so he praises Yan Hui as "a man of quality".[108] When Ji Lu "did not feel ashamed when he was in a shabby gown together with a man in luxurious fur coat", he also praised him greatly.[109] Yet, on the other hand, he thinks that personal consumption must be banded together with personal position so as not to lower oneself. For himself, he arranged his clothes according to his status.[110] In food and drink, he advised that in "choosing food, the finer, the better; in choosing meat, the more elegantly cooked, the better".[111] When fish had turned rotten he refused to eat; when food had discoloured or smelled badly, he would not eat.[112] He even declared: "After I become an official, I will not go on foot".[113] So we can see that his standard of personal consumption is class-oriented.

Xunzi's position is much the same as Confucius's as he also advocates thrift and his standard of consumption also conforms to the ethic of social rank order.

106 *Analects*, III.4.
107 Ibid., I.14, IV4.9.
108 Ibid., VI.11.
109 Ibid., IX.27.
110 Ibid., X.5.
111 Ibid., X.8.
112 Ibid., X.6.
113 Ibid., XI.8.

But Xunzi's argument on consumption has more characteristics of a theory. He regards thrift as a means to struggle with nature and make the country rich and strong: "If you encourage agriculture and are frugal in your expenditure, then Heaven cannot make you poor.... But if you neglect agriculture and spend lavishly, then Heaven cannot make you rich".[114]

Xunzi regards "enriching the people through thriftiness" as a way to enrich the country, believing that through thrift it was possible to make the country's riches pile up like mountains. Just like Confucius, however, Xunzi does not advocate excessive thrift, deeming that if it develops to such a degree as to involve eating bad food, wearing shabby clothes and having no amusements at all it would be called "too weak nourishment" or "too poor life". Starting from the presumption that the feudal hierarchy must be maintained, he emphasises that thrift is not so necessary for the ruling class. In his opinion, if the ruling class are as thrifty as common people they will lose their stateliness; when they have lost their stateliness, it will be impossible for them to execute rewards and punishments; when rewards and punishments cannot be administered, worthy people will not be promoted and unworthy people will not be demoted; people will not give full play to their special skills so production will not go smoothly and the country will not become rich. Only by the normal execution of rewards and punishments can we make everyone bring their strong points fully into play, perform good jobs in production and make the country affluent. In talking about the relationship between thrift and production, Xunzi still has in mind the dignity of feudal ranks. As for the specific standard of consumption, Xunzi suggests that the main requirement is to permit a clear distinction between the different social ranks. In clothing, therefore, there is no need to seek an extremely attractive appearance providing that a distinction can be made between high and low; similarly in habitation, the main requirements are that a dwelling should prevent dryness and humidity and distinguish between the nobility and the lowly; as for food, it will be sufficient if it provides adequate nourishment. Evidently, Xunzi's advice on consumption was directed at the ruling class rather than ordinary working people.

Daoists also advocated thrift and the removal of extravagance but in their case the arguments were based on the interpretation of natural law and "Way of Heaven" and contained no tinge of ethical preaching. As we might expect, the Daoist idea of removing extravagance and keeping thrifty was targeted at ruling-class extravagance, corruption and cruel exploitation of working people. Laozi advocates little desire and regards thrift as one of the three essentials in life. In his opinion, "In governing others and serving heaven, there is nothing like storing".[115] As for the standard of consumption, Laozi maintains that so long as we can "fill the stomach" and "strengthen the bones" it will be enough, and he argues against an extravagant life that may "weaken one's mind" and "weaken one's will". In Laozi's opinion: "The five colours turn a man's eyes blind; the

---

114 *Xunzi*, "A Discussion of Heaven".
115 *Daodejing*, 59.

five notes turn a man's ears deaf; the five tastes turn a man's palate dull; racing through fields hunting turns a man's heart wild; goods hard to obtain cause a man's progress to halt."[116] Extravagant creature comforts bewilder the will of the people.

Zhuangzi goes even further than Laozi. He advises reducing human life to the level of animals, believing that so long as we "minimise expenses, and minimise the desires, even if we have little grain, it will be enough for our living".[117]

Influence of Confucian and Daoist economic thought on later generations

We do not propose to deal with the influence of Confucian and Daoist philosophy on later generations, a topic that has received much scholarly attention elsewhere. Rather, we focus here on the legacy of Confucian and Daoist economic thinking.

Of the nine schools and ten sects of thought in the pre-Qin period, each has left some economic viewpoints to the world. Although these ideas are scattered and have not formed into complete and systematic theories of economics, they are important legacies in China's economic thought and the arguments on some issues are profound. After the Qin and Han dynasties, when feudal rulers of all ages considered managing state affairs and restoring peace to the people, and when thinkers discoursed on economic matters or carried out economic reform, most of them went back to the arguments of pre-Qin thinkers to seek inspiration and guidance. Therefore, in more than 2,000 years from the Qin and Han dynasties until the middle of the nineteenth century, China's economic thinking never broke from the fundamental categories and frameworks proposed by the pre-Qin thinkers even though the ideas were progressively enriched and developed with the passage of time. As Mr Hu Jichuang remarks, although pre-Qin economic thought did not lay out an impassable limit to the classical school of political economy, as David Ricardo did for European economics, it depicted a rough outline for the later development of economic thought in feudal times.

All schools and sects of economic thought in the pre-Qin period exerted some influence on later generations, but we have contended that there are only two major schools of significance, Confucianism and Daoism.[118] Since the Western Han dynasty, when Dong Zhongshu's suggestion of "Rejecting all schools of thought, and only respecting Confucianism" was adopted by the government, Confucianism began to take the official orthodox position in Chinese feudal society and became the dominant paradigm for managing state affairs, including financial matters. The influence of Confucian economic thought on the authorities was very great indeed, as all thinkers of all ages would quote the sayings of pre-Qin Confucian thinkers, especially Confucius's sayings on economic

116 Ibid., 12.
117 *Zhuangzi*, chapter "On Mountain Forest".
118 Hu Jichuang, *China's Economic Ideological History* Part I, p. 508.

matters, when they deliberated matters of governing and financing. The influence was mainly shown in the following respects.

First, there was the practice of using ethics to regulate economic activities, namely the so-called "justice–profit" thinking. When thinkers of subsequent generations holding Confucian ideas talked about economic activities they either said "We should seldom talk about profit" or "Why do we need to talk about profit?" or "Gentlemen understand justice while mean persons understand profit". Such a predominant idea characterised by restriction of economic activity became a major cause of the slow development of the commodity economy in China's feudal society.

Second, there was the belittling of manual labour. As representative statements of this idea from Confucius we have: "Why do we use farming?"; "Gentlemen are engaged in Dao, instead of food"; "By farming, people will still hunger, but by learning people can get reward"; "Gentlemen only worry about Dao, not about poverty". From Mencius: "Mental workers govern others while manual workers are governed by others"; "The governed feed others while the governors are fed by others". And from Xunzi: "Gentlemen live by morals while lowly persons live by strength". All those sayings represent the viewpoint of belittling manual labour and labouring people and such a perspective exerted a great influence in China's feudal society. In the minds of intellectuals of the feudal society, accordingly, such ideas came into being as "Books contain gold rooms naturally" and "Books contain beauties as pretty as jade", which became a direct reason for "attending school to become officials" in feudal society. It seems possible, therefore, that the belittling of labour in China's traditional culture was of Confucian origin.

Third, there is Confucian allocation thinking – "not worrying about poverty, but worrying about unevenness of distribution" – which was the root of equalitarianism in China's feudal society. Such thinking may be considered as an advanced idea at its inception but it was to become a barrier to economic development.

Fourth, the Confucian finance principle was to govern the economic development of feudal society, even becoming a golden rule. For example, "If the common people are rich, no emperor will be poor"; the principle of "reserving riches in the people"; the light taxation policy of "10 per cent tax" and "removing customs duties"; the economic proposition of "saving the expenses and expanding the sources" and so on, were favoured by thinkers of all dynasties and worshipped as guidelines for financing by rulers of all ages.

Fifth, there was the "Great Harmony" idea. The influence of cosmopolitism (Great Harmony) has been chiefly shown in recent times, being utilised by some progressive thinkers as a tool to rebel against the feudal ruling class. We may name Hong Xiuquan, Kang Youwei and Sun Yatsen as having been deeply influenced by cosmopolitism thinking.

Sixth, we have the idea of valuing agriculture and repressing commerce. Valuing agriculture has had no negative effect but the repression of commerce has been damaging. Although thinkers of the Legalist School, such as Shang

Yang, also adopted a policy of repressing industry and commerce, it was Confucian thinkers who explained this idea from the viewpoint of economic theory. The slow development of industry and commerce in China's feudal society was directly related to the agriculture-valuing and industry/commerce-repressing policy advocated by Confucian thinkers and implemented by rulers of successive dynasties.

As for Daoists, they were mostly out of political office and were usually hermits, critical of current politics. Their thinking influenced people in other ways. Unlike Confucian economic thought, which was advocated and spread publically and used for the management of state affairs, Daoist thought was spread silently among the common people chiefly through the folk channel, exerting a subtle influence on people's minds, habits and customs. Daoist economic thought was mostly characterised by cynicism and rejection of existing society, hence it has held a strong attraction for rebellious movements against feudal rulers.

The influence of Daoist economic thought on people of later generations is shown chiefly in the following aspects.

First, the approach of Daoist thinkers to the observation and analysis of social and economic life in terms of the "Way of Heaven and Nature" and "No doing" had a great influence in the restoration of regimes. If Daoist thought is sifted for ideas that could be used for governing a state, the chief point is quietism as epitomised in the expression, "Let the emperor sit quietly facing the south". At the beginning of the Han dynasty, after more than 200 years of fighting in the Warring States period and the great chaos at the end of the Qin dynasty, the country was in a broken state and the people's livelihood was in a miserable condition. According to Sima Qian's *Records of the Grand Historian*:

> When the Han dynasty came to power, it inherited the evils left by the Qin. The able-bodied men were all away with the army, while the old and under-aged busily transported supplies for them. There was much hard work and little wealth. The Son of Heaven himself could not find four horses of the same colour to draw his carriage, many of his generals and ministers were reduced to riding about in ox carts, and the common people had nothing to lay away in their storehouses.[119]

In such a state, the national strength and financial resources of the people could not provide for the construction of many new buildings. The rulers at the beginning period of the Han dynasty therefore adopted the "Way of [Emperor] Huang and Lao" characterised by rehabilitating together with the people. Such a kingcraft suited the administration of an agricultural society in which everything went on naturally so long as people followed the right farming seasons. The prime minister of the time, Cao Can, merely observed Huang and Lao's way of "Keeping quiet and letting the people settle things by themselves". Emperor

119 *Shi Ji*, 30, "The Treatise on the Balanced Standard".

Wen, Emperor Jing, the Empress and many other rulers were attracted to Daoism. In the seventy years at the beginning of the Han dynasty, Daoist thought was implemented in practical politics and worshipped as the national religion. Thus, the poverty-stricken country became rich; the royal barns were brimming over with grain; the coins in the national treasury were spread all over the ground when being taken as the old rope was broken; in the street, people lived a very rich life with surplus food and meat. Daoist thinking was applied to actual politics openly for the first time and was remarkably successful. Later, at the beginning of each dynasty, the way of Huang and Lao was used for actual politics from time to time, although it was not worshipped so much as it had been in the Han dynasty. For example, during the Song dynasty, Emperor Zhenzong used the quietism of Huang and Lao's politics to administrate the country. Also, Sima Guang, the famous statesman in the Song dynasty, advocated a policy of "quietness and tranquillity".

Second, there was the influence of "Inaction" on laissez-faire thought. Laozi's "Inaction (No Doing) [*wu-wei*]" thought is one of the great bases of economic laissez-faire in all ages. Sima Qian's laissez-faire thinking was directly a result of following the "Way of Huang and Lao".

Third, the critical aspects of Daoist ideas such as "sharing out riches", opposing the feudal rulers' greed and so on, were to become an enlightening influence on the progressive classes in subsequent generations as well as thinking weapons for the peasantry of all ages to criticise their cruel exploitation by the feudal ruling class. For example, the peasants' uprising at the end of the Han dynasty used precisely this Daoist viewpoint as their fighting banner. Almost all the ideas and fighting slogans of peasants' uprisings of all ages, such as "even allocation" and "sharing out riches", were products of the direct or indirect influence of Daoist thought. Daoist thinkers have a close affiliation with the common people and often sharply criticised the entire feudal system.[120] Their behavioural model includes rebellion against all kinds of tradition and custom, retiring from political life, refusing to take up any official position, and a close contact with the common people. It is understandable that their thinking was eagerly accepted by leaders of peasant uprisings.

Fourth, there has been the influence of Daoist ideas of "pure heart and few desires" and "serene life without seeking fame and wealth" upon the customs of the Chinese people. Such an influence has both active and passive aspects. The active significance is that it has helped the Chinese people to cultivate a virtue characterised by simple living, self-contentment and a peaceful life without struggling with others. Chinese people keep a simple diet and live a basic existence with few desires and little selfishness. Most people can live in peace with each other, are satisfied with what they have, keep happy and fear no hardships. In terms of the passive influence, however, it has resulted in the inert mentality of the Chinese, their lack of an aggressive spirit, which has impeded the development of a commodity economy. Especially, the influence on the state of mind

120 See Joseph Needham, *Science and Civilization in China*, pp. 36–37.

of intellectuals is very obvious. Why were there so many hermits, monks, nuns and Daoist priests in ancient China? We should say it is just a result of such thinking.

Fifth, there is the influence of the idea of "valuing the ego and respecting life". Daoism regards nature as fundamental and values human life. In Daoism, there is no distinction between high and low; as an element of the natural world, everyone is equal. Hence the saying: "Dao is great, Heaven is great, Earth is great, and Humankind is also great". In politics, Daoist thinkers oppose feudal tyranny and autocracy, emphasise the value of individual existence and advocate the full development of individuals, thus exhibiting features of democracy. The development in ancient times of China's rich and varied cuisine, as well as Qigong, acupuncture and traditional medicine, were all closely related to the Daoist idea of "Valuing the ego and respecting life".

Sixth, Daoist thinking had a significant influence on the development of science and technology as the major productive power. Many ancient branches of learning in China, such as chemistry, mineralogy, biology and medical science, originated from Daoist thinkers' explorations of nature. Daoist thinking also contributed to the protection of the natural ecological environment.

In conclusion, we can say that the economic thought of Confucianism and Daoism has influenced and dominated the economic life of feudal society in China and continues to exercise an influence and domination even to the present day. Looking to the future, however, that influence is likely to diminish as the impact of Western civilisation on China becomes gradually more prevalent.

7 The start of family economics of Chinese feudal landowners

On Jia Sixie's *Important Arts for People's Welfare*[1]

Zheng Xueyi

The landlord family economics elaborated in Jia Sixie's *Qi Min Yao Shu*[2] is composed of three parts: "Profession to Make a Living" (*Zhi Sheng Zhi Dao*[3]) is the selection of family business objects, approach and related theories; "Principles to Make a Living" (*Zhi Sheng Zhi Li*[4]) means understanding the theories and rules of private management; "Strategies to Make a Living" *(Zhi Sheng Zhi Ce*[5]) refers to the methods and measures of microeconomics. The theoretical framework constituted by the above three parts laid the foundation and pointed the direction for the formation and development of China's feudal landlord family economics.

Most of the economic thought inherited from ancient China attempted to explore the way of economic management for the purpose of increasing revenue and social wealth from the national perspective. The state-based economic thought developed in the form of the "Theory of Enriching Countries" (*Fu Guo Xue*). Compared with this thought, family-based economic thought reflected in the "Theory of Making Wealth" was not very well developed. However, China's ancient family economics still contains some valuable insights. The theory of increasing the wealth of landlords in Jia Sixie's *Qi Min Yao Shu*[6] is a case in point.

China's ancient family economics ("Theory of Increasing Wealth"[7]) was originated by the Commercialist School in the pre-Qin period with the representative figures of Tao Zhugong and Bai Gui. What they discussed was how to make a fortune by doing business. Therefore, the early "Theory of Increasing Wealth" was actually the mercantile "Theory for Making a Living" or mercantile family economics.

---

1 Originally published as "中国封建地主家庭经济学的产生 – 论贾思勰的《齐民要术》" ("The Start of Family Economics of Chinese Feudal Landowners: On Jia Sixie's *Important Arts for People's Welfare*"), *The Economist*, 1993 Issue 2, pp. 117–128.
2 齐民要术, written in Northern Wei dynasty (between 30s and 40s of the sixth century AD).
3 治生之道
4 治生之理
5 治生之策.
6 齐民要术, as explained in footnote 1.
7 治生之学.

Since merchants could not create a new mode of production, commercial and merchant capital must be incorporated into the historical track of feudal economic development. In the Western Han dynasty, with the development and consolidation of feudal landlords' ownership as well as the further growth of the forces of merchant capital, the merchants, as a subordinate class to landlords, often became landlords through buying land with the wealth obtained by business. Sima Qian summarised the process as follows: "To acquire wealth by managing business, and to keep it through acquisition of land and engagement in agriculture".[8] This position clearly reflected the requirement in the early stage of China's feudal society to transform the capital of the merchant into landed property, which indicated the transition from the mercantile "Theory of Making Wealth" to the landlord's "Theory for Making a Living".

However, Sima Qian did not offer any specific analysis or discussion of how to run the landlord economy to maintain and expand private wealth, and he did not even touch upon this issue, which means that his "Theory of Increasing Wealth" was not the landlords' "Theory for Making a Living". That transition did not occur until the publication of Jia Sixie's *Qi Min Yao Shu*[9] in the Northern Wei dynasty.

Qi Min Yao Shu comprises nine volumes and ninety-two chapters with more than 110,000 characters in total. It quoted more than 150 works from both previous and contemporary times and collected the technical knowledge of agricultural production from historical documents. Therefore, it became the earliest and most comprehensive work on agricultural science in China and occupies an important position in the history of world agriculture.

According to the explanation of Jia Sixie himself, *Qi* expresses the same meaning as "common", and *Qi Min* means "common people". *Qi Min Yao Shu* indicates the way for citizens to earn their livelihood. In feudal society, as the old saying goes, "hunger breeds discontent", and agriculture was the most important sector of production. For the livelihood of ordinary people it was not only necessary to study and understand the technical knowledge of agricultural production but also to pay attention to farm management taking the family as the unit, which was within the scope of landlords' "Theory for Make a Living". Therefore, it is not enough just to regard *Qi Min Yao Shu* as the most ancient and comprehensive work on agriculture. It is also the first work to discuss landlord family management in China's feudal society, which initiated the landlords' "Theory for Making a Living".

It was not by accident that landlord family economics in ancient China was formed in the Northern Wei dynasty. Among the landlords from the Warring States period to the early Han dynasty, a noble class with official posts together with bureaucratic landlords occupied a relatively large proportion of the society. With high status, their incomes were composed of three parts: a salary rewarded by the feudal dynasty, predatory wealth based on their status, and land rent based

---

8 *Records of the Grand Historian,* "The Biographies of the Money-Makers".
9 齐民要术, as explained in footnote 1.

on the exploitation of peasants. Although these dignitaries owned large amounts of land and earned rents from them it was easier to collect wealth and reputation through prestigious titles and salary. Besides, for these aristocrats and bureaucratic landlords with prominent identity and high status, the main duty was to "explore common sense, morality and justice", which means entering politics and governing people. "Working for food" activities, such as land management and rent extraction from dependent peasants, were carried out by their housekeepers and servants. The aristocrats, bureaucratic landlords and their counterpart intellectuals did not care about such practical matters at all. They despised "managing and increasing the wealth inherited from ancestors", let alone doing academic research on "making a living by agriculture". Under these circumstances, it was impossible for the landlords' "Theory for Making a Living" to be generated among the aristocrats, bureaucratic landlords and the representatives of their thought.

Great changes took place in the Northern Wei dynasty. After the unification of China's northern regions by the tribe of *Xian Bei Tuo Ba*, the regime of the Northern Wei dynasty was established. In order to consolidate domination in these areas, the governor of the Northern Wei dynasty issued decrees on several occasions to encourage farming and sericulture, and implemented a series of reforms on politics and economics such as repealing "the system of sovereign viceroy", setting up "The System of Three Officials" and carrying out "land equalisation". These reforms were not only a strong impetus to the revival and development of agricultural production, they also further weakened the tyrannical landlords' power, which suffered crackdowns in the Three Kingdoms Period and the Jin dynasties. The momentum for landlords to expand annexation of land and "occupy peasants" was suppressed.[10] Meanwhile, some peasants broke away from the tyrannical landlords and became "the person who was written into household register" who could live on their own land. Some of the peasants even became landlords. The number of small landlords increased and the strength of this group was enhanced. These civilian landlords without political power and status had a better understating of agricultural production and paid more attention to family economics and management issues. They often thought about how to "make a living by agriculture", how to increase yields and income through the operation of land exploitation and ultimately realise private wealth. In these circumstances, the transformation from the merchants' "Theory of Making Wealth" to the landlords' "Theory for Making a Living" was accelerated. As the typical thought of landlord family economic management in early times, Jia Sixie's *Qi*

---

10 In ancient China, peasants were the main providers of taxation, labour force and military service. Government obtained and managed the information about peasants through strict household registration. However, in some dynasties, such as the Han, big landlords would get peasants who had lost their land to work and live on their manors. These peasants were owned by landlords personally and lost their nationally registered identity. This is the process of "occupying peasants".

Min Yao Shu was the very product of these social changes and it signified the formation of landlord family economics.

The landlord family economics elaborated in Jia Sixie's *Qi Min Yao Shu* was composed of three parts. "Profession to Make a Living"[11] is the selection of family business objects, approaches and related theories; "Principles to Make a Living" refers to theories and rules of private management; and "Strategies to Make a Living" refers to the methods and measures of microeconomics.

After the determination of the business object and approach, the theoretical research is developed based on the object, followed by the exploration of operating rules and then the means and measures of management. Therefore, "Profession to Make a Living", "Principles to Make a Living" and "Strategies to Make a Living" are inseparable and mutually supportive parts which together form the whole theoretical system of "Theory for Making a Living". Among the three components, "Profession to Make a Living" plays the pivotal role. Therefore, the exploration of "Principles to Make a Living" and "Strategies to Make a Living" is based on and serves for "Profession to Make a Living".

The merchants' "Theory of Making Wealth" established by Tao Zhugong and Bai Gui in the pre-Qin Period did not involve the issue of object selection or any theoretical exploration. They took for granted that business management was the main way or means for private enrichment. Sima Qian was the first person who proposed and studied business objects in "Theory for Make a Living". He believed that the management of agriculture, forestry and animals, industry and commerce was the right way to enrich both family and country. After further analysis and comparison, the following conclusions were obtained. On the one hand, it was stable and reliable to become rich by operating land under feudal ownership and collecting rent. There was also more honour and glory in social political status, while the management of industry and commerce would suffer relatively higher risk and lower social status. Therefore, we could say: "the best kind of wealth is that which is based upon agriculture, the next best is that which is derived from the secondary occupations".[12] On the other hand, it was more rapid and effective to become rich by running commercial or service industries, especially by doing business, than by engaging in agriculture. Sima Qian linked business with farming on this basis and proposed the following point of view: "gaining wealth in the secondary occupations and holding on to it by investing in agriculture".[13] From the discussion by Sima Qian on the selection of business objects, it was obvious that he did not exclude business management from "Profession to Make a Living". On the contrary, he approved and emphasised industry and commerce as important objects or means in "Profession to Make a Living" activities.

11 "Governance for life" can be interpreted in both a broad sense and narrow sense; the former is the same as the Theory of Making Wealth, while the latter refers to the objects or the ways of management. The "Governance for life" we discuss here is in the narrow sense.
12 *Records of the Grand Historian,* "The Biographies of the Money-Makers".
13 Ibid.

For the discussion of "Profession to Make a Living" or selection of business object, Jia Sixie made a fundamental change. His main statement was "Profession to Make a Living" would be a political post or farming as there was no other choice: "If you do not know enough about agriculture, you will lead a hard life."[14] Jia Sixie associated the business objects and means in "Profession to Make a Living" with politics and farming. He considered politics and farming as the only legitimate ways to obtain, maintain and expand private wealth. Meanwhile, he emphasised that ignoring the importance of agricultural production or not focusing on feudal property management would lead to poverty.

While Sima Qian's theory on business objects represented the transformation from merchants' "Theory of Increasing Wealth" to landlords' "Theory for Making a Living", Jia Sixie's proposal of "Either Politics or Farming" excluded business management from "Profession to Make a Living". In his opinion, it was not sensible for elites to abandon agriculture and engage in business. Abandoning agriculture means being rich for a period of time and becoming poor by the end of the year, and hunger and cold would be eased only temporarily. Therefore, it was inadvisable to engage in business. In *Qi Min Yao Shu*, any trace of merchants' "Theory of Increasing Wealth" disappeared completely and turned entirely on landlords' "Theory for Making a Living".

In China's feudal times, being an official could bring both fame and fortune. The glorious status was admired by the people and the privileged income outside of fixed salary was relished and dreamed of by feudal gentlemen. What they were struggling for throughout their lifetime were the high salary and wealth by obtaining an official position. Therefore, it was not surprising for Jia Sixie to regard "being an official" as the main way "Profession to Make a Living". However, the way to become rich by entering politics or being an official was not involved in Jia Sixie's argument except for the theoretical description of "making a living by agriculture".

Jia Sixie pointed out that agriculture was the source of food and clothes for ordinary people as well as the basic condition for people's survival and development. It was of paramount importance to run the country well and give the people peace and security by reinforcing and emphasising the management of agricultural production. As he wrote: "Food is the basis for people; People are the basis for the country; Country is the basis for the lord. Therefore, the mutual cooperation of heaven, earth and people can make the society prosperous."[15]

Literally, there was nothing new in Jia Sixie's explanation. The agriculture issue was emphasised from a "macro" perspective or national economic management perspective both in his own discussion and in quotations from existing literature. In other words, it was just the theory of "enriching the country by agriculture" rather than "making a living by agriculture". In order to incorporate agriculture issues from the national perspective of "theory of enriching countries" into a personal "theory for making a living", Jia Sixie proposed the theory

14 *Qi Min Yao Shu*, "Za Shuo".
15 *Qi Min Yao Shu*, "Growing Crops III".

of "state catching the same meaning as family" as an intermediate link to solve this problem.

Jia Sixie believed that management by private landlords and the management of the feudal national economy had something in common, including various rules and principles:

> Family is the same as country, and vice versa. When a family is in poverty, a virtuous wife is expected to help manage the household. When a country is in chaos, a loyal and capable premier is expected to help manage the country. Therefore, managing a household is like managing a country.

Through this intermediate link, Jia Sixie transplanted and introduced the macro agriculture issues into "Theory for Making a Living", which provided a theoretical basis for "making a living by agriculture".

Although there were few words in Jia Sixie's theory of "state sharing the same meaning as family", with little explanation and elaboration, it provided an important reference for the later development of family economics. His way of looking for a theoretical solution from the macro "theory of enriching countries" was inherited and perfected by Zhang Lüxiang [1611–1674] and Zhang Ying [1637–1708] in the Qing dynasty.

The change of "Profession to Make a Living" led to the change of "Principles to Make a Living". Different business objects have different operating principles or rules. Tao Zhugong and Bai Gui summarised their own and other merchants' experiences and advanced various business principles on that basis. Sima Qian wrote biographies for great merchants, did intensive research based on their business activities and made a theoretical summary of the regular phenomena in the commercial and industrial fields. What Tao Zhugong and Bai Gui discussed was the merchants' "Principles to Make a Living". But the first person to explore and study the landlords' "Principles to Make a Living" was Jia Sixie. The content of his work may be summarised under various headings as follows.

Becoming rich by managing the household with diligence and thrift

Jia Sixie believed that it was of great importance to be diligent in agricultural management. Where there was no farming there was no food, and where there was no weaving there were no clothes. Arduous cultivation and productive effort are the precondition for obtaining wealth through "making a living by agriculture". As he pointed out:

> *Zuo Zhuan* said, "Live a diligent life, and you will lack nothing". As the ancient proverb said "Hard work can alleviate poverty, cautious speaking and action can help to escape disasters". Therefore, diligence can prevent poverty and caution can prevent disasters.

He also quoted the words of Zhong Changtong to indicate that given the same natural conditions, the great difference between diligence and laziness was reflected in the output of labour:

> The god arranged the seasons, but we cannot get food without cultivation. Spring comes and rain falls. From cultivation to harvest, the diligent people reap more while lazy people get less. Would it be possible to reap where one has not sown?

Jia Sixie realised that in "making a living by agriculture", we should not only work hard to accumulate wealth but should also practice thrift and "saving". He said, "It was difficult to acquire fortune or goods", which means that the fortune obtained by hard work should be cherished and saved. Extravagance would gradually lead a wealthy family into trouble:

> We will underestimate the importance of food after being full and look down upon the function of clothes after being dressed warmly. Some people do not pay attention to their savings because of a good harvest, while others easily give their clothes away as they have too many, both of which can gradually lead to poverty and distress.

The consequences will be dreadful when natural disasters occur: "People do not limit the use of their wealth.... Besides, improper policies, flooding and drought will cause crop failure and mass mortality, which are ineradicable disasters since ancient times."

From Sima Qian's point of view, in the management of industrial and commercial business one cannot rely solely on diligence to become rich. "Thinking out of the box" seems more important, because there are high risks, fierce competition and an ever-changing market environment in "making a living by doing business". Without different business skills and unconventional ideas, market competition will bring failure. However, Jia Sixie emphasised the important function of thrift in "making a living by agriculture" in accordance with different features of agriculture management. In feudal society, agricultural productivity was very low. People had little power to fight against nature. There were limited surplus products even in middle and small landlord families. Under these circumstances, the combination of arduous farming and strict thrift was the only safe way to increase wealth. Therefore, Jia Sixie proposed diligence and thrift as important principles in making a living.

Management

Jia Sixie thought that for the purpose of getting rich by thrift in the theory of "making a living by agriculture", attaching importance to the management of tenants and employees was also essential. In his view, "humans are born lazy". With improper command, which means ineffective organisation and supervision by governors of the efforts of workers engaged in agricultural production, conditions are unfavourable for landlords to maintain and expand land or increase rent. He pointed out:

> As for human nature, they will work hard under organisation and leadership, and get slack without supervision. Therefore, as Zhong Changzi said, "It is beside the jungle where the barns are to be built, and the place where fish and turtle live is where crops are grown, which should receive attention to secure the needs of people".

Jia Sixie maintained that efficient monitoring and strict management were necessary for tenants and employees:

> People whose crop is not taken good care of, mulberry tree and fruit tree are not flourishing and cattle are not strong, deserve to be lashed. People whose fence is not strong, wall is not solid and courtyard is not clean, deserve to be beaten.

On the other hand, for the purpose of preventing conflict the governors should also pay heed to compensate their tenants and employees,[16] stimulate the labourers' initiative and harmonise the exploitation relationship between landlords and peasants.

In "Principle for Making a Living", Jia Sixie thought highly of the management of tenant and employee and advocated the exploitation of peasants using a carrot and stick approach. This understanding, with its emphasis on employment, is of great significance in the development of landlord family economic management.

Pursuing efficiency by taking into account timing and location

There were plenty of ideas that paid attention to location and timing in the works of the pre-Qin period, but most of them were proposed from a "macro" perspective to enrich countries. In contrast, Jia Sixie emphasised timing and location considerations from the micro perspective of family management

Jia Sixie recognised that crops have their rules of growth, reproduction and maturity. Agricultural activity must abide by the requirement of natural rules, including the requirements of time and place. That way we can obtain twice the result with half the effort, which means achieving more economic benefit with less manpower and resources: "Following the natural rules and using the advantage of land enable us to achieve more with less effort".[17] He emphasised that acting at will and violating natural rules would result in gaining little or even

16 *Qi Min Yao Shu*, "Za Shuo".
17 *Qi Min Yao Shu*, "Growing Crops III".

nothing while consuming more labour, described vividly as follows: "Looking for timber in water or catching fish on the mountain, one will end up with empty hands, while it is difficult to sprinkle water against wind or roll the mud balls up the hillside".[18]

Based on "Profession to Make a Living", and guided by "Principles to Make a Living", Jia Sixie also introduced a relatively elaborate discussion of the specific measurement and means of landlord family management, namely "Strategy for Making a Living". The key features of this discussion may be summarised as follows.

Intensive operation and cultivation

Jia Sixie opposed extensive cultivation and strongly advocated intensive cultivation of the land. As he never tired of repeating: "As the proverb says 'Without intensive cultivation, a hectare of land will yield no more than an acre', which means high yield with low quality is no better than low yield with high quality".[19] Also: "People should engage in agricultural management according to their capability, we should choose lower production with higher quality rather than higher production with lower quality".[20] In the Warring States period, Li Kui mentioned, "Diligent and cautious management of agriculture may yield three *dou* more in an acre of land while laziness will be subject to loss".[21] And Xunzi had argued: "The land yields all kinds of crops. With proper management, more grain will be produced per *mu* and can be harvested twice a year".[22] All of the above indicate that increasing production per unit area by intensive work had been recognised. Fu Xuan in the Jin dynasty advocated "Not pursuing the acreage but efficacy".[23] He did not approve of the way of increasing agricultural production simply by expanding the area being cultivated. On the other hand, he attached importance to increasing land utilisation and agricultural benefit by inputting more labour to a given area of land. Compared with his predecessors, Jia Sixie proposed the principle of intensive cultivation in a clearer and broader way.

Jia Sixie put forward a set of systems and measures on intensive cultivation. For example, on the planting of crops he laid stress on the whole production process from land cultivation, seed selection, sowing, ploughing, harvesting and storage to processing. He also proposed strict requirements for the management of each step. He thought highly of hoeing in order to prevent pests, clear weeds, loosen soil and retain moisture. He advised not only more cultivation but also the application of different methods of hoeing in different seasons: "Spring

18 Ibid.
19 Ibid.
20 *Qi Min Yao Shu*, "Za Shuo".
21 *Book of Han Dynasty*, Records of Economics Activities and Policies.
22 *Xunzi*, "Country-Enrichment".
23 *Book of Jin Dynasty*, Biography of Fu Xuan.

hoeing is to loosen the soil, while summer hoeing is for weeding"; [24] and, "Plough deep in autumn and shallow in spring and summer".[25] These measures would make full use of natural fertility and promote the growth of crops.

Multiple operation and the carry-out trade

Jia Sixie's "making a living by agriculture" is not construed narrowly. On the contrary, within landlord family management he included an all-round development of agriculture, forestry, animal husbandry, side-line production, fishery and handicraft production. He did not narrowly emphasise food production, but also discussed planting trees, growing vegetables, fishing, and making wine and vinegar, and he paid special attention to the planting and management of cash crops.

He recognised that operating cash crops required less investment with lower risk and repaid the outlay quickly with high profits. By using actual data and comparing the profit with input in monetary terms, he pointed out the huge economic benefits from cash crops. For example, 100 acres of turnips could harvest three times a year. Putting aside the income from leaves and roots, the profits by exchanging seeds for crops could alone exceed the produce of 1,000 acres of paddy fields. Taking the planting of trees as another example, "It does not require the consumption of the cow used for ploughing, or seeds or labour, or concern about natural disasters such as flood, drought, wind and insects. It was a million times more comfortable than farming."[26] Moreover, the economic benefits were much more considerable. After satisfying their own need for firewood, people could sell the surplus branches and leaves that were obtained in the process of tree growth, which was sufficient to cover the cost. Much more sales revenue could be gained after the trees matured.[27] It is therefore obvious that Jia Sixie did not view the issue of "making a living by agriculture" from the narrow perspective of natural economy, but considered cash crop production as a significant means of becoming rich.

Operation of cash crops must have something in common with the merchandise trade, including market supply and demand as well as price fluctuations. It was mentioned above that Jia Sixie held a critical attitude towards specialisation in business. He believed that although business may generate wealth in a short time, it could not solve the longer-term problems of hunger and cold. Therefore, he made clear that he would not discuss the business issues of professional merchants. However, engaging in agricultural production and trading by the land operators themselves, which belongs to the theory of "making a living by agriculture", was different from simply trading with merchants. Therefore, he entirely approved and advocated the cash crop trade based on agricultural production.

---

24 *Qi Min Yao Shu*, "Growing Crops III".
25 *Qi Min Yao Shu*, "Plough I".
26 *Qi Min Yao Shu*, "Growing Trees".
27 Ibid.

In Chapter 62, "On Trading", in *Qi Min Yao Shu*, Jia Sixie extracted numerous business principles from Sima Qian's "Biographies of the Money-Makers" and analysed the relationship between capital and interest made by Sima Qian. In Chapter 30, "Of Various Opinions", the specific plans for landlords who were interested in market trade were also quoted from Cui Shi's *Si Min Yue Ling* from the Han dynasty. Meanwhile, he himself suggested some strategies to get rich on the cash crop trade. For example, according to the regular pattern of seasonal prices, he preferred to purchase seeds for corn and vegetables in the harvest season which was a time of higher supply and lower prices. Conversely, it would be profitable to sell seeds in the planting season because the market would be in great need of seeds at that time and the price would increase as a result. He pointed out that people engaged in the agricultural trade should pay attention to the state of supply and demand as well as price fluctuations and should seize the favourable opportunity and earn more profits through buying low and selling high. Thus:

> The profits can be doubled if corn and vegetable seeds are bought in harvest season and sold in planting season. It is natural for the price to be doubled by buying crops in winter and selling them out in summer or early autumn when heavy rains and floods occur. These are all natural rules.[28]

Improve tools and care about employees

"Strategies to Make a Living" proposed by Jia Sixie has a distinctive feature which is the emphasis on both material and human factors. As he pointed out: "Getting the tools ready is the precondition of planting crops well. Make the peasants happy and they will forget fatigue."[29] Material and human resources should be used rationally from the two aspects of improving tools and caring about employees, so promoting "making a living by agriculture".

Jia advised the use of advanced production tools to improve labour productivity. He took the actions of the prefecture chiefs Jiu Zhen and Lu Jiang as examples. At one time the people "did not know how to farm with cattle and always lacked food". But later the prefecture chiefs of both counties actively promoted cattle farming: "They taught people to cultivate the land. With plenty of reclamation each year, people became self-sufficient in food".[30] In the Dun Huang area, "people did not know about drill barrow, plough, and always reaped little millet with a high input of human resources and cattle". Local officials "taught them to make use of drill barrow and plough",[31] and increased the harvest by half, saving more than half the human resources at the same time.

Jia Sixie clarified the significance of advanced production tools in agricultural development in accordance with historical experience. Furthermore, he integrated

28 *Qi Min Yao Shu*, "Various Opinions".
29 Ibid.
30 *Qi Min Yao Shu*, Preface.
31 Ibid.

making use of advanced tools with mobilising the enthusiasm of labourers. He regarded sufficient material reserves, adequate working tools and strong animals as the prerequisite of smooth agricultural production: "Train labourers to become competent in using tools and be sure to make them nimble; feed animals and keep them healthy and strong",[32] all of which will help labourers to experience less fatigue, ease their minds, and make them more willing and efficient in the service of their employers.

Jia Sixie also discussed the implications of the seasonal nature of agricultural work. Farm work must be completed at the right time during the planting or harvest period, otherwise the growth and harvest of crops and the economic benefits will be affected adversely. These busy periods require the use of additional labourers, and according to Jia they should be hired to meet the temporary increase in demand. He took safflower picking as an example. The blossoming time of the safflower is short and it must be picked before the evaporation of dew in the early morning: "the safflower must be all picked in cool air".[33] If you do not pick at the right time and wait until the evaporation of dew it will require more labour and affect efficiency. The quality of the flowers will also suffer. That meant more temporary workers should be employed to meet the needs of farm work during the picking time:

> Picking one hectare of safflower requires hundreds of people every day. Relying solely on one family, not even one-tenth of all flowers can be completed. However, as long as you get to the edge of field, there will naturally be dozens of children, male and female servants flocking to pick.[34]

For the management of employees, Jia Sixie focused on comforting them. They should be kept always happy in spirit,[35] released as far as possible from trouble, and maintained in a good working state. He also advocated stimulating the employees' enthusiasm, efficiency and quality of work by using their interest and concern in material benefit. He therefore proposed that production sharing or payment with by-products could be used as forms of remuneration. Again taking safflower picking as the example, half of the flowers picked were allocated to each employee ("fifty-fifty between owner and employee"[36]); or, in the case of tree-felling, workers could be paid in the form of branches ("hire workers by paying firewood"). These forms of payment are closely connected with the employees' productivity. The more work employees complete, the higher the payoff they will receive. Under the encouragement of material benefits, workers become interested in the job and show willingness and initiative.

32 *Qi Min Yao Shu,* "Various Opinions".
33 *Qi Min Yao Shu,* "Growing Flowers".
34 Ibid.
35 *Qi Min Yao Shu,* "Various Opinions".
36 *Qi Min Yao Shu,* "Growing Flowers".

152   *Zheng Xueyi*

In China's feudal society, very few landlords directly organised agricultural production. Instead, they separated the land into pieces and leased them to peasants. They exploited peasants and extracted surplus products by virtue of their property, the peasants' dependence on them and non-economic coercion. The amount of their rental income depended mainly on the possession of land and the number of dependent peasants that were under their control rather than output or labour productivity. Therefore, what concerned the feudal landlords was more land acquisition and turning more peasants into tenants rather than land improvement and technical progress in agricultural production. They did not consider the comprehensive management of agriculture, forestry, animal husbandry, side-line production, fishery, handicraft industry and trade, let alone the way to attach importance to material factors and the role of people in family economic management. Jia Sixie's "Strategy of life" investigated these problems and put forward several valuable proposals.

To sum up, Jia Sixie's "Theory of Making a Living" was not composed of scattered fragments or unsystematic economic points of view, but was a whole system of landlord family economic management. The theoretical framework constituted by "Profession to Make a Living", "Principles to Make a Living" and "Strategies to Make a Living" laid the foundation and pointed a direction for the formation and development of China's feudal landlord family economics.

8 Confucian thought on the free economy[1]

Ma Tao

Confucianism was a capacious ideological system encompassing a variety of academic schools. In the area of economic management, for example, some Confucians proposed unrestrained freedom while others laid emphasis on state intervention. Moreover, Confucian culture was not an immutable system. It was constantly absorbing new content, changing and developing along with the development and progress of society. A simple summary of Confucian thought is therefore impossible. For example, "laying emphasis on the basics and curbing the nonessentials" (or "laying emphasis on agriculture and curbing industry and commerce") was the policy prescription of the Legalists (e.g. Shang Yang) in the Early Qin dynasty. After the Qin and Han dynasties, along with the confluence of Confucianism and Legalism, the above thought continued to be used by some Confucian academics. However, there were great differences between the two: early Qin Legalists were concerned about the negative impact of privately operated business activity on national interests and punitive measures were taken against such activity. The aim was to curb the expansion of wealthy businessmen's power and to replace privately operated with officially operated business. Hence, their policy of "curbing industry and commerce" was only directed at private business activity. Although the Confucians also advocated "laying emphasis on agriculture and curbing industry and commerce", their concern was mainly with the balance of interests between "scholars, farmers, artisans and merchants". Even though they considered that agriculture was the basis of social existence and development, and categorised business as nonessential, they did not reject business activity altogether and they discussed its relationship with the more basic agricultural activities. When some Confucians talked about "curbing the nonessentials and rejecting the basics", their meaning was that the state should play no part in business activity – it should not scramble for "nonessential interest", which should be left to private individuals.[2] Thus, the same slogan was given entirely different meanings

---

1 Originally published as "论儒家的自由经济思想" ("On Confucian Thought of the Liberal Economy"), *Chinese Culture: Tradition and Modernisation*, 1998 Issue 6, pp. 14–22.

2 See Wu Hui, *Chinese Ancient Commercial History* Book 1, Chinese Commercial Press Version, Beijing: Commercial Press, 1983, p. 403.

   This paper is not intended as a comprehensive study of the many traditions of Confucian economic thought. Its purpose is only to indicate their more "liberal" aspects, as mainly reflected in the economic management policy of "sparing a little will benefit another greatly".

   During the Early Qin period, in the aspect of national economic management policy there were two basic approaches: one was the approach of state intervention emphasised by the Legalists, who held that the stricter the state intervention and control over the economic life were, the better the outcome would be. After the Qin and Han dynasties, some imperial officials continued to argue for the primacy of the state in economic affairs. But they were not representative of mainstream Confucian thought. On the contrary, during the pre-Qin period it was argued by Confucius and Mencius that economic development should be left to private individuals and that the state should adopt a policy of non-interference; the common people should be allowed to own private property; the state should desist from excessive intervention; and competition should be encouraged, thus creating the conditions for profitable economic activity. After the Qin–Han period there were many Confucians who adopted a similar position, of whom representatives were Sima Qian in the Han dynasty, Li Gou and Ye Shi in the Song dynasty, Qiu Jun in the Ming dynasty, and Huang Zongxi and Tang Zhen in the late Ming and early Qing dynasties. The contention of this paper is that they represent the mainstream of Confucian economic thought. The contributions of Confucius, Mencius, Sima Qian, Ye Shi and Qiu Jun are discussed further below.

Confucius's free economy thought

The economic management system that Confucius had in mind was a kind of free and unrestrained system. In such an economic system, government intervention in the economy would be reduced to a minimum and people would be allowed to exert their intelligence and wisdom in economic activities freely and fully. Confucius had a famous saying: "Whatever does Heaven say? Yet the four seasons run their course through it all and all things are produced by it. Whatever does Heaven say?"[3] This was the description in his mind of the influence of the government on economic activities. Confucius proposed to govern with nothing that goes against nature and opposed excessive government intervention in economic life, as indicated also by the following saying: "Surely Shun was one who governed by non-action. For what action did he take? He merely adopted a courteous position and faced due south."[4] Confucius considered that the main tasks of government were only to have "enough food" and "enough soldiers".[5] With a reduced economic role for government, he further proposed

---

3 *Analects*, XVII.17.
4 Ibid., XV.5.
5 Ibid., XII.7.

that "few taxes should be collected".[6] For the student Ran You, who assisted the Ji family in increasing the tax rate, Confucius exhorted his disciples to "sound the drum and attack him".[7]

Confucius believed that "the minds of the mean men are conversant with gain", and that the pursuit of wealth and rank is the desire of everybody.[8] Hence, "the mean men" will perform economic activities providing only that they are allowed to receive benefits. But how was it possible to make the common people gain sufficient physical benefits to mobilise their efforts? The scheme designed by Confucius was expressed thus: "If he [the ruler] benefits the people on the basis of what the people will really find beneficial, then surely he is not wasteful although he is bounteous."[9] That is, let common people undertake economic activities freely to gain benefits.

Confucius also had a set of strategies for economic development. For example,

> When the Master went to Wei, Ran You drove his carriage. "How dense is the population!" exclaimed the Master. "When the people have multiplied, what more should be done for them?" said Ran You. "Enrich them," he replied. "And when they have been enriched, what more should be done for them?" "Instruct them," he replied.[10]

This may suggest that Confucius had realised that economic development could be divided into three stages: increased population; increased wealth; and education. Such a pattern of economic development is not dissimilar from the one observed by Kuznets, who identified the successive stages of population increase, increased per capita use of capital and increased labour productivity and personal consumption. Confucius's trilogy for economic development of being "numerous, rich and educated" has some similarities with Kuznets's theory. Both recognised the stages of increased population and greater riches (consumption), and the stage of education identified by Confucius may be viewed as a precondition for the development of enhanced techniques of production.

Mencius's free economy thought

Mencius inherited and developed Confucius's free economy thought. This was mainly reflected in his proposals to "conform to nature" and the emphasis that he gave to personal property rights, interests and the need for competition.

Mencius once said, "Though nothing happens that is not due to Destiny, one accepts willingly only what is one's proper Destiny."[11] "Destiny" should be

---

6 *Zuo Zhuan* (Spring and Autumn Annals).
7 *Analects*, XI.17.
8 Ibid., IV.5, IV.16.
9 Ibid., XX.2.
10 Ibid., XIII.9.
11 *Mencius*, VII.A.2.

interpreted as natural law. The meaning of the sentence is to lay emphasis on "being natural". Mencius once told a story of "pulling up seedlings to help them grow":

> There was a man from Song who pulled at his seedlings because he was worried about their failure to grow. Having done so, he went on his way home, not realising what he had done. "I am worn out today," he said to his family. "I have been helping the seedlings to grow." His sons rushed out to take a look and there the seedlings were, all shrivelled up. There are few in the world who can resist the urge to help their seedlings grow.... Not only do they fail to help them but they do the seedlings positive harm.[12]

The intention of this allegory is to emphasise that natural law should be followed in all activities. Its relevance to economic policy is that the government should follow the natural law of economic activity and not intervene mandatorily. The result of that kind of action may only be "doing harm rather than generating any advantages".

Mencius also anticipated modern theories of property rights. As he said: "The people ... will not have constant hearts if they are without constant means [of support]. Lacking constant hearts, they will go astray and fall into excesses, stopping at nothing."[13] He also said: "Benevolent government must begin with land demarcation. When boundaries are not properly drawn, the division of land ... and the yield of grain use for paying officials cannot be equitable".[14]

Mencius's economic thought laid great emphasis on individual interests. He considered that individuals constitute the fundamentals of the country: "There is a common expression, 'The Empire, the state, the family'. The Empire has its

---

12 Ibid., II.A.2.
13 Ibid., I.A.7, III.A.3. What are "property rights"? There are many definitions, but the one basically agreed by Roman law, common law, Max and Engels, as well as modern laws and economic research, is that property right does not refer to the relation between people and things, but refers to the action relation recognised by people arising out of the things' existence and their use. Property rights arrangements determine each person's code of behaviour corresponding to the things; each person must observe the relation with others, or assume the costs arising from non-compliance with such relations.

> So, as far as a house is concerned, if the group of property rights obtained by one person includes the right of not allowing establishing gasoline stations and chemical factories around the house, the value of such house to him is relatively high. Therefore, that group of different property rights held by one decision-maker towards the resources is in the utility function of the decision-maker.
>
> (E. Furubotn and S. Pejovich, "Property Rights and Economic Theory: A Survey of Recent Literature", *Journal of Economic Literature*, 10.4, 1972)

Thus, the concept of property right is not limited to "private property right". As a result, the similarity between Mencius's position and modern thinking on property rights is not affected by whether peasants have property rights under his 井-field [well-field] system.

14 Ibid., III.A.3.

own basis in the state, the state in the family, and the family in one's own self."[15] In the opinion of Mencius, individuals are the fundamental constituents of the country and the society under Heaven. Mencius also advocated "self-respect", saying:

> Anybody who wishes to cultivate a paulownia [tree] or a catalpa [tree], which may be grasped with both hands, perhaps with one, knows by what means to nourish them. In the case of their own persons, men do not know by what means to nourish them. Is it that their regard of their own persons is inferior to their regard for a paulownia or catalpa? Their lack of reflection is extreme.[16]

Such "self-respect" thought, which lays emphasis on "considering individuals as the basics", is consistent with the thought which lays emphasis on "self-benefit" in Western classical economics.

Free market ideology emphasises market competition and opposes monopoly. Mencius held a similar position and vehemently opposed market monopoly:

> In antiquity, the market was for the exchange of what one had for what one lacked. The authorities merely supervised it. There was, however, a despicable fellow who always looked for a vantage point and, going up on it, gazed into the distance to the left and to the right in order to secure for himself all the profit that was in the market. The people all thought him despicable, and, as a result, they taxed him. The taxing of traders began with this despicable fellow.[17]

Mencius also affirmed the status and influence of businessmen in social-economic life, opposed the theory advocated by Legalists of "laying emphasis on agriculture and curbing industry and commerce", and proposed that business-men should be exempt from taxes: "only inspection is conducted but no levy in imposed at border stations and market places".[18] The purpose of his proposals was to encourage free trade activities. As for monopolists, they would force up prices and reap exorbitant profits, which would not only make legitimate busi-nessmen lose opportunities, but would also force farmers to be poor and bank-rupt as the monopolising businessmen who seized market profits would use their extra wealth for merging land. This was neither consistent with the legitimate business operation principles advocated by Mencius, such as "exchanging what one has with what one does not have", "sharing out the work and cooperating with one another" and so on, nor in conformity with "letting each person have a legitimate occupation and stable income". As revealed in his story of the

15 Ibid., IV.A.5.
16 Ibid., VI.A.13.
17 Ibid., II.B.10. [Irene Bloom (*Mencius*, New York: Columbia University Press, 2009) gives "greedy" in place of "despicable".]
18 Ibid., I.B.5.

"despicable fellow" (above), he was not only against monopoly but also used the allegory to oppose wealth and rank.

Compared with Confucius, Mencius's economic development strategies are more detailed and explicit. They include the land system, rural planning, resource protection and tax reform. Mencius attached the most importance to the land system. He proposed the "nine squares" or *jing* system and described the pattern as follows:

> One large square of field was divided into nine small ones like the Chinese character "井" [the corresponding pinyin *jing* means "well"] of 900 *mu* in total. Of these, the central plot of 100 *mu* belongs to the state, while the other eight plots of 100 *mu* each are held by eight families who share the duty of caring for the plot owned by the state. Only when they have done this duty dare they turn to their own affairs.[19]

The nine squares system was not only economic, but also social:

> Neither in burying the dead, nor in changing his abode, does a man go beyond the confines of his village. If those who hold land within each *jing* befriend one another both at home and abroad, help each other to keep watch, and succour each other in illness, they will live in love and harmony.[20]

The nine squares system was also related to rural planning:

> Around the homestead within its five *mu*, the space beneath the walls is planted with mulberry trees, with which the women nourish silkworms, and thus the old are able to have silk to wear. If each family has five hens and two sows, and these do not miss their breeding season, the old can have meat to eat. The husbandmen cultivate their farms of 100 *mu* and thus their families of eight persons are secured against hunger.[21]

Mencius's resource protection strategies were also designed for an agricultural society. It was said,

> If you do not interfere with the busy seasons in the fields, then there will be more grain than the people can eat; if you do not allow nets with too fine a mesh to be used in large ponds, then there will be more fish and turtles than they can eat; if hatchets and axes are permitted in the forests and hills only in the proper seasons, then there will be more timber than they can use.[22]

19 Ibid., III.A.3.
20 Ibid.
21 Ibid., VII.A.22.
22 Ibid., I.A.3.

In the aspect of tax reform, Mencius proposed that "few taxes should be collected" and advocated the "*Zhu* method" of the Yin Dynasty, whereby private land was untaxed and farmers worked on public land to pay their tax. From the perspective of modern economics, the rationale was that labour rent does not damage the farmers' gains but only adds working hours, since there is always disguised unemployment in the countryside and the opportunity cost is extremely low. The farmers therefore benefit from the system.

Sima Qian's free economy thought

Sima Qian was an eminent historian in ancient China and also an outstanding pioneer of free economy thought. He made significant advances over the ideas of Confucius and Mencius and his contribution was to have an enormous influence on the subsequent development of free economy thinking.

Sima Qian's free economy thought was reflected in his proposed economic policy:

> the highest type of ruler accepts the nature of the people; the next best leads the people to what is beneficial; the next best gives them moral instruction; the next forces them to be orderly, and the very worst kind enters into competition with them[23]

Sima Qian's meaning was as follows.

First, "accepting the nature of the people" meant that the best economic policy in a feudal state was to be in accordance with the nature of economic development. Private persons should be permitted to carry out activities such as production, trade and so on, and intervention and restraint were unnecessary. Such a policy was the backbone of all Sima Qian's economic doctrines and may be considered as the clearest statement of a "laissez-faire" approach in the history of ancient Chinese economic thought. Second, "leading the people to what is beneficial" proposes to make the state offer guidance in order to encourage people to undertake particular kinds of economic activities. Third, "moral instruction" refers to a policy by which a feudal state would guide people to undertake certain kinds of economic activities by civilising or persuading them. Fourth, "forcing people to be orderly" means precisely that the feudal state would take administrative and legal methods to intervene in people's economic activities by restricting and coercing them. Finally, "entering into competition with the people" refers to the policy by which a feudal state would directly operate industrial and commercial business in order to make profits. Sima Qian raised strong objections to the latter two kinds of policies. In his opinion, undertaking profitable production and trade activities was something that could be left to private persons. It was unnecessary to practice excessive intervention in economic activities.

23 *Records of the Grand Historian*, "The Biographies of the Money-Makers".

Sima Qian's preference for a "free economy" had its basis in his view of human nature. He thought that all human beings prefer benefits:

> judging from what is recorded in the *Odes* and *Documents*, from the age of Emperor Shun and the Xia dynasty down to the present, ears and eyes have always longed for the ultimate in beautiful sounds and forms, mouths have desired to taste the best in grass-fed and grain-fed animals, bodies have delighted in ease and comfort[24]

These are all examples of naturally created instincts and desires. Moreover,

> When each person works away at his own occupation and delights in his own business, then, like water flowing downward, goods will naturally flow forth ceaselessly day and night without being summoned, and the people will produce commodities without having been asked.... Is this not a natural result?[25]

Hence, the best policy is to be in accordance with human nature and to harness that nature to allow people to make profits. This thought coincides with Adam Smith's theory of "self-betterment", although stated by Sima Qian more than 1,800 years earlier. Both of them believed that seeking for profit was the starting point of all economic behaviour. It was private individuals who knew the most effective measures for making the greatest profit and how to make full use of their own advantages to achieve the best result:

> Society obviously must have farmers before it can eat; foresters, fishermen, miners etc. before it can make use of natural resources; craftsmen before it can have manufactured goods; and merchants before they can be distributed. But once these exist, what need is there for government directives, mobilisations of labour, or periodic assemblies? Each man has only to be left to utilise his own abilities and exert his strength to obtain what he wishes.[26]

Seeking for profit is natural for human beings: "So it is said, 'Jostling and joyous, the whole world comes after profit; racing and rioting, after profit the whole world goes'". Of course, a competitive system in which people are given free play to pursue their own interests will have winners and losers, and this was recognised and accepted by Sima Qian: "Poverty and wealth are not the sort of things that are arbitrarily handed to men or taken away: the clever have a surplus; the stupid never have enough";

24 Ibid.
25 Ibid.
26 Ibid.

there is no fixed road to wealth, and money has no permanent master. It finds its way to the man of ability like the spokes of a wheel converging on the hub, and from the hands of the worthless it falls like shattered tiles[27]

Sima Qian also paid attention to market adjustment and the price mechanism. For example, he cited the words of King Goujian of Yue (496–465 BC):

If you study the surpluses and shortages of the market, you can judge how much a commodity will be worth. When an article has become extremely expensive, it will surely fall in price, and when it has become extremely cheap, then the price will begin to rise[28]

This indicates Sima Qian's appreciation of the operation of the law of supply and demand. According to Adam Smith, it is as if an "invisible hand" is guiding the social economy to the most appropriate outcome. Sima Qian had a wonderful description of the mechanism:

when a commodity is very cheap, it invites a rise in price; when it is very expensive, it invites a reduction. When each person works away at his own occupation and delights in his own business then, like water flowing downward, goods will natural flow ceaseless day and night[29]

Sima Qian was evidently referring to what we would call a price mechanism, and the function of this mechanism is similar to the "invisible hand" proposed by Adam Smith.

Ye Shi's free economy thought

The free economy thought of Confucius, Mencius and Sima Qian was extended and developed in the Song dynasty by Ye Shi [1150–1223]. Ye Shi criticised state interventionism and the theory of state macroeconomic control. The theory of macroeconomic control was put forward in the book *Guanzi*, which emphasised that the government should control the national economy by various means on the principle that the rights of "giving and taking away, impoverishing and enriching [should all lie] in the hands of the prince".[30] As Ye Shi remarked tersely on such policies, "if the methods are implemented, the world will be in a mess".[31]

As with Sima Qian, Ye Shi believed that seeking wealth and preferring benefit was human nature: "seeking benefits and keeping away from harm" is the

27 Ibid.
28 Ibid.
29 Ibid.
30 *Guanzi*, "Guo Xu" ("The State's Store of Grain").
31 *Collected Works of Ye Shi*, "Financial Measures I".

"same idea of all people".[32] For the purpose of pursuing benefit, the common people "go out early in the morning and come back at dusk, compete for gain with their own strength, and fearlessly take risk in pursuit of gain".[33] Therefore, Ye Shi proposed that in national economic management a feudal state should adapt to people's natural desire to seek their own benefit, allow people to manage financial matters themselves, and let private persons undertake economic activities for the purpose of realising "self-benefits".[34] Rather than hindering their activities, the government should facilitate them by providing appropriate protection. Ye Shi reckoned that allowing private persons to carry out economic activities for the purpose of realising "self-benefits" could not only make people rich but would also promote the development of the national economy.

Ye Shi also expounded on the inevitability of the free economy from the angle of historical development. He considered that in the Western Zhou dynasty, "people all had equal wealth": without private ownership there was no differentiation of wealth at that time, and the state economic management corresponding to such historical conditions was "the right of opening and closing, collecting and decentralising; economic policy was controlled by the upper rulers".[35] Whereas, with historical development, the private economy developed and along with it the differentiation of poverty and affluence: "Nowadays, all common people in the world were not and had not been equal in wealth for a long time".[36] With the development of the private economy, state economic management had to change accordingly: inequality was a matter of objective fact but the government should not control or intervene in private economic activities; on the contrary, free economy policy should be implemented, people should be encouraged to manage financial matters themselves and private persons should be encouraged to carry out all kinds of activities to seek for benefits: "rich persons and great merchants possessed the wealth of their own".[37] As proposed by Ye Shi, therefore, state economic management should be guided by free economy principles.

Qiu Jun's free economic thought

Qiu Jun [1421–1495] was a typical advocate of Confucian free economy thought in the Ming dynasty, as mainly reflected in his "self-doing theory". Qiu Jun took the position that human survival and development must be based upon physical wealth: "people rely on wealth to survive; they are not able to live without wealth even for one day".[38] In his opinion, pursuing wealth and preferring benefit were natural for human beings: "Wealth is the common pursuit of human beings".[39] Moreover, the

32 Preface to *Learning Notes – Shang Shu*. [A work completed in the Song Dynasty.]
33 *Collected Works of Ye Shi*, "Records of Liugengtang".
34 *Collected Works of Ye Shi*, "Fiscal Measures I".
35 Ibid.
36 Ibid.
37 Ibid.
38 *Daxue Yanyibu*, "General Discussion of Financial Matters Management I".
39 *Daxue Yanyibu*, "General Discussion of Imperial Courts' Politics".

desire for benefit was unlimited: "Preferring benefits is the nature of human beings, there is no limit".[40] Consequently, the state should adapt its economic management to such behaviour, desist from excessive control and intervention, and allow private persons to carry out their own activities to obtain wealth: "make the rich keep on the rails of their wealth, the poor not too impecunious, both the rich and the poor abide by the law and behave themselves, satisfy their needs, and it is done."[41] He summarised his approach as being "letting people do for their own convenience" and made it the general programme for managing the national economy.[42]

One of Qiu Jun's outstanding contributions was to consider the whole country and the whole society as the grand total of individuals: "Although the world is large, it is composed of individuals".[43] In this way, he expressed the view that the total of individual interests was equal to the interest of the whole country and the whole society, so that the pursuit of wealth and benefit by private persons was consistent with the interest and development of society as a whole. As Qiu Jun emphasised, allowing private persons carry out economic activities so that they "gain what they deserve and satisfy their desires" can improve the position of the whole society so that "the world may be peaceful".[44] This is consistent with the idea proposed by Adam Smith some 300 years later, namely that the pursuit of private benefit may promote the development of the nation.

Another manifestation of Qiu Jun's free economy thought was his encouragement of the development of industry and commerce among the common people. Qiu Jun's basic proposal was that "people have their own market".[45] Some indication of his meaning may be gleaned from Confucius's criticism of the practice of weaving mats from cattails by Zang Wenzhong's concubines as "heartless". If they weaved for sale, they must take part in market competition, striving for benefits with the people; if they weaved for their own use, they would reduce the opportunities for common people to sell their own weaved cattails. Sima Qian held a similar perspective and objected to the state's operation of industrial and commercial economic activities for the purpose of competing for benefits with the people.[46] Qiu Jun objected to officially operated business on

---

40 *Daxue Yanyibu*, "General Discussion of Financial Matters Management I".
41 *Daxue Yanyibu*, "Order of Market Food Purchase".
42 *Daxue Yanyibu*, "Control over People's Industries".
43 *Daxue Yanyibu*, "General Discussion of Financial Matters Management I".
44 Ibid.
45 *Daxue Yanyibu*, "Order of Market Food Purchase".
46 Lu Country's Prime Minister Gong Yixiu of the Spring and Autumn Period

> ate the vegetables, thought the vegetables were delicious, then pulled out all the *donghancai* [a type of vegetable] in his family's own vegetable garden. When he found out that the cloth weaved in his family was good, he immediately drove his wife out of the family and burnt the weaving machine

> Gong Yixiu had judged that the growing of vegetables and weaving of cloth by noble families would make it difficult for "peasant men and working women" to "sell their commodities" (*Shi Ji* [Records of the Grand Historian], Collected Biographies of Xun Li). His position echoes Confucius's criticism of Zang Wenzhong's "concubines weaving cattails".

the grounds that it was likely to result in unstable prices and disturbance to normal market activities through the use of "cunning tricks". He believed that competition among private persons would adjust the price, quantity and quality of commodities, thereby reaching a kind of optimum balance: "If people conduct market transactions themselves, the rules for the commodity quality and price level … could be implemented on their own".[47] In Qiu Jun's opinion, if the common trade activities were carried out freely, the supply and demand and market competition mechanisms will spontaneously adjust commodity prices, making "the price naturally not too high"[48] so that government intervention would not be required to stabilise prices. Qiu Jun would seem to have recognised the "self-adjusting" propensity of the market, similar to the "invisible hand" proposed by Adam Smith.

Similarly to Sima Qian, Qiu Jun also raised objections to the policy of state monopolies. He harshly criticised historical examples of officially operated business, such as Sang Hongyang's "equalisation" and Wang Anshi's "market transactions" as "extremely ugly" policies that were only "striving for the benefits of businessmen".[49] With regard to the "salt tax" system, through which the government monopolised the production and sale of salt, he raised a strong objection. He thought that natural resources such as salt were "the creature of nature", could not be monopolised by a minority for "appropriating their benefits", but should rather be "publicly owned" by the nation.[50] He remonstrated that the salt tax system implemented by the imperial court not only violated the "expectation of natural creation" but also went against "the intention of the god". There were also more mundane objections. Because it was easy to make profits from undertaking the production and circulation of salt, the imperial courts could "rely on salt to make profits" but the common people also "noticed the profits" which would act as an incentive for them to conduct their own clandestine operations.[51] It was therefore hard to prove that the imperial court's monopoly operation and severe penal codes were effective. The result of monopoly was only to produce high prices and low quality and cause a decrease in consumption, contrary to the original intention, and the monopoly was in any event difficult to enforce. His reform proposal was that the production and sale of salt should be operated by private persons under the supervision and management of the state. With respect to other commodities, people should be encouraged to "conduct market transactions themselves" in order to promote general prosperity.

Modern relevance of Confucian free economy thought

Confucian free economy thought generated positive influences on the ancient Chinese commodity economy. Confucian free economy thought was active in

---

47 *Daxue Yanyibu*, "Benefits of Mountains and Ponds I".
48 Ibid.
49 *Daxue Yanyibu*, "Order of Market Food Purchase".
50 *Daxue Yanyibu*, "Benefits of Mountains and Ponds I".
51 Ibid.

the Warring States period to the Qin–Han period, and in the Song–Ming period. These periods correspond to the two peaks in the development of the Chinese ancient commodity economy, the first from the Spring and Autumn period and Warring States period to the period of the Emperor Wu of the Western Han; the second from the Song dynasty to the late period of the Ming dynasty. The occurrence of each peak was related to the prevalence of Confucian free economy thought and its influence on official economic policies. During the development of the modern market economy, Confucian free economy thought has also played its part, the rising of the East Asian economy being a good example. The East Asia region is an area greatly influenced by Confucian thought. Since the 1950s, the rapid economic growth and the fast development of industrialisation in the East Asia region, as represented by Japan, South Korea, Singapore, Taiwan and Hong Kong, have prompted Chinese and foreign scholars to discuss the relation between Confucian culture and the economic development of the region. Several scholars maintain that Confucian economic thought and ethics have exerted a positive influence in the rise of the East Asian economy.[52] I agree with that viewpoint. I suggest that we may regard aspects of system and policy as the "hardware" for the rise of the East Asian economy, and the traditional cultural factors, notably including Confucian culture, as the "software". "Software" and "hardware" have supplemented and influenced each other to facilitate the growth process. In particular, Confucian traditional culture has successfully accomplished a harmonious relationship in the above-named countries between a market economy and democratic political and legal systems, which has provided momentum for the development of the East Asian economy. Professor Sheng Hong once suggested that Confucian free economy thought was transmitted to Europe by Western missionaries and thereby influenced such classical economists as Quesnay, Turgot and Smith, to that extent becoming the Chinese source of Western modern economics.[53] That point alone can be enough to attract the attention of Chinese people to the cultural heritage of Confucian free economy thought. As to the system of economic reform currently being implemented on the Chinese mainland, the theoretical resources from such a precious cultural heritage cannot be too highly regarded.

52 The American academic Herman Kahn was the scholar who first used Confucian thought to explain the "miracle of Asian economy". He argued that the reason why East Asian economies rose abruptly is that most of their people were nurtured by Confucian culture. He suggested that the East Asian peoples "had higher economic efficiency compared with other cultures" and, to that extent, Confucian culture was superior to the "protestant ethic". (Quoted from S.G. Reading, "The Role of Entrepreneurs in the Asian New Capitalism", in Peter Ludwig Berger and Hsin-Huang Michael Hsiao, *In Search of an East Asian Development Model*: Piscataway Township, NJ: Transaction Publishers, 1988.)
53 See Sheng Hong, "Chinese Sources of Modern Economics" in *Spirits of Economics*, Chengdu: Sichuan Literature & Art Publishing House, 1996.

9 Etymological studies of "Chinese economics"[1]

Ye Tan

1

In recent years, issues related to the localisation, normalisation and internationalisation of economics have aroused controversy among economists. What lies at the core of this issue is the question of whether or not Western economics can serve as the basis for a "universal" or "general" economic theory or whether it is nation-specific or class-specific. Correspondingly, we can also ask if there is a need for a "Chinese basic theory", if "Chinese economics" has ever really existed or if there should be a multiple basis for the anticipated "Chinese economics". Scholars are divided over these questions.[2] Such a controversy suggests a new trend in academic development towards the turn of the twenty-first century. The social sciences based on a modern, Western foundation have been seriously challenged in China (and not only China), a country unconnected with such a foundation. It is even more so in the area of economics. China's economic reform and practice have created the demand for theoretical and disciplinary change, a situation also encountered in many other areas where scholars are discussing disciplinary theory and methodological reform. Whether the reform will be developed out of the subject studied, or introduced from outside the discipline, or both, largely depends on an exploration of the history of local economics.[3]

"The origin and development of Chinese economics" is indeed a valuable topic. What we are really interested in is the origin of present-day economics. It is commonly accepted that economics is a discipline introduced from the West, but there are some sub-areas that are certainly not Western. One example is the history of economic thought, which explores the evolution of all types of

1 Originally published as "中国经济学寻根" ("Etymological Studies of 'Chinese Economics'"), *Social Sciences in China*, 1998 Issue 4, pp. 59–71.
2 Zhang Wenmin *et al.*, eds, *The Great Controversy Over the Chinese Economy*, vol. 2. Beijing: Jingji Guanli Publishing House, 1997.
3 See the author's "An Analysis of Research in the 1920s and 1930s on the History of Chinese Economic Thought", *Chinese Studies*, Tokyo, December 1995, January 1996. The English version is included in Aiko Ikeo, ed., *Economic Development in Twentieth Century East Asia*, London/New York: Routledge, 1997, pp. 35–54.

economic thought, opinion, concepts and theories through the ages, especially in the dynastic periods. These have entered our culture and tradition and become part of the legacy of the past. The discipline also deals with modern economic theory nurtured by the ongoing reform and development. Since the modern period it has been impossible to separate research on national life, especially in the area of economics, from international scholarship. The history of economic thought in China, in spite of its breadth, can still provide a specific perspective from which to view "Chinese economics" and related questions. An exploration of "Chinese" economics should begin with a look at the original meaning and practical use of the word *jingji*, its evolution and relationship to introduced economics, as well as the difficult journey of "Chinese economics" in the early years of this century.

2

Is the modern Chinese term *jingji* a translation of the Western term "economy", or was it derived from the archaic Chinese term *jingbang zhiguo* (to govern the country) or *jingshi jimin* (to manage the country and help the people)? We need to inquire into the origin and meaning of the word. According to *A Dictionary of Borrowed Words in Chinese* by the famous linguist Gao Mingkai, *jingji* has two origins: one is the Japanese term *keizai*, which is a translation of the English "economy" or "economics", and the other is an archaic Chinese term, found, for example, in the "Biography of Wang Anshi" in *The History of the Song Dynasty*. According to the entry for *jingjixue* (economics) in the same dictionary, the word came from the Japanese *keizeigaku*, a transliteration of the English "economics" or "political economy". The modern Chinese term *jingji* therefore has two origins, one ancient Chinese and the other Japanese; the term *jingjixue* was translated from Japanese, which in turn was from the West. The entry for *keizai* in an authoritative Japanese dictionary reads:

> (1) "Wenzhongzi" in *Rites and Music* [an ancient Chinese text]: to rule the country and save the people; to manage the country and help people. (2) economy. (3) frugality.

The explanation for *keizeigaku* is "political economy; economics; a branch of knowledge related to economic phenomena." So, the Japanese term *keizai* is derived partly from the Chinese term *jingguo jimin*. But, as an area of learning it is translated from a Western term. Illustrations of the former include Taizai Shundai's *A Record of Governing*, Kaiho Kiyotaka's *Discussion on Governing* and Sato Nobuhiro's *The Gist of Governing*, all published in the Edo period.[4] As for the latter, I can cite Kamita Kohei's 1867 translation of *Outlines of Social Economy* by W. Ellis, and Fuku Yukichi's 1868 lecture on Francis Wayland's *The Elements of Political Economy* and his translation in the same year of an

4 [1603–1868.]

economics textbook published in Scotland. Kamita Kohei was the first to introduce Western economics to Japan. The Japanese economic historian, Yamazaki
Masukichi, who was president of Taka Saki University of Economics, wrote that
it is

> commonly accepted that economics means nothing but managing the world
> and helping people, just as is said in the *Great Learning* [a Confucian
> text].... However, the real meaning of economics has been forgotten in
> modern times, and has been redefined as a rationalisation for the 'Sheer
> pursuit of wealth'.

Masukichi recommended a return to the original meaning of economics.[5] In
short, the Japanese adopted the Chinese word *jingji* in their translation of the
Western term for economics. The Japanese word was later imported back to
China and became a source of the modern Chinese term *jingji*.

Since the term *jingji* existed in archaic Chinese before its translation back into
Japanese, we need to know how the word was first used in Chinese. It is impossible to examine exhaustively the tremendous amount of ancient literature, but
according to some sources the characters *jing* and *ji* appeared as early as the Yin/
Shang period,[6] although *jingji* as a compound emerged relatively late. I have
searched through such ancient texts as the *Thirteen Classics*[7] and failed to find
any reference to jingji. However, some historical records do contain the word.
For example, in *The History of the Jin Dynasty*, a prince, Sima Yi, wrote to his
brother Sima Ying in AD 303, "[we] are both born of the royal family and enfeoffed in local areas. Neither of us can apply His Majesty's teachings nor assist in
jingji". Emperor Mingdi of the Eastern Jin dynasty praised Ji Zhan in a decree:
"He is loyal and gentle, upright and perceptive, and knows how to rule."
Emperor Jianwendi wrote in a letter to Yin Hao: "You are a man of much experience and profound knowledge, good enough to govern."[8] This fourth-century
reference to *jingji* is the earliest documentation that I know of. It is hundred
years earlier than the Sui dynasty reference to *jingji* in volume 6 of *Wenzhongzi*
by Wang Tong (584–618): "[They] all have the ability to govern but remain
unknown to the Emperor", and a reference in *History of the Song Dynasty*.

In the Northern and Southern dynasties period,[9] we read in the volume on
"Alien Peoples" in the History of the (Liu-) Song dynasty a reference to *jingji*.
Emperor Wendi praised a general who conquered Linyi, saying: "The General
of Longxiang and Governor of Jiaozhou, Sao Hezhi is loyal and resolute,

5 Yamazaki Masukichi, Preface to *The Social and Economic Thought of Yokoi Kokusu*, Tokyo:
   Taga Press, 1981.
6 [*c.*1600–1046 BC]
7 [Confucian texts that formed the basis for the imperial examinations during the Song Dynasty,
   960–1127.]
8 The biographies of Sima Yi, the King of Changsha, Ji Zhan and Yin Hao in *History of the Jin
   Dynasty*.
9 [386–589].

careful and brave, and has good ideas on *jingji*." This term was used frequently from the Tang dynasty[10] onwards. For example, historical records eulogise Emperor Xuanzong's "government full of men with *jingji* talent." The famous minister Wei Zheng praised Zheng Dajie's "talent for *jingji*. He was employed by Emperor Taizong, and his dynasties lasted for a long time." The prime minister Pei Du "had no more willingness for *jingji*, and built his residence in Jixianli in the Eastern Capital." In a poem to commemorate the departure of the brother of his friend, Li Bai wrote: "Your brother is a man with a talent for *jingji* and I would not worry about his decline." Du Fu also bemoaned the lack of a talent for *jingji* throughout history in one of his poems.[11] We also find in the biography of Emperor Zhuangzong in the ninth volume of "Tang History" in *The Old History of the Five Dynasties Period* a reference to a flood and earthquake in the third year of the Tongguang reign. Duan Hui corresponded to the emperor that previous "emperors wrote in the imperial hand in red ink for an interview with their ministers when they needed to seek the truth of *jingji*." From the Song dynasty onwards, the concept of *jingji* was used more extensively. The Confucian master Zhu Xi once commented that Wang Anshi "was not merely remarkable for his prominent writing and behaviour, but also for his commitment to *jingji*." According to historical records, Ye Shi "was ambitious and regarded himself as a man with a talent for *jingji*." Chen Liang was also a man "with *jingji* aspirations and was always ready to do as he had promised."[12] In all these cases, *jingji* roughly means "governing." In addition, *jingji* could also be used as an element in an official title. One example is provided by the *jingjishi* referred to in the biography of Fu Shenwei in *The History of the Jin Dynasty*.

It is noteworthy that from the Song dynasty onwards, the term *jingji* was not only widely used, but also made its way into numerous book titles. For example, Liu Yan's work "The Essence of *Jingji*" is referred to in his biography *History of the Song Dynasty*, and in volume 7 of "Art and Literature" in *The History of the Song Dynasty* it is recorded that Ma Cun produced *Essays on Jingji* in twelve volumes. Other instances include:

- *Essays on Jingji* by Teng Gong (Song dynasty) in fifty volumes, plus a sequel in twenty-two volumes;
- *Essays on Jingji* in six volumes by Li Shizhan (Yuan dynasty), edited by his great-grandson Li Shen;
- *Essays on Jingji* in thirty-two volumes by Chen Oisu (Ming dynasty);
- A Record of Famous Ministers' Governing Deeds of the Ming Dynasty in fifty-three volumes by Huang Xun (Ming dynasty);

10 [619–907.]
11 The biographies of Emperor Xuanzong and Wei Zheng in *The Old History of the Tang Dynasty*; The biography of Pei Du in *The New History of the Tang Dynasty*; *A Complete Anthology of the Tang Dynasty*.
12 The biographies of Wang Anshi, Ye Shi and Chen Liang in *History of the Song Dynasty*.

- *A Classified Book of Jingji* in 100 volumes compiled by Feng Oi (Ming dynasty);
- *Discussion on Jingji* in twelve volumes compiled by Chen Zizhuang (Ming dynasty);
- *Essays on Jingji* compiled by Zhang Wenyan (Ming dynasty);
- *Record of Jingji* by Li Yuzhang (Ming dynasty);
- *Record of Jingji* by Zhang Lian (Ming dynasty);
- *Famous Ministers with Jingji Deeds* by He Zhongnan (Ming dynasty);
- *Grand Words on Jingji* compiled by Wang Xuexin and Wang Yishi (Ming dynasty);
- *Grand Words on Jingji* compiled by Shen Yiguan.

In addition, the "Art and Literature" section of *History of the Ming Dynasty* also refers to Huang Pu's Ming dynasty *Record of Jingji*, Wang Jie's *A Complete Account of Jingji*, and Chen Renxi's *Classified Jingji* in eight parts. A huge number of publications on *jingji* were produced during the Ming dynasty, most of which were used as reference works by candidates for the imperial examinations.

A Complete Collection of Books through the Ages published in the Qing dynasty consists of six parts; the section on *jingji* includes eighty-three volumes on business and commerce. *Collected Writings on Jingji of the Imperial Dynasty* in 128 volumes compiled by Master of the Self Strong Study and published in 1901, contain a new subject, "Western politics". The same year saw the publication of *A New Version of Collected Writings on Jingji of the Imperial Dynasty* in sixty-two volumes compiled by the Master of Yijin Study, a work devoted to the exposition of *jingji*.[13] In the Qing dynasty, *jingji* referred to an engagement with politics, and books related to *jingji* were less frequently used for examination purposes than in the Ming.

The fact that *jingji* was defined as political engagement, and served the purposes of those taking official examinations, reveals that knowledge of *jingji* was a requirement for prospective officials. In fact, words with more specific economic connotations than *jingji*, for example, *shihuo*, *huozhi*, *licai* and *fuguo*, had already existed in the Chinese language for a long time. However, the use of the term *jingji* with its much broader meaning than simply "economics" was understandable at a time when the economy was subordinate to politics and references to wealth and profit were culturally taboo. This also holds true for other countries. However, as history progressed, the connotations of *jingji* became richer and it became a matter of course to group similar concepts under the single term "*jingji*". Although this could not be referred to as a "discipline" it was nevertheless not simply a matter of terminology. Of course, the use of the term *jingji* to mean economics only occurred after the introduction of Western learning. However, it is not correct to trace the term *jingji*, meaning economics, solely back to Western learning.

13 See *A Complete Catalogue of the Library of the Four Treasures*, juan 92, 124, 136, 138, 139 and 167; also related reference in Professor Zhao Naituan's *Sifting Sand*, Beijing: Beijing University Press, 1980.

3

Since another origin of *"jingji"* was the translation into Japanese of a Western term, the question could be asked, where does "economics" come from? It is widely accepted among scholars that it came from the Greek, although we need to look at the meaning and evolution of the word in Greek.

The word first appeared in Xenophon's *On Economy*, the Greek title of which is οἰκονομικός. It is generally agreed that οἶκος refers to "home" while νομός refers to "law" or "domination". The two components combine to mean "family economy" (family, domestic or family affairs). That is why the title of this work has also been translated as *Home Economics*. The English term "economy" was derived from this Greek word. In ancient Greece, the home was the unit of production based on slavery and therefore issues related to the management of the economy fell into the category of "home economics."

Another work, the pseudo-Aristotelian *On Economy*, was written at the end of the fourth century BC during Alexander's expedition to the East. This work, by an unidentified author, has been discussed by modern scholars including Ulrich Wilcken and M. Rostovtzeff.[14] It consists of two volumes. The first volume discusses home economics and used the term *"οἰκονομίκα"* in reference to the administration of home affairs in the same way as Xenophon. The second, however, goes further and deals with public finance.

Aristotle's concept of economics is mainly to be found in his *Politics* and *Ethics*. According to *A History of Economic Thought* by Eric Roll [1938], Aristotle contributed to economics in three ways: by defining the boundaries of the subject, the analysis of exchange and the theory of currency. Aristotle believed that economics was concerned with the art of acquiring money and becoming rich. Acquiring money for the family and the state, and the pursuit of increased wealth, were the main content of economics. It is in this way that home management and state administration come together.

The birth of Western "economics" from home economics differs from the case in China, where *jingji* was first related to rule of the country. However, as pointed out above, it also meant administration of the state and had both moral and emotional connotations. One example is provided by Adam Smith's *An Inquiry into the Nature and Causes of the Wealth of Nations* [1776], which was published after his *Theory of the Moral Sentiments* [1759]. It could be said that both the Chinese and Western words for "economics" contained a humanitarian element in their early use and that a disparity exists between their former and current definitions, hence the emergence of a "strategy for enriching a country" in Chinese and "political economy" in Western languages. The term "political economy" was first used by the Frenchman A. De Montchrétien in his *Political Economy Presented to My King and My Dowager Empress* [1615]. The book is written for policymakers. An Englishman, William Petty, used the term "political

---

14 Wu Baosan, ed., *Selected Readings on the Economic Thought of Ancient Greece and Rome*, Beijing: Commercial Press, 1990, p. 178.

economy" in his *The Political Anatomy of Ireland* published in 1672. Jean Jacques Rousseau wrote an entry on "political economy" for a French encyclopaedia in 1755 in which he drew a distinction between political economy and home economics. The first appearance of the term political economy in the title of a British book was in J.D. Steuart's *An Inquiry into the Principles of Political Economy* published in 1767. The term was later widely used. The publication of Adam Smith's *The Wealth of Nations* in 1776 signified the establishment of classical political economy, which was completed by David Ricardo whose representative work was *On the Principles of Political Economy and Taxation* published in 1817.

The emphasis of political economy was not only on the area of circulation but also on statecraft in the mercantilist period. In Physiocracy and classical political economy in Britain, emphasis shifted to reproduction, which included both production and circulation, and it was thus engaged with the law of the increase in wealth and economic development. Classical political economy came to be somewhat divorced from politics and philosophy and from the seventeenth to the end of the nineteenth century the term political economy gradually came to be used to refer to the theory-oriented science that explored economic activities and relationships. It was further developed by Karl Marx, who expanded it to cover various modes of production in human society and by whom it was called "generalised political economy". In the closing years of the nineteenth century there was a trend in economics towards the discussion of economic phenomena rather than policy-related analysis. Politics gradually faded out, and in the preface to the second edition of his *The Theory of Political Economy* [1871] W.S. Jevons claimed to have replaced political economy with "economics". In 1890, the chief exponent of the new classical school, Alfred Marshall, published his *Principles of Economics*. The redefinition of political economy is evinced by the omission of the word "politics" from the book's title. In the twentieth century, political economy was replaced by economics in the West. In spite of recurrent discussions about the revival of the term "political economy" since the 1960s, no agreement has yet been reached on precisely which areas it incorporates.

Is economics universal or general? To answer this question we need to draw a distinction both between the basic principles and practical application of economics, and between its classical and modern versions. There has been no consensus among economists of different periods and countries. Economics in one country may differ from that in another, not just in the object of research but also in the researcher. The Italian economist Luigi Cossa and the Irish economist J.K. Ingram used the terms "British economics", "German economics" and "French economics" in their studies on the history of economic theories. Engels also observed in his "Karl Marx's *A Contribution to the Critique of Political Economy*" that, "it was from the emergence of this [German proletarian] party that German political economy as an independent science also dates".[15]

---

15 *Collected Works of Karl Marx and Frederick Engels*, Moscow/London/New York: Progress Publishers, vol. 16, 1980, p. 469.

Economics varies with the economy as well as with the academic research. The jigsaw interaction between the universalization and diversification of world economies (or globalisation and regionalisation), between the integration and compartmentalisation of academic research (or synthesis or deepening), and the interaction between the development of a basic theory and its accommodation to the specific environment of a certain country, have combined to broaden the scope of economics and helped to improve economic theory and methodology.

In addition to the Chinese translation of the term "economics" via Japanese, the Chinese also coined other words which sound more native. Examples include *fuguo ce* (way of enriching a country), *shengji xue* (learning for living), *jixue* (learning for accounting), and so on. In 1867, the American missionary W.A.P. Martin taught classes on economics at a *Tongwenguan* (foreign language school) under the heading of *fuguo ce*. The textbook for the course was the 1863 edition of *Manual of Political Economy* by H. Fawcett, the Chinese translation of which was printed under the title *Fuguo ce* in 1880. This *Fuguo ce* marked the beginning of Chinese translations of Western economic works. In 1886, the tax department of the Shanghai customs printed a Chinese translation of Jevons's *Primer of Political Economy* under the title of *Fuguo yangmin ce* ("Ways of Enriching the Country and Supporting People"). According to incomplete statistics, by 1898 a total of twelve books or twenty-six volumes had been translated into Chinese. Works by Chinese authors carried titles similar to *Fuguo ce*; for example, Chen Zhi claimed that his *A Sequel to Fuguo ce* was a sister work to that by Adam Smith. He wrote that "a good man [Adam Smith] produced a *Fuguo ce*, which has helped Britain to be wealthy and strong", and his work called for following Britain's example.[16] *Fuguo ce* in this context is no longer the same as its ancient version, since it also incorporates the meaning of "economics".

Why did they not use the term "economics"? Liang Qichao wrote in his "Current Exposition of the 'Volume on Business and Commerce'" in [Sima Qian's] *Records of the Grand Historian* (1897), that "Western *fuguo* learning is becoming a popular topic here.... It is a new learning, but has old roots".[17] By means of comparative studies, he found that Western economics had parallels in *Guanzi* and *The Book of History*. At this time, Liang continued to use the terms *fuguo ce* or *shengji xue* rather than "economics." In 1902 he published *A Short History of the Evolution of Shengji Xue*, a book devoted to the introduction of the Western history of economic thought. In 1901, Yan Fu translated Adam Smith's *The Wealth of Nations*, to which Yan gave a Chinese title *Yuanfu* ("The Origin of Wealth"). In the "translator's preface" he wrote that the term

> *jixue* (learning for accounting), or "economy" in English, was derived from the Greek. The first part "eco" means "home", and the second, "management". The two together imply that initially *jixue* meant "home management", but later came to refer to things such as measurement, management,

16 Chen Zhi, preface to *A Supplement to Fuguo Ce*, revised edition, 1897–1898.
17 Liang Qichao, "Essays", *Writings of the Yinbing Study*, vol. 2.

prudence, expense and income, and was later expanded to mean the way of running and feeding the country and the world. It therefore had a wide range of meanings. The Japanese translation is *jingji*, while the Chinese is *licai* (management of wealth).

"The word *jingji*," he argued, "is too broad, whereas *licai* is too narrow. Therefore, I have coined the term *jixue*.... The Origin of Wealth is thus a work on *jixue*".[18] Yan also believed that the framework of *jixue* existed in ancient China although it was not an independent area of learning.

4

According to Professor Zhao Jing, the term *jingjixue* made its debut in the Chinese language no later than the eighth century during the Tang dynasty. For example, the Tang poet Yan Wei wrote the line "Taking my *jingjixue* to monk master Dao An for his instruction." But *jingjixue* in this context refers to ideas about governing society, totally different from modern economics.[19] I believe that its appearance as a formal area of learning took place sometime later, and that the content differed from that of modern economics. In fact, all *shixue* (tangible or practical learning), *shigong zhi xue* (the study of deeds and merits), and *jingshi zhi xue* (learning for management of society) in traditional learning were somehow related to economics. But however macroscopic, blurred or relative they were, they cannot be seen as an independent area of study. Neither was *jingji zhi xue*, although *jingji zhi xue* is a special case.

As far as my reading goes, the term *jingji zhi xue* was used for the first time by Zhu Xi[20] in his comment on "Lu Xuan Gong's Memorial to the Throne", which is included in his *Classified Sayings of Master Zhu Xi* volume 136: "Discussing tax in minute detail is nothing but *jingji zhi xue*." A later example is provided by "Volume 1 of Selections" from *The History of the Ming Dynasty* which relates how the Taizu emperor of the Ming dynasty selected brilliant men from the *Guozi Xue* (The School for the Sons of the State), whom he asked to read extensively and study the learning of the *daode* and *jingji* for doing great service to the state. "The Biography of Zhang Lüxiang" in *Manuscripts of the History of the Qing Dynasty* relates that Zhang Lüxiang (1610–1674) once "told his disciples to study *jingji zhi xue*." Zhang also wrote *A Supplement to the Book of Agriculture* (1658), an important document on the agricultural techniques of the Taihu Lake area. Reference to *jingji zhi xue* are also quite often found in Qing dynasty literature, for example, the "Biography of Zeng Zhao" in *Manuscripts of the History of the Qing Dynasty* tells us that Zeng "was good at *jingji zhi xue*."

18 Yan Fu trans., "The Translator's Comments", *On the Origin of Wealth, Noted Western Works Translated by Van Fu*, No. 2, Shanghai: Commercial Press, 1931.
19 Zhao Jing, ed., *A General History of Economic Thoughts in China*, vol. 1, Beijing: Beijing University Press, 1991, p. 4, footnote 1.
20 [1130–1200.]

The increasing influence of economic connotations in traditional learning is demonstrated by the fact that ethical and metaphysical *xingming* studies no longer ran counter to the practical learning of *jingji* and *shigong*, but all existed in harmony. Chen Qianhe (1639–1714), who was active in the early years of the Qing dynasty published *Chu gong* ("The Merit of Saving"), in which he wrote that "learning about *xingming* and learning about *jingji* are two sides of the same coin ... when *jingji* declines, *xingming* is as useless as deadly Zen sitting." Wang Jiaxi, who lived in the Qianlong–Jiaqing periods of the Qing dynasty, wrote in a letter to Chen Fuya that

> the most needed learning today is *jingji* and *zhanggu* (anecdotes, happening, etc.). The former has a practical function and the latter will furnish one with literature. Without a talent for *jingji*, one will fill a book with empty words, and without knowledge of *zhanggu*, what can one say in a book?[21]

In "Encouraging Students of Zhili to Study Hard", Zeng Guofan, who was lauded by the emperor on his death as a great Confucian, divided Confucian learning into four classes: *yili* (ethics and philosophy), *kaoju* (textual criticism), *cizhang* (literature and writing) and *jingji*. "*Jingji*," he wrote, "is state affairs in the Confucian system. All past codes, rites and government documents as well as present-day anecdotes fall into this category". He believed that "having grasped *yili*, one knows everything about *jingji* ".[22] Sun Yatsen also wrote in a letter to Zhen Zaoru (dated the fifteenth year of the Guangxu reign period [1889]), the earliest of his writings found to date, that "I have been interested in learning about *jingji* for ten years or so, touching on the current changes in the European political situation and the institutional evolution through the ages in China".[23] This document is of great historical value.

It is noteworthy that *jingji* existed as a learning not only nominally but also in reality during the Qing dynasty. It was a subject taught in schools and as a special category in the civil service examinations. For example, the volume "Selection of Manuscripts" in *History of the Qing Dynasty* relates that in the twenty-fourth year of the Guangxu reign period (1898), "a special category of *jingji*" was established at the request of Yanxiu, the official in charge of education in Guizhou. The category was, however, cancelled as a result of the failure of the 1898 reform, but was reintroduced three years later. As late as 1903 candidates in the special category of *jingji* took the imperial examinations in the palace; according to his biography in *Manuscripts of the History of the Qing Dynasty*, Zhang Zhidong was the examiner on this occasion.

In the above section I discussed the indigenous learning of *jingji* and below I will move on to the question of when Western economics first appeared in China.

---

21 Essays on *Jingshi* in the Imperial Dynasty.
22 "Poems and essays", *Complete Works of Zeng Guofan*.
23 *Complete Works of Sun Yatsen*, vol. 1, Zhonghua Book Company, 1981.

5

In 1903, the Japanese Sugiei Kazuo (1873–1965) was invited to teach economics at Capital University, and the *Textbook of Economics* which he compiled may have marked the beginning of the use of the term in Chinese. This term also appeared in the titles of Chinese translations, for example, Wang Jingfang's translation of *Economics* by the Japanese writer Misaki Kakujiroyuki, in that of a lecture on "economics" given by Misaki Kakujiroyuki and compiled by Wang Shaozeng in 1906, Zhu Baoshou's 1908 translation of *The Working Principles of Political Economy* by S.M. Macvane, which was given the Chinese title *Jingji yuanlun* ("On the Origin of *Jingji*"), and Xiong Songxi and others' translation of *Outlines of Economics* by Richard T. Ely, which was published in 1910 and reprinted many times. The number of books with titles containing the term *jingji* later increased. This is especially true of Chinese translations of Japanese works, for example, *A General Account of Economics* by Abe Tamakio, and *Principles of Economics* by Fukuta Tokuzo. It has been estimated that between the Reform Movement of 1898 and the Revolution of 1911, fifteen important Chinese books introducing the history of Western economic thought were produced in addition to forty-two translated books and fifty-four volumes on Western economics.[24]

In addition to its use in translated works, the Chinese also used the term *jingjixue* according to its modern definition. As far as I know, the earliest example is that provided by Liang Qichao in his "Criticism of the State Employment of Land as Promoted in Certain Newspapers", written in 1905. In this essay, Liang argued that "a student of *jingji* must aim at national *jingji*." He believed that the German economist E. Philippovic was the most convincing of contemporary economists.[25] He also used terms such as "economic behaviour", "economic law", "economic organisation" and "economic motive". Liang fled to Japan after the failure of the 1898 reform and was inevitably exposed to the influence of the Japanese language. (In passing, his essay was published in *Xinmin congbao*, and later included in his anthology of writings *Yinbingshi heji* [Selected Works of Liang Qichao].) Another example is provided by the fourth article of the stated aims of the 1906 *Shangwu guanbao* (Business Gazette), which declares that articles should be based on *jingjixue* [economic] theory and should be used as a practical method.[26] Some authors, including in particular Li Zuoting (1907), Xiong Yuanhan (1911),

24 With regard to translations, consult the entry "The Spread of Western Bourgeois Economics in Old China", "Economics Volume", Beijing: Encyclopedia of China Publishing House, 1995, p. 636 footnote 2 and p. 712, footnotes 1–3. I mentioned in my "Some Notes on *Jingji*" published in *Dushu*, 1997, no. 11 that Wang's translation of Misaki Kakujiroyuki's book was the earliest titled *Jingjixue*. I recently learned from Wu Shuo's note published in *Dushu* 1998, no. 4 that Shangwu Bao (Business) sponsored by the office of the Governor of Hubei and Hunan Provinces serialised *Trade Economics*, translated by Chen Yan and his Japanese employee. However, this short essay is a little too simple, and we need to check the history of newspapers more carefully.
25 Ibid., "Essays", *Writings of the Yinbing Study*, vol. 18.
26 Ge Gongzhen, *A History of Newspapers in China*, Shanghai: Shanghai Bookstore Publishing House, reprinted in 1990, p. 49.

Liu Binglin and Zhao Lanping, used *Jingjixue* as the title of their books. These works dealt with economics in an entirely Western sense.

At the same time, Chinese scholars were not satisfied with merely introducing and accepting Western learning and continued their own investigation of local economics. Throughout the past century, thinkers have continued their efforts to construct a Chinese economics that differs from the traditional *jingjixue*. In 1902, Liang Qichao wrote in his *Changing Trends in Chinese Academic Thought*: "I planned to create *A History of Shengjixue in China*, a book to be devoted to comparative research on previous thinkers' opinions and Western theories." In this context, *shengjixue* means nothing less than economics. Liang believed that "such learning existed in pre-Qin China".[27] Liang Qichao's stay in Japan and exposure to Western learning, his belief that Western economics has parallels in ancient China, and his attempt to write an economic history of China, combined to make him worthy of the title "founder of 'Chinese economics'." During the 1920s and 1930s, the search aimed at the construction of a systematic discipline of Chinese economics consisted mainly of an examination and editing of previous economic ideas and theories.

6

The construction of indigenous economics consists of an enquiry into basic economic theories and exploration of the history of economic thought. In the former, research is based on a combination of basic economic theories (mainly Marxism) and studies of Chinese economic history. The aim is to construct a new theory governing research on China's economic problems. In the latter, emphasis is placed on the study of economic thought, theory and opinion from ancient times, and tracing the evolution of economic thought and theory in China, in order to provide a reference point for an analysis of current problems.

There are numerous published works on basic theory,[28] the most influential example of which is by Wang Yanan, an advocate of "Chinese economics". Wang was trained in traditional learning and was very familiar with classical economics and Marxist economy. Wang and Guo Dali were co-authors of the first complete translation of Karl Marx's *Das Kapital* (1938). They recommended studying the Chinese economy from a Marxist perspective and thus constructing "Chinese economics". Wang said that "The emphasis of my research is Chinese economics."[29] His representative work, *On the Origin of the Chinese*

---

27 Ibid., "Essays", *Writings of the Yinbing Study*, vols. 2 and 7.
28 For example, Wang Yucun's *Outlines of Social and Economic History in China* (1936), Huo Yixian's *Evolution of the Economic System in China* (1936), Yu Jingyi's *Social and Economic Development in China and the West* (1944), Fu Zhufu *et al.*, *Questions Related to Primitive Accumulation in China* (1957), Wu Dakun's *Outline Discussion on Slave and Feudal Economies in China* (1963), Hu Rulei's *Studies on the Feudal Social Form in China* (1979), and Sunjian's *The Socio-Economic System Before Capitalism* (1980).
29 Economics Institute, Xiamen University ed., *Essays on the History of Economic Thought* by Wang Yanan, Shanghai: Shanghai People's Publishing House, 1981, p. 148.

Economy (1946), which was later renamed *Studies on Economic Form in Semi-Feudal and Semi-Colonial China* (1957, also in Japanese and Russian versions), is a theoretical and empirical study. Wang was also the author of *Outlines of Feudalism in the Chinese Landlord Economy* (1954).

Another example is Xu Dixin's pioneering effort in localising political economy. He stated in his *Generalised Political Economy* published in Hong Kong at the end of the 1940s that he meant to write a Chinese political economy, "to satisfy those who find the current books on political economy useless in answering problems in reality." He wanted to produce a book "that combines the universal truth of Marxism–Leninism with the specific context of the Chinese economy." The revised edition of this book in three volumes was published by the People's Publishing House in the 1980s. The author believed that Volume 3, "The Economy of New Democracy", which followed the previously published first and second volumes, was unsuccessful since New Democracy was not an independent social system. In the winter of 1982 he was determined to rewrite the whole book using Engels's concept of "generalised political economy". Xu looked not only at the socialist economy, but also various economic relationships within the capitalist, imperialist and pre-capitalist modes of production. According to Xu, a "generalised political economy" would have theoretical, academic and practical value".[30]

Systematic research on Chinese economic thought began in the 1920s and 1930s.[31] This was a period of dramatic social change and intellectual development in China, and the desire for a strong country provided the impetus for economic development and theoretical construction. The introduction of Western economics and Marxism provided an academic reference point for Chinese economic research. Students trained in Western universities, yet with a commitment to the development of the motherland, became the main force in indigenous economics. This period witnessed the emergence of the history of Chinese economic thought as a sub-discipline of economics and was marked by the publication of numerous research results and the unprecedented opening of classes in Chinese economic thought in most universities. For example, Gan Naiguang's *History of Pre-Qin Economic Thought* published in 1926 was based on Gan's lectures at Lingnan University.[32] The first volume of Tang Qingzeng's *The History of Economic Thought in China* was also based on his teaching notes. Tang wrote in the author's preface,

---

30 Xu Dixin, Prefaces to the first and revised editions of *Generalized Political Economy*, revised edition, vol. 1, Shanghai: People's Publishing House, 1984.

31 For more details about the initial stage of research on the history of economic thought in China and on international research, see the author's "An Analysis of Research in the 1920s and 1930s on the History of Economic Thought in China". For later developments see the author's "Research on the History of Economic Thought in China: A Retrospective and Prospects, "and the author's (Kishimoto Yoshioko, trans.,) "The Current Situation and Topics of Research on the History of Economic Thought in China, "*China: Her Society and Culture*, 1994, no. 9.

32 Gan Naiguang, "Preface" to *The History of Pre-Qin Economic Thought*, Shanghai: Commercial Press, 1926.

in the seventeenth year of the Republic, I taught a class at the invitation of my friend Xu Shuliu at Jiaotong University. From this time on I began to write this book.... I taught the class thirty or forty times at various universities in Shanghai and Nanjing.[33]

Tang taught at Jiaotong University, Jinan University, Zhejiang University, Guanghua University and Fudan University. The final example is provided by Hou Wailu, who in 1931 taught a class on "the history of Chinese economic thought" at the Law School in Harbin and wrote "lecture notes of a research nature". Hou relates that "during this time I taught at a number of universities in Beiping [Beijing] but did not directly take part in the debate in the newspapers."[34] We can see from these examples that classes on the history of Chinese economic thought were taught at most universities.

Not only Chinese, but also overseas scholars – mainly Japanese – were involved in research on the history of Chinese economic thought at this time. Western scholars chiefly translated related Chinese texts. S.Y. Lee's studies (1936) on ancient Chinese economic thought appear to be the only research conducted by Western scholars.[35] Japanese scholars' initial contributions include Tazaki Masayoshi's *The Economic Thought and System of Ancient China* (1924), Tashima Kinji's *A History of Oriental Economics – The Economic Thought of Ancient China* (1935), and Oshima Yuma's *Chinese Thought: Social and Economic Thought* (1936). Special mention should also be made of Tashima Kinji's essays published in 1894 and his lectures on the history of Chinese economic thought given in the Economics Department of Kyoto University. Tashima's students later compiled and edited his lecture notes and published them as a book. It is a pity that the history of Chinese economic thought has yet to exist as an independent discipline in Japan, with researchers in this field spread across the disciplines of oriental history, economic history and so on.

The main books by Chinese authors of this period include Gan Naiguang's *The History of Pre-Qin Economic Thought* (1926), Li Quanshi's *A Short History of Chinese Economic Thought* (1927), *A History of Late Zhou Masters' Economic Thought* (1930) by Xiong Meng, Zhao Keren's *Economic Theory of Mr Sunyatsen* (1935), Tang Qingzeng's *The History of Chinese Economic Thought* (vol. 1, 1936), Huang Han's *Economic Thought of Master Guan Zhong* (1936), and Zhao Fengtian's *Economic Thought in the Last Fifty Years of the Qing Dynasty* (1939). It is worth noting that before these there were virtually no books with the title *History of Economic Thought*, and according to incomplete statistics more than 90 per cent of the 450 essays written on the subject before 1949 were published after 1926.[36]

33 Tang Qingzeng, "Preface" to *The History of Economic Thought in China*, vol. I, Shanghai: Commercial Press, 1936.
34 Hou Wailu, *Persistent Pursuit*, Shanghai: Sanlian Bookstore, 1935, p. 224.
35 J.A. Schumpeter's *History of Economic Analysis* has a reference to this book, see the Chinese translation, vol. I, Beijing: Commercial Press, 1991, p. 86, footnote 1.
36 Zhao Jing ed., *A General History of Economic Thought in China*, vol. I, Beijing: Beijing University Publishing House, 1991, p. 10.

Tang Qingzeng's work signifies the highest level of scholarship at this time. Born into a family of scholars, Tang received his training in finance and the history of Western economic thought at Harvard. He returned to China in 1925 and taught at numerous universities. He wrote in the preface to his book that "different countries have their own conditions and totally different histories. Therefore, constructing an economic science appropriate for China, we need to confront our own conditions". He also believed that "without a consideration of our own intellectual background, we are not ready to build a systematic economic science." Tang set out to "prepare for the creation of the new economic thought of our country." In the three prefaces to this work, the authors, Ma Yinchu, Zhao Renjun and Li Quanshi, discuss the splendour of economic thought in ancient China and the urgent need for research. They trusted Tang to edit this legacy from the past and create new economic concepts specifically for China.[37] Tang Qingzeng's book consists of ten sections dealing with Confucian, Daoist, Mohist, and Legalist economic concepts and those of the agricultural schools, politicians, merchants and in historical texts, with a special section devoted to a discussion of the influence of Chinese economic thought on Western nations. "The prosperity of economic thought," he pointed out, "existed earlier in China than in Western countries." Therefore, "the spread of ancient Chinese economic thought to the West must be a fact."[38]

Tang's opinion was shared by many. For example, numerous Chinese and overseas scholars wrote on the relationship between the French Physiocrats and ancient Chinese thought.[39] The noted Japanese economic historian Takimoto Shijekazu's book *A History of European Economic Theories* (1931) is subtitled "Modern Western Economic Thought had its Root in Chinese Theories."

In short, the origins and development of Chinese and Western economics are complex and diverse, as is the Chinese–Japanese term *jingji*, and we should avoid oversimplification in our research.

37 Tang Qingzeng, *A History of Economic Thought in China*, vol. I, see the prefaces by the author, Ma Yinchu, Zhao Renjun and Li Quanshi.
38 Ibid., p. 362.
39 In relation to this question see Tan Min's *The Chinese Origin of the French Physiocracy*, Shanghai: Shanghai People's Publishing House, 1992.

10 The theory of division of labour in Chinese history[1]

Yan Qinghua

Division of labour is the foundation for management. The two are mutually interdependent in that management would have no importance without the division of labour and, at the same time, efficient management can refine the division of labour.

Division of labour has been in existence for centuries. During ancient times, when there were no modern technologies and management techniques, division of labour was the primary source of productivity development as well as the key factor in rationalising the production process. It is therefore unsurprising that it should have attracted the attention of thinkers in those times.

"History is the starting point of modern scientific theories".[2] Division of labour was a central topic when Classical Plutonomy was gradually developed in the Western world. Adam Smith contributed his own work on this topic. Besides Xenophon, Plato and Adam Smith, many other scholars had expatiated on the division of labour, including Thomas More, William Petty and Charles Babbage. The theory of the division of labour was an essential component of economic theories even before economics became an independent discipline.

Similarly in ancient China, especially during the Spring and Autumn and Warring States periods, there were many views expressed on the theory of the division of labour, some of which were quite sophisticated. In general, the Chinese theories could be categorised in terms of the following aspects.

The necessity of the division of labour

In Chinese history, any scholar who touched on the division of labour had more or less to discuss its importance and necessity; among all these discussions, Mencius's stands out as the most influential.

1 Originally published as "中国历史上的分工理论" ("The Theory of Division of Labour in Chinese History"), in "中国经济管理思想概要" (*A Synopsis of Chinese Economic and Managerial Thought*), Wuhan: Wuhan University Press, 1989, pp. 19–36.
2 *Marx and Engels, Selected Works*, vol. 3, Beijing: People's Publishing House, 1972, p. 268.

Mencius brought up the topic in his refutation of the opinion of Xing Xu[3] who argued that the "wise ruler shares the work of tilling the land with his people".[4] Xing Xu believed that the ruling class should also engage in agricultural work: they should be self-sufficient instead of exploiting the people. Xing Xu's idea, to a certain extent, reflects the needs of working people, but it is incorrect from the viewpoint of the division of labour. Mencius detected the weak point in Xing Xu's position and later refuted it using the theory of the social division of labour. Mencius states that one could not master all kinds of jobs but one has all kinds of needs, hence the necessity for the division of labour.

Mencius posed the question to Xiang Chen, Xing Xu's student: "Does Xing eat only the grain he has grown himself?" Xiang answered: "Yes." Mencius then asked: "Does Xing only wear cloth he has woven himself" Xiang answered: "No, he wears unwoven hemp." Mencius then asked: "Does Xing wear a cap?" Xiang answered: "Yes." Mencius asked: "What kind of cap does he wear?" Xiang answered: "Plain raw silk." Mencius asked: "Does he weave it himself?" Xiang answered: "No, he trades grain for it." Mencius then asked: "Why does Xing not weave it himself?" Xiang answered: "Because it interferes with his work in the fields." Mencius asked: "Does Xing use an iron pot and an earthenware steamer for cooking rice and iron implements for ploughing the fields?" Xiang answered: "Yes." Mencius asked: "Does he make them himself?" Xiang answered: "No, he trades grain for them."[5]

Mencius questioned Xing's statement in this conversation. Even though Xing Xu grows his own rice, he does not necessarily have to produce clothes, hats or farming equipment. A farmer could not possibly manage to produce other handicrafts. As the old Chinese saying goes, "The equipment used by a farmer is prepared by people from all walks of life."

Mencius also discusses barter. He pointed out that only through barter could an individual satisfy all his needs without hurting other person's welfare. Hence:

> To trade grain for implements is not to inflict hardship on the potter and the blacksmith. The potter and the blacksmith, for their part, also trade their wares for grain. In doing this, surely they are not inflicting hardship on the farmer either[6]

Mencius believed that through barter people could develop their own specialisation and then exchange the necessities of life using their own surplus production. Without barter there will be excess production in each industry which

---

3 [Xing Xu is described by Mencius as "a follower of Shen Nong", the cultural hero who is fabled as the inventor of agriculture and commerce in the third millennium BC.]

4 *Mencius*, III.A.4.

5 Ibid.

6 Ibid.

nobody could obtain even if they needed it. In his view, then, exchange (barter) based on the division of labour is mutually beneficial.

Mencius also mentioned that the division of labour should include an appropriate ratio of people among different occupations. He gave an example: "In a city of ten thousand households, would it be enough to have a single potter?" In the situation where pottery was a household necessity at the time, one potter for ten thousand households was certainly not enough. Hence the answer: "No, there will be a shortage of earthenware".[7] Although he talked in this example about a situation in which taxes are too low to support public finance, he managed to convey the idea that the number of people engaged in a certain occupation should depend on the social need for that occupation's products and also be proportional to the population size. In fact, he had demonstrated the necessity for the division of labour in terms of a proportional relationship.

In the late Warring States period, Xunzi also discussed the necessity of the division of labour. His ideas were more straightforward. In his view, a person's daily necessities consisted of all kinds of products which simply could not be produced by a single person. Thus: "In history, there is no one who could truly master two skills at the same time." And that is the reason for the division of labour, so that everyone can specialise in a certain industry: "choose one and be one", meaning to choose a career and dedicate one's life to it.[8]

The famous Tang dynasty writer, Han Yu, also had a clear understanding of the necessity for the division of labour. His views were summarised in the article, "Masonry Wang Chengfu's Biography". He expressed himself in the article through the character of a mason. As he pointed out, rice is grown by some people, cloth and silk are produced by other people, and so on for other daily necessities. We cannot survive without these items. However, it is impossible to create all these daily necessities by ourselves. Then the most appropriate approach is to make the best use of everyone's ability to cooperate with each other in order to survive. This argument clearly demonstrates the need for division of labour.

Plato and other ancient Greece philosophers had also discussed the necessity of the division of labour. As Karl Marx put it, Plato illustrated division of labour "from the point of the diversity of human needs and the limitation of individual talents".[9] Essentially, Mencius and others in ancient China were using the same arguments, that the diversity of human needs and the limitation of individual talents is the major contradiction that needs to be solved in the theory of the division of labour. These ancient thinkers had precisely and insightfully addressed the same question.

7 *Mencius*, VI.B.10.
8 *Xunzi*, "Dispelling Obsession".
9 Marx and Engels, Complete Works, vol. 23, Beijing: People's Publishing House, 1972, p. 405, n. 80.

The role of the division of labour

Guan Zhong, Minister of the Qi State in the early Spring and Autumn period, was the first systematically to discuss the division of labour. He suggested that people of the same profession should live in close proximity to each other, the reasons being, first, that people within the same profession could communicate in daily conversation to exchange ideas about production techniques and product quality; second, that they could also talk about revenues, profits and prices within their industry so that there was less information asymmetry; and third, that the arrangement would help the next generation within the profession to carry on their heritage easily because they would have been exposed to the occupational environment since their childhood. As Guan Zhong explained: "Skills learned from the family could be learned without strict training; experience gained since childhood does not require diligent efforts." To sum up, division of labour is conducive to technology innovation, information exchange and accumulation of knowledge among the same profession.[10]

Xunzi exposited further on the effects of division of labour on innovation in technology. He believed that division of labour could polish workers' skills to a higher level:

> Many men have loved the art of writing, but Cang Jie alone is honoured by later ages as its master, because he concentrated upon it. Many men have loved husbandry, but Lord Millet alone is honoured by later ages as its master, because he concentrated upon it. Many men have loved music, but Kai alone in honoured by later ages as its master, because he concentrated upon it.[11]

In short, division of labour could greatly improve technology.

In addition to Guan Zhong and Xunzi, the famous thinker of the late Warring States period, Han Fei, added his opinions on the theory of the division of labour. In economic terms, Han Fei thought that division of labour can increase economic efficiency and avoid the losses caused by workers changing their jobs. He said: "Workers who change their careers several times will lose their expertise, farmers who move their fields many times will not reap abundant rice."[12] Here, he made use of the word *gong* which means "high yields, low costs."[13] *Gong* has the same meaning as the economic term "efficiency" and relates to input–output analysis. We could therefore interpret his view as follows: workers who change their jobs too often will not get the expected economic profits. He also made the following calculation:

10 [See *Guoyu* ("Discourses on the States"), *Qi Yu* ("Discourse on the State of Qi").]
11 *Xunzi*, "Dispelling Obsession".
12 *Hanfeizi*, "Commentary on the teachings of Laozi".
13 *Hanfeizi*, "Facing South". ["An achievement can be called successful only if the income is large and the outlay is small." Ibid.]

If one man loses half a day's accomplishment per day, in ten days he will lose five men's accomplishment. If ten thousand men each lose half a day's accomplishment per day, in ten days they will lose fifty thousand men's accomplishment.[14]

This means that the more frequently workers change their jobs, the greater the losses that are incurred. Only through division of labour, allowing workers to specialise in certain professions, will such losses be minimised.

After Han Fei, the author of the book *Huainanzi* during the Western Han dynasty, and Fu Xuan during the Western Jin dynasty, also contributed to the theory of the division of labour, believing that it could help to create a harmonious society. The author of *Huainanzi* claimed that the division of labour can make

Farmers talk about farming with each other, officials talk about virtue with each other, workers talk about skills with each other, and merchants talk about prices with each other. In this way, officials will avoid misbehaviour, farmers will not waste their efforts, workers will not need to do unnecessary work, businessmen will not have excess production, and therefore everybody is satisfied.[15]

Fu Xuan pointed out: "Wise governors lead their people by putting them into different professions so that they can focus; and hence society will be stable, and everyone can specialise in a certain field."[16] Stability and specialisation both emphasise the important role of division of labour in coordinating social and economic life.

In the history of Western economic thought, Adam Smith made a comparatively thorough exposition on the role of division of labour. He commented on its effect in improving labour productivity and summarised as follows: first, division of labour can lead to specialisation of labour and thus enhance workers' efficiency; second, division of labour can avoid the loss if a worker switches to another occupation; third, workers specialising in a certain field are more likely to create new machines and technologies. We have seen that at least the first two points identified by Adam Smith were discussed in some detail by ancient Chinese thinkers. Moreover, ideas that were not discussed by Adam Smith had received consideration by Chinese thinkers, as with Fu Xuan's emphasis on the role of the division of labour in coordinating social and economic life. In sum, ancient Chinese thinkers had a comprehensive and profound understanding of the role of the division of labour.

14 *Hanfeizi*, "Commentary on the teachings of Laozi".
15 *Huainanzi*, "Vulgar training".
16 *Fuzi*, "Stabilise the People".

How to divide labour

On how to divide labour, the mainstream methods in Chinese history can be cat-egorised under the following headings.

Guan Zhong's theory of dividing labour according to profession

Guan Zhong stated that people should be divided into four groups according to their professions, which he called "four kinds of people" (intellectuals, farmers, workers and businessmen). He proposed that the government should locate these four kinds of people in distinct areas according to their profession and rule them separately. He referred to this as "Fixing the people's residence" and "Not mixing people with different occupations". He also advocated that occupations should be passed down from generation to generation, that is to say, "The intel-lectuals' offspring should also be intellectuals", "The famers' offspring should also be famers", "The workers' offspring should also be workers" and "The businessmen' offspring should also be businessmen".[17]

There are three significant stages of the division of labour in human history. The first stage is to separate farming from stockbreeding; the second stage is to separate handwork from farming; the third stage is the emergence of the class of businessmen, along with the separation of manual work and brain work. Zhong Guan's classification of professions basically conformed to the situation of the social structure at that time so it was universally accepted by later thinkers and became a typical mode of dividing social careers. However, he only analysed the occupational division of labour from the macro perspective and failed to mention micro considerations.

Mo Di's theory of division of labour

Mo Di (from the Warring States period) attached importance to understanding the production activities of the working class and gave his own elaboration on the division of labour. First, he proposed that division of labour should be based on gender. That is, division of labour should be in accordance with the special-ties of males and females which requires men to concentrate on "ploughing and planting" and women on "weaving and spinning".[18] Second, he suggested that division of labour should be based on differences in expertise. Thus: "The ancient sage-kings authorised the code of laws, pronouncing: 'All you artisans and workers, carpenters and tanners, potters and smiths, do the work of which you are capable. Stop when the needs of the people are satisfied'."[19] That is to say, various kinds of handicraftsmen should focus on their own specific job. Third, he claimed that division of labour should be based on the type of work,

17 *Guoyu*; *Qi Yu*.
18 *Mozi*, "Against Music".
19 *Mozi*, "Gengzhu".

that is, we should divide labour according to different types of work within the same industry: "It is like the building of a wall. Let those who can lay the bricks lay the bricks, let those who can fill the mortar fill the mortar, and let those who can carry the materials carry the materials. Then the wall can be completed."[20] Mo Di thus advocated that all workers involved in building walls should participate in only one of the procedures according to their own expertise. His opinions were detailed, concrete and practical.

Huainanzi *and Han Yu's opinions on rational division of labour*

Neither the author of *Huainanzi* nor Han Yu had proposals for how to conduct division of labour, but both of them mentioned the important principles of division of labour, that is, the rational division of labour.

Huainanzi stated that everyone has his or her strengths and weakness, thus individual distinctions should be considered when dividing the labour so as to foster strengths and circumvent weaknesses. The author gave some examples: "When the deer go uphill, even the roebucks cannot catch them. However, when they go downhill, even children can catch them. It means that animals have merits and drawbacks." The same applies to human being:

Both Tang [Shang emperor] and Wu [Zhou emperor] are smart monarchs, but they cannot sail on the lake in a small boat like southern people from the Yue area. Yi Yin is a clever [Shang] minister, but he cannot ride and tame the wild horses; Confucius and Mozi are knowledgeable and versatile, but they cannot cross over mountains as freely as the mountaineers.[21]

The author argued that rational division of labour should enable everyone to maximise his or her talents:

people who have strategic vision should not work on bagatelle, while people who only know petty tricks should not be entrusted with important tasks. Different people have different specialisms, just as different objects have different shapes. Some could not even bear one job, while some would easily handle a hundred jobs at the same time.[22]

The author pointed out that Yi Yin, the Shang minister, did well in allocating different tasks to different people:

So when Yi Yin is engaged in construction, he appoints people with long legs to carry hoes, people with strong backs to carry soil, the people with

20 Ibid.
21 *Huainanzi*, "Zhu Shu Xun".
22 Ibid.

one blind eye to measure, and the humpbacked people to pave and plaster the floor. Everyone's specialty could be fully explored.[23]

The author emphasised that "everyone's specialty should be fully explored" so he claimed that individual characteristics should be considered when dividing the labour in order to maximise individual talents.

Han Yu also talked about the issue of rational division of labour. He argued that people should treat their own professions from the perspective of the social division of labour and fulfil themselves accordingly: "The most suitable way is allowing everyone to fulfil themselves and at the same time produce enough output to satisfy everyone." In his opinion, the process of the social division of labour is built on interdependencies between people. Although some people bear more tasks than others, everyone is a component of the whole social organism. That is, "Tasks are different in their level of difficulty; one can only work within one's ability, just like a container is limited to holding its own volume." People should therefore choose their occupation according to their ability; they should not do something "desperately, even though you know you cannot manage", but rather "choose what you are capable of doing".[24]

The author of *Huainanzi* proposed to determine professions according to social conventions while Han Yu proposed to determine them according to capability. Though they differed somewhat in their approaches, they ended up with essentially the same idea of the rational division of labour.

Fu Xuan's proposal on planning the division of labour

There were several objective reasons for the proposal to divide the labour force in a planned way. At the beginning of Western Jin dynasty, after the long-term chaos at the end of the Han dynasty and in the Three Kingdoms period, the immediate tasks facing the Western Jin were stabilising society, settling the homeless and recovering and developing the economy. Fu Xuan's ideas were developed under such circumstances. The details of his arguments were expressed as follows:

> I think it is urgent to work out a system in which we should first calculate the national population, then allocate a part of the whole population to be intellectuals in order to assist the government; allocate a second part to be farmers in order to maintain enough food storage; allocate a third part to be workers in order to maximise the supply of tools; and allocate a fourth part to be businessmen in order to provide sufficient commodities.

That is to say, intellectuals, farmers, workers and businessmen should be supplied according to the social demand. He emphasised that the agricultural

---

23 Ibid.
24 This quotation comes from "Collection of Mr Changli. Biography of a bricklayer named Wangchengfu".

population should be prioritised because the social demand for intellectuals, workers and businessmen was limited and should not be overrated, while agriculture could accommodate a large number of people. Hence, government should first allocate a fixed number of people as intellectuals, workers and businessmen and put the rest of the population into agriculture. He advised that "we should allocate enough people to assist the government and let them study; the rest should be allocated to agriculture. If the population of workers and businessmen is excessive, the extra persons should also be allocated to agriculture."[25]

At the time, the terrible social turmoil had disturbed the proportions between the different occupations and Fu Xuan's proposal had positive effects in securing the agricultural population and restoring the economy. However, in a society based on private ownership it was almost impossible to allocate labour proportionally according to the actual demands. In the end, Fu Xuan's plan reflected the wish of the feudal ruling class to secure their reign by restoring and developing the economy.

Dong Tuanxiao's theory of division of labour based on a production line

Dong Tuanxiao was an army general in the late Yuan dynasty. In the year 1356, the sixteenth year of the Zhi Zheng period of emperor Hui, he led the army to Haining. In order to obtain supplies he put forward a suggestion called "Deliver food for 100 *Li* [1 *Li*=0.3105 miles] in one day". These are the details:

> The way of transporting by land is as follows. If each person walks ten paces, thirty-six persons could cover one *Li*, 360 persons could cover ten *Li*, 3,600 persons could cover 100 *Li*. Let each person carry four pecks of rice [1 peck=6.25 kilograms]. If the people carry the rice, form a line and walk 500 round trips per day, the total distance would be twenty-eight *Li*. One would walk with a load for fourteen *Li*, walk without a load for the remaining fourteen *Li*, and they could deliver 200 *Dan* of rice each day [1 *Dan*=59.2 kilograms]. If everyone carries a litre of rice at a time, the total amount could satisfy the need of 20,000 people. And this is the way to deliver food for 100 *Li* in one day.

That is, within a distance of 100 *Li*, let 3,600 people stand in a line with an interval of ten paces in between; if one person carries four pecks of rice each time without stopping, he could deliver 200 *Dan* of rice every day in 500 round trips.[26]

This military way of transporting is designed for special purposes which could not be applied generally, but it does contain some elements of modern management principles, particularly the production line method. First, it subdivides the "production process" into several sections and arranges the workers to

---

25 This quotation comes from *Jin Shu* [Book of the Jin Dynasty, "Biography of Fu Xuan"].
26 *The History of the Yuan Dynasty*, "Biography of Dong Tuanxiao".

work repeatedly on the same section: this coincides with basic division of labour theory. Second, it deals with the productivity of individual workers by requiring them to carry the rice non-stop, which could eliminate the redundant operation process and increase time efficiency. Third, the workers are required to stand in a straight line, which makes the production process continual and rhythmic. Lastly, workers walk half their time with a load and half their time half time without; and if they only walk ten steps per time with a load of four pecks of rice, the total distance covered in one day is twenty-eight *Li*. Hence, this method not only takes account of the endurance limit of the workers but also minimises the workload; therefore, it not only applies the theory of the division of labour but also develops it further.

The above proposals are the mainstream opinions on division theory in Chinese history. They share two distinctive features: they carefully investigate the problems, and their suggestions and projects are concrete and applicable. Overall, these proposals are a generalised summary of the economic and management principles that were applied to meet actual social demands in Chinese history.

On the division of manual work and brain work

Confucius presented his views clearly on the division of manual work and brain work. He argued that the governors' duties are different from those of manual workers since it was only the governors who should develop leadership and management skills. Fan Chi, a student of Confucius, once asked his master how to grow crops and vegetables. Confucius was extremely displeased, saying, "I am not as good as an old farmer", and "I am not as good as an old vegetable-grower."[27] In his eyes, food production should belong to the manual workers and should not involve the brain workers at all. He proposed that "a gentleman should seek for doctrine, not for food".[28] As we can see, he had a clear position on the division of manual work and brain work.

Mo Di elaborated on the same issue: "Those good at arguing should engage in arguing; those good at educating should engage in educating; and those good at administering should administer. Then righteousness is achieved."[29] He proposed to separate manual work from brain work so that morality could be developed. Mo believed in the equivalence between governing the country and ploughing the field, which were merely different professions. He said:

> The rulers and ministers must appear at court early and retire late, hearing lawsuits and attending to the affairs of government – this is their duty. The gentlemen must exhaust the strength of their limbs and employ to the fullest the wisdom of their minds, directing bureaus within the government and

27 *Analects*, XIII.4.
28 *Analects*, XV.32.
29 *Mozi*, "Gengzhu".

abroad, collecting taxes on the barriers and markets and on the [natural] resources ... this is their duty.[30]

From the perspective of social class theory, the governors are exploiting the people and the process is essentially different from the production activities of the working people; but these activities could still be viewed as part of the division of labour.

In Chinese history, the most typical viewpoint on the division of manual work and brain work was expressed by Mencius:

> Some use their minds, some use their hands. The ones using their minds govern others, while the ones using their hands are governed by others. The governed ones will produce the food, while the governing ones will feed on the food produced by others. This is the golden rule.[31]

Mencius's conclusion on the division of manual work and brain work was quite innovative and conclusive. The profoundness and preciseness of his ideas made him an outstanding figure on this issue, not only in China but also in the rest of the world.

After Mencius, Xun Kuang discussed the issue from the angle of management. He also believed that the rulers and the ruled should undertake different roles. As he said, "A noble man rules with his virtues, while a manual worker will use his labour." The ruling class's responsibility is to rule and educate the people, while the people's responsibility is to work; the former dominates the latter, which is called "virtue dominates labour".[32] In Xun Kuang's eyes, even though the manual workers are experts in their field they could not act as leaders in their profession:

> The farmer is well versed in the work of the fields, but he cannot become a director of agriculture. The merchant is well versed in the ways of the market, but he cannot become a director of commerce. The artisan is well versed in the process of manufacture, but he cannot become a director of crafts[33]

Rulers, on the other hand, may not be good at farming, business or artistry: "there are men who, though they possess none of these three skills, are still able to fill the offices that direct them" How is that so? Instead of mastering the specifics, rulers master "the Way", the general rules and approaches of organising and administrating. Thus, those who are proficient at the specifics are only qualified for specific jobs while those who master the doctrine succeed in managing

---

30 *Mozi*, "Against Music".
31 *Mencius* III.A.4.
32 *Xunzi*, "The Regulations of a King".
33 *Xunzi*, "Dispelling Obsession".

different tasks at the same time.[34] Generally, an expert in merely one field is limited by his scope of knowledge whereas a successful leader overcomes this limitation by taking a general view. Therefore, Xun Kuang's points were quite reasonable. Of course, it was somewhat partial for him to believe that expert knowledge in specific fields was unnecessary for a managerial leader. But we cannot deny that Xun Kuang's contribution was positive.

The division between the manual worker and the brain worker is not only the necessary outcome of the development of social productivity but also a great contributing force to the enhancement of social productivity and the progress of science and culture. "This division (of manual worker and brain worker) is the result of past development and the reason for future progress" – this was a sentence translated by a French commentator from Adam Smith and quoted by Karl Marx in *Capital*.[35]

The efforts of Mencius and Xun Kuang were valuable because they stated the necessity of the division and asserted its influence in the development of society. On the other hand, these two thinkers could not escape from the limitations of their time and could not help but defend their ruling class. As pointed out by Friedrich Engels, "the last reason to defend classism is always that it is inevitable for one of the classes to evade from tiring themselves to make a living so that they are able to do the mental work for all."[36] And this was exactly the perspective that Mencius and Xun Kuang adopted in their theories.

As mentioned at the beginning of this essay, Greek thinkers had also stated views on division of labour, and their ideas "in the context of history, became the starting point of modern scientific theories", and were a representation of "genius and innovation".[37] However, these perspectives, which were greatly applauded by Karl Marx, were not more brilliant than those of Chinese thinkers. Take Plato, for example. In his ideal republic, the society is divided into three classes: citizens (including farmers, merchants and craftsmen), soldiers and philosopher-bureaucrats. As for Xenophon, he discussed the importance of division by referring to a perfect meal cooked for the king. He gave the reason why a king's meal could always be more delicious than that of others, because it was relatively easy in the big city to find chefs who were experts in some specific courses. Xenophon believed that no one would be capable of making a perfect meal by handling all the specifics on his own, but if each course was assigned to experts – some expert in stewing meat, some at roasting meat and others at boiling fish – then all jobs would be undertaken efficiently and perfectly.[38] We could not deny the importance of these Greek thinkers' views, but we also cannot ignore the theories on division of labour in Chinese history.

34 Xunzi, "Dispelling Obsession".
35 *Marx and Engels, Complete Works*, vol. 23, pp. 401–402.
36 *Marx and Engels, Selected Works*, vol. 2, p. 479.
37 *Marx and Engels, Selected Works*, vol. 3, Beijing: People's Publishing House, 1972, p. 268.
38 Xenophon: "Education of Cyrus". See *Marx and Engels, Complete Works*, vol. 47, Beijing: People's Publishing House, 1979, pp. 321–322.

Certainly, there were differences between the theories of division of labour in Chinese history and those of the modern capitalist period. According to the latter,

> social division of labour is regarded as an effective way to enhance productivity given the same amount of labour; therefore, it reduces product prices and accelerates capital accumulation. In contrast to this view, which emphasises quantity and trade value, ancient thinkers concentrated more on quality and user value[39]

In ancient China, thinkers were indeed concerned mostly with the effects of enhancing productivity and product quality, which were mostly views on user value. All in all, theories on division of labour in Chinese history should not be overly applauded given their historical limitations.

39 *Marx and Engels, Complete Works*, vol. 23, Beijing: People's Publishing House, 1972, p. 404.

11 Harmony of Diversity and Great Uniformity

Two trains of thought in the economics of ancient China[1]

Zhong Xiangcai

Construction of a harmonious socialist society is where the goal of the political system in our country lies and is also a new proposition brought about by the ever-deepening process of market-oriented economic reform since 1978. The modern market economy is an important product of the development of human civilisation and has no essential contradiction with the pursuit of a harmonious society. In the history of China, two trains of thought in economics for building an ideal society have appeared: one is the idea of economic diversity based on the harmonious philosophy; the other is the "Great Uniformity" social pattern advocating the abolition of private ownership. These two trains of thought in economics are the result of different philosophical approaches and have generated different policy proposals as well as different social influences and historic functions.

Economic diversity based on the harmonious philosophy

A harmonious society in the modern sense has six major features: democracy, the rule of law, fairness, justice, stable and orderly development, and harmonious coexistence between people and nature. We find many similar ideas in China's ancient economic literature.

Some historians believe that Mencius's thinking exhibits a clear awareness of democracy. He writes, for example: "The people are of supreme importance; the altars to the gods of earth and grain come next; last comes the ruler".[2] He also says: "If a prince treats his subjects as his horses and hounds, they will treat him as a mere fellow-countryman. If he treats them as mud and weeds, they will treat him as an enemy."[3] Xun Kuang compares the monarch to the "boat" and the populace to "water", pointing out: "Water can hold the boat, and can also capsize the boat".[4] In his view:

---

1 Originally published as "和谐与大同：中国古代两种经济发展思路" ("Harmony of Diversity and Great Uniformity: Two Trains of Thought in Economics of Ancient China"), *Journal of Finance and Economics*, 2007 33.9, pp. 28–37.

2 *Mencius*, VII.B.14.

3 *Mencius*, IV.B.3.

4 *Xunzi*, "The Regulations of a King" [*Xunzi: Basic Writings*, B. Watson tr., New York: Colombia University Press, 2003, p. 39.]

If the emperor does not love his people and benefit his people, he cannot get the love of people. If the people do not love him, it is impossible for the emperor to use his people and get them to die for him. If the people cannot be used by the emperor and refuse to die for him, it is impossible to build a strong army and a strong castle.[5]

What is justice? Ancient Chinese thinkers have expressed their opinions from the point of view of Dao (Way). Rui Liangfu, an intellectual in the Western Zhou dynasty, opposed any monopolisation of wealth, saying: "The wealth in the world is from all kinds of natural resources"; but some people want to occupy it themselves, and such a practice is very harmful: "Everyone has the right to take things in the world, how can some people hold them to themselves?"; and, "Those who monopolise things are just like robbers. If a king holds everything to himself, few people can obey him."[6] From *Laozi* we find the opinion that every member of the society has an equal right to material wealth: "Is the way of heaven not unlike the stretching of a bow?... The way of heaven takes from what has too much to provide for what does not have enough"; "Only those holding Dao can offer the surplus to the whole world".[7] But, according to *Laozi*, the economic system has violated natural law: "The way of the people is, however, not like this: it takes from those who do not have enough to offer to those who have too much."[8]

Dong Zhongshu used ideas from nature to criticise the unjust phenomenon of vested interests using their privilege to appropriate wealth. His argument was that the lawful income of any individual or class is specified by a natural rule of allocation:

> Heaven allocates creatures their shares: those gifted with teeth cannot get horns, those gifted with wings can only have two feet. That shows, if you have got the big, you will not get the small as well. People who receive their salary from the state do not live by physical strength, so their bodily strength is less. That means, those who have got the big may not get the small at the same time. It is the same rule as the Heavenly law. Even in the natural world, those already gifted with the big may not get the small as well, and it is Heaven that makes things, so how can people be exceptions!

Hence:

> Those who receive a salary should live on their salary and may not vie for interests with common people. In this way, interests can be allocated evenly and the common people can have enough to support their family. This is the

5 Ibid.
6 Part I of Zhou Yu of *Guo Yu* (Stories of States).
7 Ibid., 77.
8 Ibid., 32, 77.

way of Heaven and also the way of our remote antiquity. The emperor should make laws on that basis and everyone should follow those rules in their behaviour.[9]

As for good faith, fraternity, stability and orderliness, Confucian thinkers have expressed many opinions. Confucius himself favoured the construction of an economic system with a high level of social security. Zilu asked him: "Suppose there was someone who conferred benefits upon the common people far and wide and was capable of bringing salvation to the multitude, what would you think of his? Might he be called humane?" Confucius answered: "Why only humane? He would undoubtedly be a sage. Did not even Yao and Shun have to take pains over this?"[10] Zilu asked further: "I should like to hear your aspirations, Master". Confucius replied: "To bring comfort to the old, to be of good faith, and to cherish the young", thus indicating his preference for a social state that exhibited such characteristics.[11]

Mencius believed that the basis for social stability is that workers own means of production and have a stable living environment. As he emphasised:

> The way of common people is like this: Those with constant means of support will have constant hearts, while those without constant means will not have constant hearts. Lacking constant hearts, they will go astray and get into excesses, stopping at nothing[12]

The standard of "constant means of support" (or "constant assets") was stipulated in these terms:

> If the mulberry is planted in every homestead of five *mu* of land, then those who are fifty can wear silk; if chickens, pigs and dogs do not miss their breeding season, then those who are seventy can eat meat; if each lot of a hundred *mu* is not deprived of labour during the busy season, then families with several mouths to feed will not go hungry. Exercise due care over the education provided by village schools, and reinforce this by teaching them the duties proper to sons and younger brothers, and those whose heads have turned hoary will not be carrying loads on the roads. When the aged wear silk and eat meat and the masses are neither cold nor hungry, it is impossible for their prince not to be a true king.[13]

As long as the members of society "can support both their parents and their wives and children, can always have sufficient food in good years and escape

9 Biography of Dong Zhongshu, *Han Shu* ("Records of Han Dynasty").
10 *Analects*, VI.29.
11 Ibid., V.26.
12 *Mencius*, III.A.3.
13 Ibid., I.A.7.

starvation in bad",[14] human relations will be greatly improved. Moreover, Mencius advocates aiding the disadvantaged, pointing out:

> Old men without wives, old women without husbands, old people without children, young children without fathers – all these four types of people are most destitute and have no one to turn to for help. When King Wen put benevolent measures into effect, he always gave them first consideration[15]

Mencius's position is reflected in the records of political systems. *Li Ji* ("Book of Rites") states:

> Those who have lost their parents when young are called *gu*, those who have lost their children when old are called *du* [a "solitary"], those who have lost their wives when old are called *jin*, and those who have lost their husbands are called *gua*. These four kinds of people are poor and helpless, and all of them can get proper support from the government.... The dumb, the deaf, the lame ... are all fed according to what work they are capable of doing.[16]

The state has a role to assist misfortunate people, including the handicapped who should be offered opportunities to use their skills in order to earn their own living.

In order to promote a vital social life there is also a need to establish a loose and free economic system that can encourage people to acquire wealth. Ancient thinkers were clearly aware of this point. Confucius said (in paraphrase), "Is not benefiting by doing things beneficial to the common people the most helpful and economical way of governing?"[17] *Guanzi* suggests: "It is ever so that the way to maintain good order in a state is to be certain, first of all, to make its people prosperous. When the people are prosperous, they are easy to keep in order".[18] Sima Qian classifies political-economic policies into five levels:

> the highest type ... accepts the nature of the people, the next best leads the people to what is beneficial, the next best gives them moral instruction, the next best forces them ... and the very worst kind enters into competition with them.[19]

Examples of an understanding of the need to cultivate a harmonious relationship between humankind and nature are plentiful in Chinese history. Legend has it that Emperor Wen of the Zhou Dynasty put forward the following policy:

---

14 Ibid.
15 Ibid., I.B.5.
16 *Li Ji*, "The Royal Regulations" [IV, Section V, 13–14. Legge edition – James Legge (tr.) [1885] (2008) *The Li Ji or Book of Rites*, republished by Forgotten Books at www.forgottenbooks.org].
17 *Analects*, XX.2.
18 *Guanzi*, "Zhi Guo" ("Maintaining the state in Good Order").
19 *Records of the Grand Historian*, "Biographies of the Money-Makers".

For mountain forests, no felling should be done when the time is not proper, so as to let the vegetation grow. For rivers and lakes, no fishing should be done when the time is not proper, so as to let the fish and turtles grow to maturity. Do not hunt the young, so as to let animals grow big.[20]

Xun Kuang thinks that following the farming seasons and protecting natural resources are organic parts of "the rule of sagacious kings". Thus:

When the vegetation is flourishing, no felling or cutting should be done, so that the plants may grow normally. When the fish or turtles are pregnant, no net or poison should enter the waters, so that they may keep multiplying. By strictly observing the four seasons, by ploughing in spring, weeding in summer, harvesting in summer, and storing in winter, the food crops may grow ceaselessly, and the common people may have surplus food to eat. By strictly banning exploitation of pools, rivers and lakes, the fish and turtles may abound, and the people may have a rich supply all the time. By cutting trees at the proper time, we can keep the mountain forest flourishing forever, so that the people can have endless supply of timber.[21]

Guanzi suggests rigid requirements for management of water resources: "By dredging rivers and ravines, building irrigation works and storing water properly, we can prevent water from harming food crops in all kinds of weather and ensure a good harvest."[22] *Guanzi* even records the saying that "the sage's transformation of the world lay in understanding water".[23]

Although the above evidence is fragmentary, and some of it is only suggestive, not forming a strict system, it does suggest the goal of working towards a harmonious society. But, more exactly, what is meant by "harmonious" in this context?

The Chinese word *hexie* (harmony) first appeared in print in the book *Zuo Zhuan* ("Spring and Autumn Annals") – "just as in music, harmony is everywhere"[24] – and suggested an analogy with a sweet musical effect. Similar ideas can also be found in later literature. For example, "when metals and stones are played together, a harmonious music emerges."[25] By further study, we discover that the Chinese character *he* is itself related to music. *Shuo Wen Jie Zi*

---

20 *Yi Zhou Shu* (Records of the Zhou Dynasty), "Note to Wen Zhuan".
21 *Xunzi*, "The Regulations of a King".
22 Guanzi, "Politics".
23 *Guanzi*, "Water and Earth".

> [What is it that is complete in its virtue? It is water.... It is the root of all things and the ancestral hall of all life. It is that from which beauty and ugliness, worthiness and unworthiness, stupidity and giftedness are produced.]

24 *Zuo Zhuan*, Eleventh Year of Xiang Gong.
25 *Jin Shu* (Records of Jin State), "Biography of Zhi Yu".

explains 龢 as "mixing of sounds of all kinds".[26] In the inscriptions on oracle bones, the pictograph 龠 indicates a kind of musical instrument, such as a piccolo or wind instrument with two or three holes. Later, 禾 was added, reflecting the features of an agricultural society. Music can express different feelings, such as anger, grief, fervour or profundity, but what *he* (harmony) conveys is "love". As it is said in *Li Ji*: "When love is deep, the sound (music) will be harmonious and tender."[27]

It is interesting to observe that there are points of similarity between Eastern and Western cultures in the understanding of "harmony". According to Qian Zhongshu's research, ancient Greek sages had the saying,

> Musical harmony comes from the mutual complementing of five sounds and seven tones, not merely the singleness of monotonous sound. Without the differences of high and low sounds or tones, there will be no harmony. Thus, sameness will not lead to harmony whereas harmony stems from variety.[28]

When Plato talks of "abstinence", he says:

> It runs through all the citizens, and combines the strongest, the weakest and the moderate (whether in terms of wisdom or, if you please, in terms of force, or in terms of other aspects such as number of people, wealth and so on), to create harmony, just like the musical scale running through the whole process of music, blending together all kinds of strong or weak musical notes to produce a harmonious symphony.[29]

Chinese thinkers in the pre-Qin period expounded on the meaning of "harmony" in various ways. Commenting on King You at the end of the Western Zhou dynasty, Taishi Bo said:

> The present king ... has given up "harmony" for the sake of "sameness". Harmony can produce everything, but sameness cannot. Balancing all things together is called "harmony" and can lead to prosperity and growth. If you use sameness to replace harmony, you will give up all good things.[30]

Yan Ying in the Spring and Autumn period not only mentioned diversity but also stressed variety. He gave the following analogy:

---

26 [*Shuo Wen Jie Zi* is a dictionary, completed in AD 121.]
27 *Li Ji* (Book of Rites), *Yue Ji* ("Record of Music").
28 Qian Zhongshu: Volume I of Guanzui Bian, Beijing: Zhonghua Book Company, 1979, p. 237.
29 Plato: *Utopia*, translated by Guo Fuhe and Zhang Zhuming, Beijing: Commercial Press, 1995, p. 152.
30 *Guo Yu* ("Stories of States"), Chapter *Zheng Yu* ("Story of the state of Zheng").

Just like the potage, we use water, fire, salt and all kinds of seasonings to cook the fish. The cook adjusts the taste in a subtle way. When we eat it, we can balance our mood. The same is true of the relationship between king and ministers. When the king says yes, his ministers may say no. The ministers say no to supplement the king's yes. When the king says no, his ministers may say yes. The ministers say yes to supplement the king's no. In this way, politics will go on smoothly, and the people will be calm. As the saying in *Shi Jingi*[31] goes: "There is a harmonious potage, proper in all kinds of taste. When we offer it to the god, the world will be in harmony without discontent." The late king adjusted the five tastes and balanced the five tones to achieve a tranquil mood and make a perfect government. The sounds are just like the tastes and may be combined to make perfect music. All kinds of opposition complement each other: clear and turbid, great and small, short and long, fast and slow, glad and sad, hard and soft, late and early, high and low, in and out, expanding and contracting, and so on. When we hear it, we can balance our mood. When our mood is well balanced, good morals will prevail. As the saying in *Shi Jing* relates: "The sound of morality is perfect". But the present state is not so ideal. When the king says yes, his subjects also say yes. When the king says no, his subjects also say no.... If we make the sounds of the lyre into a single sound, who will like to listen to it? Thus, sameness is not the best way.[32]

Confucius's follower, You Ruo, asserts:

> The key to courtesy lies in harmony. The most precious point in the ruling way of our late sagacious kings is just this. But we cannot just let all things go without conflict. Sometimes we must use rules [ritual] to control things.[33]

In his opinion, we cannot have both "harmony" and "sameness" together, and wise people should seek "harmony" and reject "sameness": "Noble people are in harmony but not in sameness, whereas mean people are in sameness but not in harmony".[34]

When these ideas of "harmony" containing diversity were implemented into economics, various ideas came into being such as a viewpoint on allocation. For example, Confucius says:

> Those having a country or a family do not worry about the size of their wealth, but only worry about unevenness in the allocation of wealth.... If

---

31 ["The Book of Songs", the first Chinese anthology of poetry composed from the eleventh to the sixth century BC.]
32 Yan Zi Spring and Autumn, Part I of Outer Chapter,
33 Analects, I.12.
34 Analects, XIII.23.

the wealth is allocated evenly, there will be no poverty.... If peace prevails, the country will not be in danger.[35]

In Confucius's opinion, "harmony" is an ideal pattern for economic interests. Although there are differences in the economic status of individuals or groups, it does not mean unjustness has appeared in the society, or that social chaos will ensue.

Xun Kuang's ideas on allocation are similar. In *Shang Shu*,[36] there is the saying *Wei Qi Fei Qi*,[37] which means that if we want to realise or maintain the state of *Qi* (accord, uniformity), the best approach is to recognise or allow the existence of *Fei Qi* (non-accord, or non-uniformity). If we only seek the "uniformity" in form, the result will inevitably lead to "non-uniformity". Xun Kuang quotes the saying in support of social inequality in various aspects:

> When ranks are all equal, there will not be enough goods to go around; where power is equally distributed, there will be a lack of unity; where there is equality among the masses, it will be impossible to employ them. The very existence of Heaven and Earth exemplifies the principle of higher and lower, but only when an enlightened king appears on the throne can the nation be governed according to regulation. Two men of equal eminence cannot govern each other; two men of equally humble station cannot employ each other. This is the rule of Heaven.... This is what [the *Shang Shu*] means when it says, "Equality is based upon inequality".[38]

Evidently, the harmonious philosophy of melding variety and diversity into one can only appear and be spread in the pre-Qin period characterised by free contention of all schools of thought. After unified feudal autarchy was established it could not help but give way to another quite different trend of social thought.

The conception of the Great Uniformity society characterised by abolition of private ownership

In comparison with the harmonious philosophy, "Great Uniformity" was undoubtedly the mainstream ideal social pattern of ancient China. The characteristics of the "Great Uniformity" society are described as follows: "The Great Way" lies in all things in the world being publically owned, choosing the worthy and able persons as officials, and fostering harmonious relations and good faith. Thus, people will not only love and care for their own family, the old will spend their years without worry, the vigorous will have their chances to use their

35 Analects, XVI.1.[On this translation see above, p. 10.]
36 [A record of imperial documents in the Shang and Zhou periods.]
37 Lü Xing, *Shang Shu.*
38 *Xunzi*, "The Regulations of a King".

strength, the young will get proper support, all kinds of misfortunate persons such as widowers, widows, childless old people, handicapped people, and the ill and infirmed, will get proper care and support. Males will have their status, and females will have their homes. There will be no theft or unrest, so everyone can keep his door open without fear. That is the picture of a society of "Great Uniformity."[39]

It is generally agreed that the literature on cosmopolitism (Great Uniformity) was produced at the end of the Warring States period (480–221 BC) or the period between the Qin and Han dynasties,[40] although we can find some elements of the ideology in earlier works. Mozi (*c.*479–372 BC) advocates "upholding uniformity". In his opinion, before the country came into being, "The world was as chaotic as though it were inhabited by birds and beasts alone".[41] Then, people chose "the most worthy and able man in the world ... as Son of Heaven [i.e. emperor]".[42] Once there was an emperor, other leaders could be selected from the top downward, by which means "the Son of Heaven was able to unify the standards of judgement throughout the world, and this resulted in order".[43] Thus, the country received proper administration. Such a saying is identical with the cosmopolitism ideal of "choosing the worthy and able as officials, and fostering harmonious relations and good faith". As for "All things in the world belong to the public", the book *Wei Liaozi* (*c.* fourth century BC) says:

> Ruling means making the people selfless. When the people are selfless, the whole country will become one family. There will be no private farming or weaving, and all the people will share the same destiny. Thus, if there are ten children in the family, there is no need to add food; if there is one child in the family, there is no need to reduce food, either.... If any person violates a ban, he (or she) will be punished. There will be no people above others.[44]

Mozi thinks that the root of social unrest is that everyone "tries to benefit by taking others' interests". If we want to make the country peaceful, we must make people "love and benefit others"; we should "promote what is beneficial to the world and ... eliminate what is harmful". Therefore,

> by taking universality as our standard, those with sharp ears and clear eyes will see and hear for others, those with sturdy limbs will work for others,

39 *Li Ji* (Book of Rites"), Book *Li Yun* ("The Conveyance of Rites"). ["Great Uniformity" is also sometimes translated as "Great Harmony", "Grand Harmony", or "Great Tranquillity". Cf. James Legge's translation of the relevant passage in the *Li Ji*, given above at p. 26.]

40 Hou Wailu as editor-in-chief: *Great Uniformity Ideals of All Ages of China*, Beijing: Science Press, 1959, p. 11.

41 *Mozi*, "Identifying with One's Superior".

42 Ibid.

43 Ibid.

44 Wei Liaozi.

and those with knowledge of the Way will endeavour to teach others. Those who are old and without wives or children will find means of support ... the young and orphaned ... will find someone to care for them[45]

and, moreover, "those who possess wealth will share it with others."[46]

The conception of the "Great Uniformity" theory provided an important ideological basis for later generations to expound their ideas on the ideal social system. In the Western Han dynasty, many books contained depictions of the ideal society, such as *Master Lü's Spring and Autumn, Six Arts of War, Huainanzi, Wenzi,* and so on. What they have in common is a yearning for an ideal society without exploitation and conflict. In such a society, the rulers manage state affairs justly and private ownership is abandoned. People work diligently, their life is rich, economic development respects the natural environment. Such arguments were to resurface periodically. Even in the late Ming and early Qing dynasties, the famous scholar Huang Zongxi still described such a society on the basis of the ancient descriptions:

> At the beginning of the human world, everyone was selfish and worked only for himself. No one would do what was good for all the world and no one would do away with what was harmful to the whole world, either. Then a wise man appeared, suggesting we should not only work for our own interests, but should work for the benefit of the world. We should not only consider what is harmful to ourselves as harmful, but should do away with anything harmful to the world. So, this wise man's merits will surely be thousands of times greater than those of the common people.[47]

If we say that the idea of Great Uniformity is chiefly a wish of scholars in ancient China, the ideal pursued by the peasant revolutionaries in feudal society is more straightforward and daring.

Tai Ping Jing ("Scripture on Great Peace"), also entitled *Tai Ping Qing Ling Shu,* was the ideological weapon of Zhang Jiao of the Eastern Han dynasty for his promotion of the peasant uprising.[48] What is *Tai Ping?* The book explains:

> *Tai* means "great", indicating the world is as great as Heaven. Nothing in the world is greater than Heaven. *Ping* means peace and equality. In such a state, there is no longer any evil and selfishness. *Ping* is just like the plain ground, holding everything equally and peacefully.[49]

---

45 *Mozi,* "Universal Love".
46 *Mozi,* "The Will of Heaven".
47 *Mingyi Dai Fang Lu* [Waiting for the Dawn], "Yuan Jun".
48 [The "Yellow Turban Rebellion", which broke out in AD 184.]
49 *Tai Ping Jing,* Part 65 of "*San He Xiang Tong* Rhymes", Shanghai: Shanghai Press of Ancient Books, 1993, p. 215.

We can see here that *Ping* means more than simply equality,[50] but refers to a sort of state of harmony with natural law. "There is no longer any evil and selfishness" means doing away with all acquisition through self-interest so as to realise "eternal peace and tranquillity".

Tai Ping Jing enumerates six major crimes of the human world that will surely lead to nemesis, of which two are related to the economy: not living by one's own labour and not helping the poor. With regard to the former, *Tai Ping Jing* points out:

> Heaven gives birth to people, and gifts them with physical power so that they can live by their own labour. Yet, they do not work hard, but even suffer from hunger and cold, so they are unworthy of the body offered by their forefathers. They do not work by themselves to earn a living, but often complain about poverty and often rely on wealthy people for a living. It is a great crime indeed.... Why? Heaven bestows enough wealth to support all people, hence, everyone ought to make the effort to get it, and in this way no one can be poor. But some people do not use their natural strength and belittle themselves, or try to get things in ill ways by robbing others and so on. Naturally, such a crime should lead to death.[51]

As for not helping the poor, *Tai Ping Jing* asserts:

> Some people store up hundreds of millions of assets, but they refuse to help poor people or those in dire need, causing many people's death from hunger and cold. Such a crime is great indeed.... Why? All wealth belongs to Heaven. Heaven uses it to benefit all creatures so that people can be free of poverty. Yet, these people gather it and stop it from flowing everywhere, opposing the will of Heaven and Earth. They either spend it themselves, or leave it to their offspring, but no wealth can be kept forever.[52]

Afterwards, the even distribution of wealth became the battle cry of peasant revolutions. At the end of the Tang dynasty, the leader of the peasant uprising, Wang Xianzhi, called himself "Imperator of Even Distribution for Heaven". In the Northern Song dynasty, when Wang Xiaobo called on the tenant farmers and tea growers to join his uprising, he exclaimed: "I hate the uneven allocation between rich and poor, and now I am going to even it for you!"[53] Later, Zhong Xiang, the peasant uprising leader, pronounced: "If a law discriminates between

---

50 In *Tai Ping Jing*, there is a clear reflection of the sense of hierarchy in the society. For example, it says the minister "is the good son of the king", "helps the king to administrate the world"; the people "are the king's unfilial sons", "are in charge of farming for the king" (100th Law of the King, *Tai Ping Jing*, Shanghai: Shanghai Press of Ancient Books, 1993, p. 262.)

51 The 103rd of Six Crimes and Ten Punishments, *Tai Ping Jing*, Shanghai: Shanghai Press of Ancient Books, 1993, p. 272.

52 Ibid.

53 Wang Pizhi: *Mian Shui Yan Tan Lu.*

high and low and between poor and rich, it is not a good law. If I make a new law, I will equalise high and low, and even poor and rich".[54] In the slogans raised in the great peasant uprising at the end of the Ming dynasty there were also such sayings as: "politics of even allocation of farmland"[55] and "equal distribution of farmland and exemption from grain taxation".[56]

Those slogans were put into practice to a greater or lesser degree. For example, in Fang La's uprising in the Song dynasty, when the populace "began to join it, there were very poor people. Others helped them with money, and later they became better-to-do"; "whenever the uprising army passed a place, they would open the barn to divide grain to poor people and everyone could use the assets equally and freely, just like living in one family[57]; "Whenever one family is in trouble, all the people in the army would help".[58] When Li Zicheng started an uprising there were popular rhymes such as:

> We are striving for a living every day, but now it is hard for poor people to survive for a single day; open your door to welcome Chuang Wang (Li Zicheng), and we ensure every one of you will be happy and gay[59]

and, "Eat freely and wear freely. Chuang Wang will give you an endless supply of food and clothing. You will have no need to serve the government and nor will you need to pay taxes."[60] In the time of Zhong Xiang's uprising, "they called the state law an evil law, and called people killing as executing the law, and called robbing as equal allocation".[61] Some peasant armies

> declared their "robbing the rich to feed the poor" policy to all people in the street ... any farmland could be claimed by a new owner. Thus, a century-old house or thousands of pieces of gold might be claimed by someone else as its owner, so the poor person could get rich overnight. There were also bullying neighbours who plundered properties from others, some felled others' trees or grabbed others' grain or took others' valuables and ran away. The whole town fell into a great chaos and everyone lost their stable job.[62]

It should be pointed out that in the history of pursuance of the Great Uniform-

---

54 Xu Meng Xin: Volume 137 of *San Chou Bei Meng Hui Bian*, 17 February, 4th Year of Jianyan Period.
55 Cha Jizuo: Volume 17 of *Guilt Repenting Record*, "Stories of Emperor Yi Zong Lie".
56 Cha Jizuo: Volume 31 of *Guilt Repenting Record*, "Biography of Li Zicheng".
57 Zhuang Jiyu, Part I of Chapter "Of Chicken Ribs".
58 Volume 76 of *Records of Years since Jian Yan Period*.
59 Volume 23 of *Ming Ji Bei Lve*.
60 Volume 9 of *Sui Kou Ji Lve*.
61 Volume 137 of *San Chou Bei Meng Hui Bian*.
62 Ding Yaokang: *Chu Jie Ji Lüe* (transcript), quoted from Hou Wailu (ed.) *Great Uniformity Ideals of All Ages of China*, Beijing: Science Press, 1959, p. 21.

ity ideal in ancient China there are two paths: one is the literary thinkers' subjective description of living conditions characterised by affluence, stability and selfless love; the other is the poverty-stricken labourers' revolutionary practice to realise a society of equal allocation of wealth and public ownership. The realisation approaches of the two are different, but they have something in common in terms of philosophical thinking, economic system and social pattern.

Theoretical analysis

As stated above, Chinese ancient harmony philosophy is characterised by diversity and variety, which is closely related to various ideas in the pre-Qin period that tally with the economic theory of the construction of a harmonious society. In terms of modern economic method, we find that all these viewpoints have one common assumption: the self-benefiting nature of mankind.

Recognising the self-benefiting nature of mankind is the scientific starting point for considering socioeconomic issues. According to traditional political economy, "economic man" is a self-dissimilation of the individual in a capitalist society. Weber asserts that economic rationalism is a unique phenomenon of modern capitalism. But Chinese ancient literature does not support this opinion, and research findings in world history do not agree with it either.[63] If we regard the modern market economy as a symptom of mankind's progress towards the harmonious society; and if the assumption of "economic man" is a major theoretical precondition for this progress; then we can say that economic ideas of ancient China such as recognition of mankind's self-benefiting nature, pursuance of natural justice, upholding of free competition and advocating fraternity, are indeed positive factors for progress towards civilisation and harmony.

However, China's ancient economy did not evolve in the direction of a natural expansion of the market order but stepped into the inefficiency trap of a despotic centralisation of state power. This cannot be separated from other aspects of economic thought in the pre-Qin period. Recognition that everyone has a self-benefiting nature may be a necessary condition for establishing a market economy, but the recognition by itself may also lead to a different system. For example, Shang Yang, starting from the *Ming Li Lun* ("Way of Interest") theory, carried out the policy of "interest coming out of one hole" through a far-reaching policy of state control over economic affairs. The

---

63

For example, Dominic Rathbone, in his book *Economic Rationalism and the Egyptian Farming Community in the 3rd Century AD*, studied the documentary materials of a village, such as the account book of business operations, and he has discovered that farm-production was market-oriented and, moreover, its management also considered cost issues very closely. Therefore he concluded that what guided the production of the farm was a rational economic objective to maximise profit. That means that the economic behaviour of ancient people was not primitive, but quite rational.

(Quoted from a secondary source by Huang Yang: Modernity and Study on European History of Ancient Economy, Wen Hui Daily, 15 April 2007.)

author(s) of *Guanzi* (part of Western Han) likewise realised that "Both those on high and those below, will concentrate where profits are to be found. Once there is profit, goods can circulate [and] a ruler may establish a true state,"[64] but cautioned:

> When interest comes from one hole, the state will be invincible; when interest comes out of two holes, the army can be strong; when interest comes out of three holes, no army can be used; when interest comes out of four holes, the state will be lost.[65]

The so-called "interest coming out of one hole" means simply that we should let commercial profit belong to the state as much as possible so that "the full-time merchants [lose] their advantage in doing business".[66] Wealth-seeking activity by individuals is therefore restricted by the national will. *Guanzi*'s economic pattern is chiefly characterised by the state control of fiscal revenue. If we consider Mozi's *shang tong* (upholding uniformity) theory, we will find that it is quite natural for the Great Uniformity conception to appear at the beginning of the Western Han dynasty, whose chief idea is governing the state by virtuous and talented persons. The Great Uniformity society stresses that "All things in the world belong to the public", people "should not only love and care for their own family", properties "need not be kept to individuals", people "need not serve themselves". All such ideas go against the self-benefiting nature of mankind.

The two trains of thought for the construction of an ideal economic society have actually embodied different philosophical approaches. As stated above, the harmony philosophy and economic propositions in the pre-Qin period are based on an understanding of individual differences and recognition of the self-benefiting aspect of human nature and hope to use interpersonal free competition to reach the goal of economic development and social harmony. But the Great Uniformity ideas after the Western Han dynasty are quite different. According to these later ideas, people belong to a social group with the same desires, gifts and diligence and should therefore have equal rights to wealth. Individuals are equated with the community, hence it is asserted that as long as the community is organised with the public interest as its objective, the individuals in the community will work for the group, just as they work for themselves. In this way, private ownership can be ruled out, and so long as there are managers with excellent moral characters and superior wisdom, generally recognised by the public as possessing those qualities, everything will proceed smoothly. It is just such a vision that has made Great Uniformity so attractive to the patriarchal management system and the controlled economy.

Judging from the level of productivity development, the negation of private

---

64 *Guanzi*, "Chi Mi" ("On Extravagance in Spending").
65 *Guanzi*, "Guo Xu" ("The State's Store of Grain").
66 *Guanzi*, "Qing Zhing Yi" ("Qing Zhong Economic Policies: B").

ownership is a reflection of a primitive awareness of the socially collective nature of agricultural labour. And judging from political philosophy, it originates from the belief in traditional Chinese culture that "human nature can be changed". For example, the Confucian thought of *Nei Sheng Wai Wang* (virtuous governing) became the cultural spirit of the whole nation after the Western Han dynasty. Its meaning may be described like this:

> Not only the emperor as the head of state can receive the will of Heaven and set up an authoritative centre in politics and society. Anybody can also "realise the will of Heaven" and "serve Heaven" directly by their own moral transformation, by setting up an internal authority independent of the emperor and the society.[67]

Thus, humankind's "self-benefiting nature" can be transformed through subjective morality, and in this way modern legal institutions such as equality, freedom and democracy based on such human nature assumption will lose their necessity to exist. It is just in this sense that some scholars think that "The sagacious king's optimistic spirit implies a strong utopian trend."[68] Ancient Chinese thinkers

> were always imagining the faraway future ideal society, instead of designing or seeking solutions to handle actual socio-political problems. That has determined on the whole the characteristic of Chinese political thinkers; that is, they always avoid talking of actual politics and are only fond of conceiving an empty utopian politics[69]

As to why such a holistic economic philosophy has become the predominant ideology in China's feudal society, Hayek's analysis is very convincing. In his view, the reason why Utopia are dangerous is that "the so-called economic freedom promised by it just means relieving us of the trouble to solve our own economic problems, and means the choice that should be made in such matters can be made by others instead of ourselves".[70] However, although this choice seems to conform to the nature of "economic man", it often makes people lose some virtues, such as "independence and self-reliance, personal originality and local self-responsibility, relying on voluntary activities successfully, non-intervention of others' matters and tolerance of heresies, respect of customs and traditions, and proper doubt about power and authority".[71] These are just the

---

67 Zhang Hao: *Transcending Awareness and Gloomy Awareness: Recognition and Reflective Thinking on Confucian Thought of Internal Wisdom and External Governing*, quoted from Zhang Hao's *Self-selected Works*, Shanghai: Shanghai Educational Publishing House, 2002, pp. 27, 42.
68 Ibid.
69 Ren Jiantao, *Liberalism in Thought Development of Ancient China*, Beijing: Peking University Press, 2004, pp. 77, 91, 204.
70 Ibid.
71 Ibid.

basic ideas and norms of behaviour for mankind's progress to the harmonious society. The popularity of the Utopian trend of thought has explained from one aspect why China's feudal society could continue for so long. Meanwhile, the social environment of despotic centralisation of state power had deformed the original philosophy of harmony so that, for example, the Confucian idea of diversity became the basis for the atrophying feudal hierarchy after the Western Han dynasty.

Evidently, the reason why this proposition of diversification of the economy based on the harmony philosophy was replaced after the Western Han dynasty by the Great Uniformity conception and a despotic economic theory has something to do with the dependence on a train of thought. Objectively, such an ideological evolution impeded China's society from escaping from the middle ages. The replacement also indicates that the evolution of thought was not linear. Before the market economy became a standard system, the philosophy of harmony of variety and diversity only provided a possibility for the sustainable development of the society. Such a possibility was aborted because of a holistic trend of thought that ignores personal motivation and blindly worships the patriarchal system. Even in the present time, characterised by increasing appreciation of the harmonious value of a market economy, the traditional Great Uniformity Utopia still shows signs of returning. The inertia of the traditional culture and opportunistic choice have determined that strengthening government intervention is again a practical danger. But the lucky thing is that after experiencing the failure of the new form of the Great Uniformity conception, namely, the planned economic system, Chinese people have resolutely begun to tread the road towards establishing a socialist market economy and have taken substantial steps in economic growth and social progress. We can be sure that the historic mission of constructing a harmonious socialist society will greatly advance the progress of modernisation and the transformation of Chinese society and will continue to help us contribute our wisdom to the development of human civilisation.

12 The influence of ancient Chinese thought on the Ever-Normal Granary of Henry A. Wallace and the Agricultural Adjustment Act in the New Deal[1]

Li Chaomin

The influence of Chinese civilisation on the West is a major research area. With the revitalisation of China in the second half of the twentieth century, the contribution to the world of Chinese civilisation in general, and of Confucian economics and economic policies in particular, has regained people's attention.[2] For example, the republication of Chen Huanzhang's *The Economic Principles of Confucius and his School*[3] has ignited a lively debate on the influence of Confucian ideas in the West.[4]

One such debate related to Chen's study concerns the influence of Chinese thought on the American agricultural system. Henry A. Wallace, former vice president of the United States, commented in 1944 that the legislation of the Ever-Normal Granary, an ancient Chinese agricultural policy he had learned from Chen Huanzhang, was "an action of which I was most proud".[5] However, the Chinese influence on Wallace has long been a matter of debate among both American and Chinese scholars,[6] who have variously proposed as his source of inspiration a "China hypothesis", a mixed "China–Bible hypothesis"[7] and a

---

1 Originally published as "中国古代常平仓思想对美国新政农业立法的影响" (The Influence of the Idea of Ever-Normal Granary on Henry A. Wallace and the Agricultural Adjustment Act in the New Deal), *Fu Dan Journal (Social Sciences)*, 2000 No. 3, pp. 42–50.
2 Zheng Zemin, "Chen Huanzhang" (the modernised pinyin of "Chen Huan-chang"), in Li Xin and Sun Sibai (eds), *Biographies of Figures in 1911–1949*, vol. 2, Beijing: Zhonghua Book Company, 1980, pp. 393–398.
3 Originally published in 1911 by Columbia University Press.
4 Liang Jie, "The Correct Way To Manage Wealth: Chen Huanzhang and His Book of *The Economic Principles Of Confucius And His School*", *Chinese Book Review Monthly*, 2007, 4: 18–22; Ye Tan, "*The Economic Principles of Confucius and His School*: The Start of China Economics to the World in a Centennial", *Chinese Social Sciences Today*, 26 August 2010, p. 8; Hu Wenhui, "Some Sources of Old Chinese System Impacting the U.S.", *Southern Weekend*, 20 April 2011.
5 "Mr. Wallace's Speech at the Luncheon Party Given by Admiral Shen", 22 June 1944, in Wei Ming ed. and annotated, *Wallace in China*, Chongqing: The World Press, October 1944, pp. 30–32.
6 For Chinese studies, see Li Chaomin, *The Ever-Normal Granary: A Chinese Idea in the American System*, Shanghai: The Far East Press, 2002.
7 Leuchtenberg thought that the source of Wallace's measures was partly from the Bible and partly from China. See William E. Leuchtenberg, *FDR and New Deal, 1932–1940*, New York: Harper & Row, 1963. p. 255.

"pure Bible hypothesis".[8] As to the "China hypothesis", it has been suggested that Wallace's Ever-Normal Granary programme was inspired by reform measures proposed by Wang Anshi in the Song dynasty. Derek Bodde raised the possibility of such an influence directly to Henry Wallace but was led to reject it flatly after receiving Wallace's reply.[9] Bodde went on to argue that the American idea of the Ever-Normal Granary did not derive from Wang Anshi and that Chen's book was a propagandising attempt to exaggerate the influence of Chinese culture.

This paper explores the nature and extent of Chinese influences on Wallace's proposals. It is argued that the idea of the Ever-Normal Granary is indeed a case of Chinese influence on American agricultural policy.

The transformation of the Ever-Normal Granary system in China

1 The Sijia system: the origin of the Ever-Normal Granary idea

The granary system was unique in ancient China's public finances. The basic role of "the Ever-Normal Granary was to stabilise prices."[10] In *Zhou Rites*, there was an administrator with the title of *Sijia* (Superintendent of Grain) whose responsibilities were given as follows:[11]

> The *Sijia* is an official who travels the country to observe crops, and to distinguish different grains and areas on which certain grain is suitable, and to keep the record of surveys as planting instructions for farmers. The *Sijia* regulates taxation by his survey of the annual yields and seeks to stabilise food supplies. In lean years he manages to increase supplies to suppress high prices.

The above shows that one role of the *Sijia* in the Zhou dynasty was to stabilise food prices. This was the germ of the later Ever-Normal Granary. *Sijia*-like

---

8 Higgins argued that Wallace's influence was from the Bible. See Andrew C. Higgins, *The Life of Henry A. Wallace: 1888–1965*, formerly available at: www1.american.edu/epiphany/bio.html, 1998.
9 Wallace replied,

> I first learned about the Ever-Normal Granary by reading a doctor's degree thesis written by Chen Huan-chang, a Chinese scholar at Columbia University. The title of his thesis was "The Economic Principles of Confucius and His School". As a result I wrote several editorials for *Wallace's Farmer* during the decade of the twenties entitled "The Ever-Normal Granary". I didn't become familiar with Wang An-shih until late 1933 or early 1934.... While I am a great admirer of Wang An-shih's work, I don't think I carried out any measures as the result of reading about him. The term "Ever-Normal Granary" traces not to Wang An-shih but to the thesis to which I have earlier referred.
> See Derek Bodde, "Henry A. Wallace and the Ever-Normal Granary", *The Far Eastern Quarterly*, 5(4): 412, 1946

10 See "Occupations and Officials, II", in *Old Book of Tang History* (《旧唐书·职官二》).
11 See Section II of "The Official Situ in the Land Administration System", *The System of Zhou*, vol. IV (《地官·司徒下》).

policies can also be found in *Guanzi* and in the state policies of Fan Li in the Spring and Autumn period, Li Kui in the Warring States period, and Sang Hongyang in the Han dynasty.

2 The Ever-Normal Granary: institutionalisation of the idea of food stability

The Ever-Normal Granary system is based on the idea of stability in food supplies. The evolution of policies for food stability from Li Kui's Food Stabilising Rule to Geng Shouchang's Ever-Normal Granary system in the Han dynasty is well documented in the *Royal Library Book of Lessons*.[12] In the fourth year of Emperor Xuandi of the Western Han (54 BC), Minister of Agriculture Geng Shouchang made a request to establish a granary system in frontier provinces in order to stabilise prices by purchasing food when abundant and selling when harvests were poor: a policy entitled *Changping* or "constantly normal price". This was the beginning of the Ever-Normal Granary system[13] which basically sought to stabilise the supply of food.[14] In the royal history book, however, another record states that the purpose of the *Changping* was "to establish the Ever-Normal Granary system to provide national defence along the northern border, so as to minimise financial cost."[15] This was a by-product of the system. Qiu Jun (1421–1495) gave this system the simpler but clearer explanation that it aimed to benefit both farmers and citizens in good years and in bad years.[16] In addition, there are also recorded cases of the Ever-Normal Granary being used to guarantee "the source of royal taxation".[17] Thus, the Ever-Normal Granary was developed by Geng Shouchang as the basis of Li food stability measures in the Warring States period and later transformed into a system of stabilising prices and food supplies and of bringing financial convenience to bordering people. However, "the basic role for the system to stabilise food price and supplies",[18] a heritage of *Sijia* in the Zhou dynasty,

12 See "Section of State Finance: Price Stability, Volume 502" ("邦计部.平籴") in Wang Qinruo *et al.*, *Prime Tortoise of the Record Bureau* (《册府元龟》), Beijing: Zhonghua Book Company, 1989. 册府 is the royal library in the Song dynasty, 元龟 is a big tortoise, an ancient Chinese custom being to tell fortunes by turtle bones. 《册府元龟》 indicates the practice of emperors taking lessons from the books of history edited in the royal library.
13 See "Book I: Volume 26: The Regulator of State Finance" (太府卿) in Du You, *General History of System* (《通典》). Also see "Volume 20: Ministry of Finance" (太府寺) in *Code of Tang Regulations* (《唐六典》).
14 See "Record of Economy and Finance", in *History of Han Dynasty* (《汉书.食货志》).
15 See "Emperor Xuandi", in *History of Han Dynasty* (《汉书.宣帝记》).
16 See "Volume XVI: Fortifying the State Foundation: People's Relief" ("固邦本, 恤民之患") in Qiu Jun, *The Derivative Supplements to the Book of Daxue*, Book I, annotated by Lin Guanqun and Zhou Jifu, Beijing: Jinghua Press, 1999. p. 158.
17 Zhang Gong, *A Simple Inquiry into the Tang Granary System*. Beijing: Zhonghua Book Company, 1986, p. 104.
18 Hu Jichuang, *A History of Chinese Economic Thought*, Shanghai: Shanghai University of Finance and Economics Press, 1962. Book II, p. 130.

was unchanged. Until the 1940s, the Ever-Normal Granary system was retained by local governments to regulate food prices.[19]

3 The Green Sprout Money: financialisation of the Ever-Normal Granary

A monetary economy became dominant and paper money circulated in China from the time of the Tang–Song transition (*c.*750–1250):[20] a period of revolutionary social, political, demographic and economic change, marking the transition from medieval to early modern society.[21] Candice Goucher *et al.* argue that the Chinese commercial revolution between 750 and 1250 did not take place in isolation, since it was situated at the eastern end of trading networks linking peoples across Eurasia. It did, however, result in enormous changes for people at all levels in Chinese society, especially from the growth of cities and changes in gender roles.[22]

The Eve-Normal Granary was developed into the Green Sprout Money, a government loan system, by the Wang Anshi Reform (1068–1093).[23] In the monetary economy the granaries were central to public finance and taxes were paid either physically in terms of grain or in valuable goods named *Zhese* (折色), or in currency.[24] As reported by Ma Duanlin (1245–1323), a historian in the

19 See "Rule of Purchasing Grain by the Ever-Normal Granaries of Zhejiang Province in 1941", *The Government Bulletin of Zhejiang Province*, 1941, No. 3312 ("浙江省三十年度常平仓穀收购办法",《浙江省政府公报》, 1941年第3312期); "Shanghai Plans to Operate the Ever-Normal Granaries", *The Bank Weekly*, 32(18): 6–7, 1948.

20 Gao Mingshi, "The Debates on the Timely Properties of the Tang–Song Transition", in *The Post-War Chinese History Studies in Japan*, Taipei: Mingwen Press, 1987; Zhang Guangda, "Naitō Konan's Tang–Song Transition Hypothesis and Its Impacts", in *Historians, Historiography and Modern Scholarship*, Guilin: Guangxi Normal University Press, 2008.

21 James T.C. Liu & Peter J. Golas (eds), *Change in Sung China*, Lexington, MA: D.C. Heath and Co., 1969. pp. 4–8.

22 See Chapter 11, "Commerce and Change in Asia, Europe, and Africa", in Candice Goucher, Charles Le Guin, and Linda Walton, *In the Balance: Themes in Global History*, Boston, MA: McGraw-Hill, 1998.

23 It is very interesting that we have found many translations of this Chinese system, such as: "*the Green Sprouts farming-loans*" (Robert P. Hymes and Conrad Schirokauer, eds, *Ordering the World: Approaches to State and Society in Sung Dynasty China*, Berkeley, CA: University Of California Press, 1993, p. 90), and "*the Green Sprouts program*", "*the Green Sprouts reforms*", "*the crop loan program*", "*the Green Sprouts Act*", "*the green sprouts' loan policy*", "*the green-sprout loans*", "*the Green Sprout Money Law*", "*the Green Sprouts Law*", "*the green sprouts regulation*" etc. In the above references many scholars believe that the measure was a loan paid by nature.

24 In ancient China's physical asset economy, the taxes could be paid partially in money, cloth, silk or other items instead of grain. *Zhese* also means that salaries to civil servants were paid with cash and various tangible products. In the third section of Book I, "Record of Economy and Finance" in History of Song, we find:

A local governor requested that because in his country there was a huge surplus in granaries … he wished that the opening of the grain market on border should be permitted annually, so that the peasant farmer would pay their normal taxation more by cash ("有司言其地沃民勤, 颇多积穀, 请每岁和市, 随常赋输送, 其直多折色给之。"见《宋史》: 食货志上三).

Song dynasty, local Shaanxi authorities bought food from the farmer by means of a prepayment that was made before the annual planting season had begun. The prepayment was named the Green Sprout Money.[25] Zhao Yi (1727–1814) discussed the transition of the Ever-Normal Granary to the Green Sprout Money. According to his account, in AD 766 the Tang Emperor had paid his officials with a green sprout tax. This was the beginning of the "green sprout system" but it differed from the system in the Song dynasty when citizens could receive a low-rate interest loan of Green Sprout Money. In the Tang dynasty, the Green Sprout Money was a system of taxing according to the peasant's land. In contrast, the grain sprout money in the Song dynasty was initiated by local administrators with the aim of benefiting farmers.[26] Actually, the Green Sprout Money was individually operated by transportation administrators; it was loaned in spring and repaid in autumn, similar to Wang Anshi's proposal in the Song dynasty. To that extent, Wang Anshi's proposal for a Green Sprout Money system was a transformation of the system in the Tang dynasty;[27] it was entitled the "New Ever-Normal Granary Law" or "Green Sprout Law".[28]

The operation of the Green Sprout Money was modern and effective. According to the new law, the government stored grain in the ever-normal and protection granaries and loaned it to farmers in spring and in autumn. At harvest, the loan was repaid together with tax and repayment with grain was permissible. In years of famine the repayment of the loan could be postponed to the following year. When the grain price rose, borrowers were permitted to repay up to 30 per cent in cash at the previous price, with the remainder to be pain in grain at price negotiated between the government and farmers.[29]

The development of the Ever-Normal Granary to the Green Sprout Money was hugely significant. Wang's reform was attacked by the conservatives. Zhu Xi (1130–1200) wrote:

> It is sure that the farmers benefit from the Green Sprout Money. But the shortcomings of the Green Sprout Money were apparent, because its credit was by currency rather than grain; its location was in cities rather than in

25 See "Volume 21: The Second Research on Grain Trading: The Ever-Normal Granary and the Free Granary" (《文献通考》：市籴考二：常平义仓), in Ma Duanlin, *General Research on Literatures and Authorities*.

26 See Zhao Yi, "The Green Sprout Money was not Initiated by Wang Anshi", in *A Mindful Scratch of Twenty-two Histories*, Beijing: Zhonghua Book Company, 1963, pp. 509–511.

27 See "Record 129, Section I, Part 4: Frontier Land Plough, the Ever-Normal Granary and Free Granary" in *History of Song*, Volume 176 (《宋史》：卷一百七十六：志第一百二十九食货上四："屯田常平义仓").

28 Wang Anshi, "An Integrated Request to His Majesty Explaining of the New Ever-Normal Granary Law in the Third Month of the Year 1070", in *Wang Anshi Collected Works*, Volume 210 ("画一申明常平新法奏（熙宁三年三月）",《王安石集》：卷二百十).

29 See "Record 129, Section I, Part 4: Frontier Land Plough, the Ever-Normal Granary and Free Granary" in *History of Song*, Volume 176 (《宋史》：志第一百二十九：食货上四：屯田常平义仓).

villages; its control was by the officials rather than the people; and its operation was with the aim of revenue rather than the motive of charity.[30]

However, from a modern perspective, Wang Anshi was really a great statesman, but he lived at the wrong time: "Had his whole plan been carried out, China would have been a modern state one thousand years ago", wrote Chen Huanzhang.[31] Ray Huang is of a similar opinion, pointing also to the historically unprecedented and extensive role that Wang ascribed to central government in the performance of financial regulation.[32]

Wallace and his Ever-Normal Granary idea

The Ever-Normal Granary idea had an impact on American farm policies. Henry A. Wallace himself associated the reform of American farm policies with the idea of an Ever-Normal Granary and his Agricultural Adjustment Acts of 1933 and 1938 were aimed specifically at establishing agricultural stability and paving the way for the defeat of the Great Depression. The source of inspiration for Wallace's Ever-Normal Granary has attracted much scholarly attention, the three contenders being the "China hypothesis", the "China–Bible hypothesis" and the "pure Bible hypothesis".

The "China hypothesis" affirms that the inspiration for the American Ever-Normal Granary came from China. This hypothesis is the most popular and receives support from Wallace himself. He wrote:

> February 25, 1943
> Madame Chiang told me how deeply interested she was in agriculture, that she had been told by the President that part of our agricultural program was based on Chinese philosophy. I told her the story of how I gotten the phrase 'Ever-Normal Granary' out of a book, *Economic Principles of Confucius*.[33]

Wallace's diaries, from which the above extract is taken, provide valuable autobiographical evidence.[34]

The diaries indicate that that the New Deal farm policy was based on the Ever-Normal Granary of Chinese provenance. In preparation for his 1944 state visit to China it is clear that Wallace had been thinking about the Chinese Ever-Normal Granary. As he noted in his diary on 28 April 1944:

30 See Zhu Xi, "About Jinhua County's Village Granary in Wuzhou", in *Zhu Xi Collected Works*. Shanghai: Commercial Press, April 1937. Book II, pp. 381–383 ("婺州金华社仓记", 见《朱子文集（中）》：卷九：记).
31 Chen Huan-chang, *The Economic Principles of Confucius and His School*, pp. 596–597.
32 Ray Huang, *China: A Macro History*. Beijing: Sanlian Bookstore, 1997, pp. 140–141.
33 John Morton Blum (ed.), *The Price of Vision: The Diary of Henry A. Wallace, 1942–1946*. Boston, MA: Houghton Mifflin Company, 1973, p. 196.
34 Ibid., p. 24.

Vincent, head of the Department of Chinese Affairs in the State Department, seems to be very glad to go to China with me. He seems like a fine fellow in every way. We talked about minor details of the trip together and I gave him a copy of Chinese extracts of the Confucius Economics on the constantly normal granary. I outlined to him some of the things I might want to say in the only carefully prepared speech I expected to make in China.[35]

Wallace's interest at this time in Wang Anshi and the Ever-Normal Granary receives further support from a diary entry by Wang Shijie, former KMT Secretary of Propaganda Department, recounting a meeting held with Wallace on 24 February 1944: "I went to pay a visit to the U.S. Vice President Wallace in the Senate this morning. The gentleman is a key member in Roosevelt's New Deal. He talked a lot with me about Wang Anshi's New Policies."[36] Wang Shijie's diary entry was made during his visit to America in early 1944. After his return to China, Wang accompanied Wallace on his tour in China, writing on 19 June:

In the library of the school for women was stored *The Complete Works of Wang Anshi*. I knew Mr. Wallace admired Wang Anshi, so I told him about the spirit of that former Duke of Jing State as "bold enough to face any unforeseeable event, to ignore any protests, and not to abide by conservative disciplines" in ratifying the new laws. In the impromptu speech to students, Wallace said that under the guidance of such a spirit, Mr. Chiang Kai-shek would overcome any difficulties to come in China.[37]

For the "China hypothesis", however, the most compelling evidence comes from Wallace's speech at the luncheon party hosted by the National Government on 22 June 1944. Wallace spoke as follows:

For more than thirty years the Chinese farmer has aroused my deep interest. It was in 1911 – the year of the Chinese Revolution – that I read Professor F.H. King's book about China, *Farmers of Forty Centuries*. This book gave me a stronger feeling about the intimate relation between the soil and the people who work the soil by hand than any book which I have ever read...
   Soon after I became Secretary of Agriculture I asked the Congress at the earliest possible moment to put into the legislation of the United States an ancient practice of Chinese agricultural statesmanship, the "Ever-Normal Granary" I obtained from a book on *"The Economic Principles of Confucius and His School"* by Chen Huanzhang...
   It was ten years ago that I learned for the first time about the famous

35 Ibid., p. 326.
36 Xiaowei, *The Selected Diaries of Wang Shijie* (1944), in The CASS Institute of Modern History Studies, ed., *Reference Files of Modern History of China*. Beijing: The CASS Press, 2004, Vol. 110, p. 188.
37 Ibid., p. 201.

Chinese New Dealer who lived about 900 years ago, Wang An-shih. Under very great difficulties he was faced in the year of 1068 with problems which, allowing for the difference between historical periods, were almost identical with the problems met by Franklin D. Roosevelt in 1933. The methods which he employed were strikingly similar. Wang An-shih inaugurated a system of crop plan, taxation adjusted to the capacity to pay, a public works program and a number of other acts which were to the interest of the common man.[38]

Wallace had quite categorically affirmed the Chinese inspiration for his agricultural legislation and had also alluded to Wang Anshi's reform with its core plan of the New Ever-Normal Granary Law, in which the aim of farm loans was to benefit peasants. But, as time went by, the truth of Wallace's inspiration became effaced to a greater or lesser degree in historical studies and new hypotheses emerged.

One such was the "China–Bible hypothesis". Louis Bean, a former USDA official, and Joseph Davis of Stanford University, averred that both Chinese history *and* the Bible had inspired Henry Wallace to develop his Ever-Normal Granary system. Bean suggested that the idea of the Ever-Normal Granary came to Wallace from two sources, one the Bible, the other China, although it was admitted that the phrase "Ever-Normal Granary" derived from Wallace's reading of a doctoral thesis on the Confucian School by a Chinese student and that Wallace had sustained an interest in the idea for years and had written about it in *Wallace's Farmer*.[39]

Davis found that the "Ever-Normal Granary" was a phrase coined by Wallace as early as 1926 to describe an ancient Chinese practice. The idea increasingly became a central element in Wallace's agro-political thinking. Davis also mentioned "the biblical tale of Joseph in prehistoric Egypt and the asserted use of an ever normal granary in China for over 1,400 years."[40]

Leuchtenberg at the University of North Carolina wrote that, like Joseph of the Old Testament, Wallace hoped to create an Ever-Normal Granary by storing surplus when yields were good and distributing them in lean years. But Leuchtenberg also believed that "the idea of the ever-normal granary came to Wallace in part from reading a Columbia dissertation on Confucian economics written by a Chinese student."[41]

Accordingly, proponents of the "China–Bible hypothesis" did not completely neglect the Chinese historical practice of the Ever-Normal Granary, nor did they

---

38 "Mr. Wallace's Speech at the Luncheon Party Given by Admiral Shen".
39 Louis H. Bean, Reminiscence, *Columbia Oral History Collection*, p. 150.
40 Joseph S. Davis, "The Economics of the Ever-Normal Granary", *Journal of Farm Economics*, February 1938, 20(1: 8) p. 13.
41 William E. Leuchtenberg, *FDR and New Deal, 1932–1940*. New York: Harper & Row, 1963 p. 255.

deny that Chen Huanzhang's Columbia dissertation was the bridge between the China-source and Wallace.

In contrast, Andrew C. Higgins argued that the inspiration for Wallace's Ever-Normal Granary system had come solely from the Bible.[42] Specifically, the Book of Genesis relates a story in which a pharaoh dreams that a relief system should be established in Egypt.[43] But this only says that people should collect food in good years and store it as a reserve for bad years. It is interesting that Bean found "Ever-Normal Granary"-like practices even in Peru. But he recalled that the difference between the Chinese and the modern versions was the non-recourse nature of the loan in Wallace's Ever-Normal Granary.[44]

It is not denied that the Bible may have had some influence in Wallace's development of the idea of the Ever-Normal Granary. As a pious Christian, it was hardly surprising that Wallace should have invoked the Book of Genesis in support of the Ever-Normal Granary idea, even though the idea had derived primarily from his understanding of ancient Chinese experience. Further, it seemed that Wallace never fully appreciated the evolution of the Ever-Normal Granary to Wang Anshi's system of the Green Sprout Money (for reasons discussed below).

Finally, it should be noted that different translations of the Chinese expression *Changpingcang* (常平仓) as the "Constantly Normal Granary" and the "Ever-Normal Granary" may have given rise to some confusion. It is Wallace who coined the phrase "Ever-Normal Granary" based on the "Constantly Normal Granary" of Dr Chen, although Wallace did on occasion refer to the "Constantly Normal Granary" as well.[45] Arthur M. Schlesinger Jr., the American historian and social critic, perceptively observed that Wallace had borrowed the phrase from Confucius and expressed it as the "Ever-Normal Granary."[46] Mr Bean also believed "it is the 'Constantly Ever-Normal Granary' that appears in that Columbia study which Wallace in our language called the Ever-Normal Granary."[47]

Wallace's Ever-Normal Granary and Wang Anshi's Green Sprout Money

Bodde argued that Wallace's Ever-Normal Granary did not derive from Wang Anshi, even though Wallace had studied Wang Anshi over many years.[48] However, Wallace had disclosed in his speech in China that FDR's New Deal was "strikingly similar" to the proposals of Wang Anshi, whose core policy was

42 Andrew C. Higgins, *The Life of Henry A. Wallace: 1888–1965, Henry A. Wallace Biography*, formerly available at: www.hawiaa.org.
43 Genesis 41, "Pharaoh's Dreams", New International Version, http://niv.scripturetext.com/genesis/41.htm, accessed 18 October 2011.
44 Bean, Reminiscence, *Columbia Oral History Collection*, pp. 150–151.
45 See Blum (ed.) *The Price of Vision: The Diary of Henry A. Wallace, 1942–1946*, p. 326.
46 Arthur M. Schlesinger, Jr. *The Coming of the New Deal*, Boston, MA: Mifflin, 1958, p. 29.
47 Louis H. Bean, Reminiscence, *Columbia Oral History Collection*, p. 151.
48 Derek Bodde, "Henry A. Wallace and the Ever-normal Granary", pp. 411–426.

the Green Sprout Money, or the New Ever-Normal Law.[49] Yet, his speech about Wang Anshi in 1944 was contrary to his letter to Bodde in which he denied the connection between Wang Anshi and the Ever-Normal Granary, even though he granted that he was familiar with Chen Huanzhang's Columbia study. The question of how this discrepancy may be explained is addressed in the following sections.

1 Chen Huanzhang and his scholarly aspiration

Chen Huanzhang's overarching ambition was to celebrate the value of Chinese culture. He was a *Jinshi* of the late Qing dynasty and was promoted to the position of Secretary of the Grand Secretariat before his study at Columbia University.[50] His dissertation was written on Confucian economic principles by which he hoped to introduce the glories of Chinese economic thought and Confucian religion within a Western economics framework[51] and proclaim the merits of Chinese morality, literature and language. He believed that taking the history of China as a whole, and comparing it with that of the West, Chinese people had nothing to be ashamed of. The future of China was bright and the country would become a strong nation in virtue of the intelligence, diligence, prudence and vigour of its people, its endowment of a vast territory and abundant natural resources, and its centralised government, uniform language, highly developed religion and a concept of national identity that had been forged over many thousands of years.

His Confucian study was also viewed more narrowly as a contribution to economics. The system of Confucian ideas was reorganised within a framework of "consumption–production–public finance", embodying the idea that economic policy should aim to increase production and allocate wealth equally.[52] But it was the Confucian production principle that formed the central part in Chen's book, accounting for more than 40 per cent of its content.

Chen wanted to translate his book into his mother language with the title of *Kongmen Licaixue* (孔门理财学), that is, *The Principles of Wealth Management of the Confucian School*, where *Kongmen* means the "the Confucian School", and *Licaixue* refers literally to "the principles of wealth management". He defined *Licaixue* as "a true science of wealth management to help people live in society" (以义理财之科学，使人类得相聚以生者也). He wrote:

49 "Mr. Wallace's Speech at the Luncheon Party given by Admiral Shen", p. 34.
50 See Zheng Zemin, "Chen Huanzhang".
51 "This book was written with western way of writing". Chen Huanzhang, *On Confucianism* (孔教论), Shanghai: The Commercial Press, 1912, p. 66.
52 Chen Huanzhang wrote that there were two parts of the book of the *Economic Principles of Confucius and His School*, one was production, the other was consumption, and this was the structure of Clark's economics. Clark's opinion was the same as Daxue, the Great Learning, noting the production of wealth must be by correct ways, and this was coincident of the two. See Chen Huanzhang, *On Confucianism*, p. 75.

Wealth management originated in the Chapter *Xici* (系辞) of the Book of
Zhouyi [*Book of Changes*] which states that it is wealth that unites people.
However, the only right way to manage wealth is by prohibiting people
from unproductive business. This is the truth. Thus, *Licaixue* should be
translated accurately into Chinese as "Economics".[53]

This well explained his goal of studying Confucian economic principles and dis-
playing the splendour of the Chinese economic heritage to the world. He also
wrote that his book could be entitled *A History of Chinese Economics* (中国理财
学史) if supplemented with a biography of pre-Qin scholars. Moreover, by
"referring mainly to Chinese Classics without ignoring the Twenty-Four Histories" (以经为主、以史为辅), this book could also be entitled *A Chinese History
of Livelihood* (中国生计史), which studied the essence of history of economic
thought.[54] As it is not the purpose of this article to review Chen's book in detail,
readers could refer to John Maynard Keynes, Max Weber and Joseph Schumpeter for a Western understanding of ancient China's economics based on Chen
Huanzhang's work.[55] Evidently, it was not only Henry Wallace who learned
about Confucian economic ideas from Chen's studies.

2 *Chen Huanzhang on Green Sprout Money*

Chen Huanzhang studied the history of the Constantly Normal Granary as part
of China's public finance system. According to his account, whenever the price
of grain was considered too low, the government granaries bought in at a higher
price to benefit the farmer. And whenever the price was too high, the government sold out at the normal price, lower than the market price, to benefit the
consumer. Such was the Constantly Normal Granary. This system existed con-
tinuously from the time it was established in the Han dynasty to the present day
and its name had remained the same throughout the ages. Despite frequent modi-
fications, the fundamental principle, to stabilise food price, had remained
unchanged since the time of Geng Shouchang in the Han dynasty.

The relationship between Wang Anshi and the Green Sprout Money was paid
less attention in Chen's study. The government's "control of demand and
supply", "control of grain" and "loan and public relief" were all described as
notable "socialistic policies" of Confucian production principles, but the Constantly Normal Granary *qua* economic stability measure was not clearly

---

53 "理财二字，始于繫辞，其文曰：何以聚人曰财，理财正辞，禁民为非曰义，故理财学三
   字，实当西文之Economics". See Chen Huanzhang, *On Confucianism*, p. 69.
54 Chen Huanzhang, *On Confucianism*, pp. 65–77.
55 Ye Tan, "The Economic Principles of Confucius and His School: The Start of China Economics
   to the World in a Centennial", p. 8; E.A. Ross, "Economic Principles of Confucius", *The American Economic Review*, March, 1912, 2(1); J.M. Keynes, "The Economic Principles of Confucius
   and his School", *Economic Journal*, December 1912, 22 (88): 584–588; Joseph A. Schumpeter,
   History of Economic Analysis, twelfth impression 1981, Taylor & Francis E-Library, 2006. p. 49.

expressed to Western readers, with no attention paid to differences in the way the system was implemented in different historical periods.[56]

In particular, Chen's study did not reveal the development of the Constantly Normal Granary in the Tang–Song transition from a grain-based system to a monetary system, i.e. the Green Sprout Money system. It seemed that the Constantly Normal Granary in Chapter 30 of Chen's work was totally distinct from the Green Sprout Money in Chapter 31, thus giving the impression that Wang Anshi had put forward the idea of Green Sprout Money as an alternative to the Constantly Normal Granary. In fact, the Constantly Normal Granary had been diversified in the Song dynasty into village granaries *and* the Green Sprout Money. The Green Sprout Money was similar to a modern government loan system. According to Chen, however, the origins of the Green Sprout Money were to be found in *Sijia*, a system to control demand and supply, and *Quanfu*, loans to farmers and citizens in the Zhou dynasties. Before the planting season, peasants were allowed to borrow from the authority, and when farmers repaid the loan after harvest with tax they were permitted to pay with grain instead of money. Whenever the price of grain was high they could borrow grain instead of money and return money instead of grain. For summer planting the money was loaned in the first lunar month and for autumn planting in the fifth lunar month. Whenever the crop was bad and food price higher at harvest the farmers were allowed to pay back at a lower price in a good year. This law was intended to enable farmers to begin planting without delay and to prevent private money-lenders from taking advantage of the interval of the harvest to make huge profit.[57]

The role of the Constantly Normal Granary was to stabilise food prices according to Chen and this was the point that was latched onto by Wallace. But the Green Sprout Money was depicted as nothing more than a government bank. However, in spite of the Chinese origin of the Constantly Normal Granary, it was expedient to persuade the American farmer by associating the idea with a biblical reference, as Wallace did, and with a reference to the Peruvian Ever-Normal Granary by Bean. Both Wallace and Bean kept on referring to the Constantly Normal Granary during the agricultural depression, which Bean referred to as Ever-Normal Granary until it was finally accepted.[58]

Confusion also resulted from Chen's duplication of the incorrect English translation of passages from *The Sacred Books of the East* by James Legge (1815–1897).[59] Chen concluded his study with opinions learned from the New

---

56 Chen Huanzhang, *The Economic Principles of Confucius and His School*, pp. 571–572.
57 Ibid., p. 590.
58 Bean, Reminiscence, *Columbia Oral History Collection*, pp. 150–151.
59 James Legge was the first professor of Chinese at Oxford University (1876–1897). In association with Max Müller, he prepared the monumental *Sacred Books of the East* series, published in fifty volumes between 1879 and 1891.

Texts School.[60] This led to confusion. So it is quite reasonable that Wallace brought books of the Ever-Normal Granary to China[61] where he was to discover more about Wang Anshi than he knew previously.[62] There is, however, a great deal written about Wang Anshi and his policies of the Green Sprout Money and the New Ever-Normal Law in Chen's book.[63] Considering that Wallace started to learn about the Constantly Normal Granary in 1912,[64] it seems reasonable to infer that if the history from the Constantly Normal Granary to the Green Sprout Money had been more clearly and correctly explained in Chen's study, Wallace would have better understood Wang Anshi and his policies of the Green Sprout Money before 1934.

3   *Wallace's American Ever-Normal Granary*

The essence of the ideas of the American Ever-Normal Granary was from China. As Bean mentioned, however, it was supplemented with the policy of the non-recourse loan.[65] The American Ever-Normal Granary in the Agricultural Adjustment Act (AAA) had as its goal not only the stabilisation of commodity prices, as deriving from ancient Chinese practice, but also a farm income goal overseen by the Commodity Credit Corp (CCC) and a mechanism in the form of the non-recourse loan.[66] This amounted to a modernised version of the Ever-Normal Granary and the Green Sprout Money scheme proposed by Wang Anshi.[67]

The mechanisms of the American Ever-Normal Granary were similar to Wang Anshi's scheme although the goals were different. The non-recourse loan is made by collateral in terms of crops, initially applied in the American farm

60 Or called the Present Characters Confucianism. See Liang Jie, "The Correct Way to Manage Wealth: Chen Huanzhang and His Book of *The Economic Principles of Confucius and His School*". The New Texts School is a Han Confucian School based upon the New Texts of Confucian Classical Works rewritten in the Han dynasty. In the Qin period all nongovernmental records were destroyed, and a short time afterwards the Royal Libraries were set on fire by Xiang Yu. The result was the disappearance of classical Confucian works. After the Han dynasty, the New Texts School, with its reinterpretation of Confucian principles and views on government and policy, became the sole official source of Confucianism. But with the rediscovery of original Confucian Classics in the late Western Han, the School of Original Texts was founded, represented by Liu Xin (*c.* 50 BC–AD 23). There followed a long debate between the two Schools. In the Qing dynasty, with the decline of China, there was a Revival Movement of the New Texts School, which advocated the search for truth from the West and reforming the traditional system in China. This thought was reflected in Chen Huanzhang's dissertation.

61 Entry for April 29, 1944 in John Morton Blum, ed. *The Price of Vision: The Diary of Henry A. Wallace, 1942–1946.* Boston, MA: Houghton Mifflin Company, 1973, p. 326.

62 Qin Qing, "Henry Wallace and China Agriculture", *Journal of the Agricultural Extension Communication*, 6 (8): 42, 1944.

63 Chen Huanzhang, *The Economic Principles of Confucius and His School*, pp. 45, 563–567, 584–585, 589–593, 666–667, 673–676.

64 Leland L. Sage, *A History of Iowa*, Ames, IA: The Iowa State University Press, 1974. p. 306.

65 Louis H. Bean, Reminiscence, *Columbia Oral History Collection*, p. 150.

66 U.S. Code, Title 15, Chapter 15, Subchapter II, p. 714: "Creation and Purpose of Corporation".

67 Ray Huang, *China: A Macro History*, p. 142.

belt and later made available to all US farmers. Such loans to farmers were made in accordance with the AAA to stabilise food prices and farm income. The CCC loses its right to recourse the loan once it is made. In order to obtain loans, farmers contract with the CCC on area planning, using crops as collateral. Either the loans are repaid with interest or the crops are taken by the CCC if the market price is lower than the target price. For the CCC, food price stability is the primary goal, and it decreases the loan amount whenever the interest rate is low and vice versa. Therefore, the interest rate is capped and the loan risk is borne by the CCC.

Wallace paid his own glowing tribute to Wang Anshi. He said that Wang had been confronted by problems that were almost identical to those faced by Roosevelt in 1933 and that the methods Wang employed were strikingly similar. Wang Anshi's reforms ended up being frustrated in their implementation; nevertheless, Wallace thought that Wang Anshi had left an enduring impression in the Chinese tradition of statecraft and that what was beyond the reach of paternalistic statesmanship nine centuries ago was within the reach of democratic statesmanship today.[68] How striking it is, as J.M. Keynes remarked, that

> the ideas of economists and political philosophers, both when they are right and when they are wrong, are more powerful than is commonly understood. Indeed the world is ruled by little else. Practical men, who believe themselves to be quite exempt from any intellectual influence, are usually the slaves of some defunct economist.[69]

Conclusion

The Chinese philosophy of the Ever-Normal Granary, as derived from Chen Huanchang, became encapsulated in Henry Wallace's agricultural programme in which the non-recourse loan took the place of the Green Sprout Money proposed by Wang Anshi in the Song dynasty. In Wang Anshi's Green Sprout Money system, the lack of government loan contracts with farmers to limit planting areas and the imposition of policies to profit the public finances led to the frustration of the original programme with its aim of benefiting farmers. The failure of Wang Anshi provided lessons for Wallace in the formulation of his own programme.

Wallace was influenced by Wang Anshi's ideas from reading Chen Huanzhang's study. But because of Chen Huanzhang's incorrect explanation of the origin of the Ever-Normal Granary idea and its evolution to the Green Sprout Money system, and Chen's adherence to the ideas of the New Texts School, Wallace was misled about the true nature of Wang Anshi's reform policies, believing only that there were broad similarities between his policy and Wang's

68 "Mr. Wallace's Speech at the Luncheon Party Given by Admiral Shen", pp. 32–34.
69 J.M. Keynes, *General Theory of Employment, Interest and Money*, Book 4, Chapter 12, Section 5 (London: Macmillan, 1936).

New Law, and that the Chinese Ever-Normal Granary was merely a policy to stabilise the prices and supply of farm products. The importance of Green Sprout Money as introducing a credit revolution in the Ever-Normal Granary system in Song China was thereby overlooked. However, the influence upon Henry Wallace came not only from Chen's study, with its confusing explanation of the evolution from the Ever-Normal Granary to the Green Sprout Money system, but also from other sources[70] as noted in Wallace's letter to Bodde.[71] Bodde studied the history of the Ever-Normal Granary and reported accurately his own understanding of the influence of Chinese thought on Wallace, but he failed to appreciate the significance of Wang Anshi. The fact that the evolution of the Ever-Normal Granary to the Green Sprout Money had not been clearly explained by Chen Huanzhang had led to confusion in Wallace's idea of the Ever-Normal Granary. Thus, while it seems that Wallace took the Ever-Normal Granary as the prototype for his own proposals, the real prototype is Wang Anshi's Green Sprout Money.

70 See note 8 of this paper.
71 H. Raymond Williamson, *Wang An-Shi: A Chinese Statesman and Educationalist of the Sung Dynasty*. Cambridge, MA: Harvard University Press, 2 vols, 1935, 1937.

Index

Printed in the United States
by Baker & Taylor Publisher Services